Studies in Writing & Rhetoric

Other Books in the Studies in Writing & Rhetoric Series

Archives of Instruction

Archives of Instruction

Nineteenth-Century Rhetorics,
Readers, and Composition Books
in the United States

Jean Ferguson Carr
Stephen L. Carr
Lucille M. Schultz

SOUTHERN ILLINOIS UNIVERSITY PRESS

Carbondale

Publication partially funded by a subvention grant from The Conference on College
Composition and Communication of the National Council of Teachers of English.

Library of Congress Cataloging-in-Publication Data
Carr, Jean Ferguson.
Archives of instruction : nineteenth-century rhetorics, readers, and composition
books in the United States / Jean Ferguson Carr, Stephen L. Carr, Lucille M.
Schultz.
   p. cm. — (Studies in writing & rhetoric)
Includes bibliographical references (p.) and index.
1. English language—Rhetoric—Study and teaching—United States—History—
19th century. 2. English language—Composition and exercises—Study and teaching—United States—History—19th century. 3. English language—Textbooks—
History—19th century. 4. Textbooks—United States—History—19th century.
5. Readers—History and criticism. I. Carr, Stephen L., 1950– II. Schultz, Lucille M.,
1943– III. Title. IV. Series.
PE1405.U6C37 2005
808'.042'07107309034—dc22
ISBN 0-8093-2611-6   2004014497

For
David Smith
Mary Anne Ferguson
Maggie and Julia Carr

Contents

Figures

Preface

At the beginning of the nineteenth century, few people in the United States had access to significant school education or to the materials for instruction. By century's end, education was a mass though not universal experience, and literacy textbooks were ubiquitous artifacts, used both at home and at school by a growing number of learners from quite diverse backgrounds. Some textbooks circulated throughout the population across generations. Others, less well known, nonetheless offered new ways of teaching reading and writing. These textbooks became the common property of the nation, drawn upon in various ways to foster widely shared cultures of literacy. Many of these books have been forgotten and their contributions slighted or dismissed. Or they are remembered through a haze of nostalgia, as tokens of an idyllic form of schooling.

Archives of Instruction, a study of nineteenth-century rhetorics, readers, and composition books in the United States, seeks to unsettle this forgetfulness. It is in part a historical project of recovery and in part a critical project of rethinking the functions, cultural work, and signifying practices of textbooks. We trace the sedimented histories of widespread educational practices; we treat the textbook as an important means of cultural formation; and we develop a critical history of influential traditions of textbooks that restores a sense of their distinguished and peculiar contributions to the history of literacy. Underpinning this project is our commitment to investigate the cultural work of books by locating them in a larger field of textual production, by reading them, that is, as parts of an archive.

We came together to write this book because of our shared interest in nineteenth-century literacy textbooks, bringing our different knowledges and experience of archives and our diverse concerns, interests, and commitments. Each of our chapters, to be sure, reflects personal preoccupations, but our various approaches to archival study also reflect alternative methodological emphases prompted in part by substantive differences in the size, organization, and prior history of each category of books as well as in the traditions of secondary criticism about them. Our chapters all pay close attention to selected key texts; they offer, in various ways, a systematic mapping of a textbook category; they provide critical accounts of publishing history; and they seek to respect different conditions of use and circulation.

The books we investigate mark importantly different ways of conceiving of literacy instruction at different times in the past, as well as across different parts of the population. Rhetoric has long had a privileged status in the academy; readers achieved an unparalleled mass distribution, disseminating literacy concerns across a wide population; and composition has reshaped the participation of students in their own learning and the disciplinary practices in the academy. We see the books in these three categories of literacy instruction, as well as the categories themselves, as particularly important, then as now, to the teaching of reading and writing in schools and colleges.

We wrote this book for a range of uses and readerships. We have in mind composition teachers, who use the descendants of these books without necessarily recognizing the traditions and traces of the past. To our colleagues already immersed in historical literacy studies, we offer a revisionist and critical history of the formations of nineteenth-century literacy textbooks. To graduate students in composition or rhetoric, or others beginning historical or literary studies, we provide an overview of the literacy books used in nineteenth-century schools and colleges, we demonstrate various ways of mapping the field in dialogue with though not identical to previous mappings, and we try to be explicit about methodological questions and procedures. We imagine also the person who leafs through a single nineteenth-century textbook and wants to know how to appreciate its strangeness and situate it in a larger context. And we believe that colleagues working in other parts of English studies will find this a useful articulation of the various strands of the discipline and the ways that textbooks can illuminate that history. We hope the material inquiry into such an archive will prove valuable to those in related fields—in the history of the book and in the history of education.

Steve Carr wrote chapter 1, "Reproducing Rhetorics"; Jean Ferguson Carr wrote chapter 2, "Reading School Readers"; and Lucy Schultz wrote chapter 3, "Constructing Composition Books." We have all contributed to one another's sections, both in conversation and through written feedback, and we wrote "An Introduction to Textbooks and the Cultures of Literacy," the coda, and this preface together, at a dining room table in Pittsburgh and in the virtual spaces of telephone and e-mail.

We all teach composition, and we have all taught the teaching of writing and trained new teaching assistants. We have all administered and developed institutional programs and been responsible for textbook selections. Our graduate work was primarily in literature and textual study, and we have published on a range of literary, rhetorical, and cultural topics. As graduate students and beginning in our early professional lives, we were immersed in composition and in pedagogical inquiry and in forging for ourselves links with our formal training. We are, then, inside and outside of the disciplinary formation of composition, and this eclectic slant informs our work.

We have all found that early formulations were often challenged by subsequent discoveries. We have all come across books that nudged the general claims under which we worked, that exceeded our expectations, or took a narrative in a different direction. We have all rediscovered books we had once set aside as central to new questions or lines of inquiry, and with each traversal of the archive, we have found new materials and ways of reading to enrich the history we are composing. Even though our ongoing work in the archives and that of our colleagues keep prompting new questions and opening new lines of research, this project has come to its necessary closure. Here, then, is a primer of what we have learned.

Acknowledgments

The research for this book is grounded in the many hundreds of nineteenth-century literacy textbooks that we have read in a range of special collections and archives. Our debt, therefore, to librarians and archivists who helped us to navigate holdings and retrieve hard-to-find works is large. We offer particular and ongoing thanks to Charles E. Aston Jr., Head, Special Collections Department, and Curator, John A. Nietz Old Schoolbook Collection, University of Pittsburgh Library System; to Marylène Altieri, Curator of Books and Printed Materials at Harvard University's Schlesinger Library, formerly Special Collections Librarian/Archivist at Harvard's Gutman Library; and to Kathy Woodrell, Reference Specialist at the Library of Congress. Each of these librarians, time and again, and often at a moment's notice, has helped solve one of the many problems that can emerge during a lengthy research project.

From our home institutions, we have received departmental and institutional support in a number of ways. Jean and Stephen Carr thank the University of Pittsburgh for research and travel funds. Lucy Schultz thanks the University of Cincinnati's Taft Faculty Memorial Fund and the Faculty Development Fund, which made possible the research travel that undergirds her work in the archive.

Along the way, we have benefited from conversations with colleagues and friends. The Carrs thank the many colleagues in Pittsburgh who share conversations on teaching, history, and books, especially David Bartholomae, Nancy Glazener, Paul Kameen, Peggy and James Knapp, Mariolina Salvatori, Phil and Susan Smith; students in various graduate seminars, especially Stephen Arch, Kirstin Collins, Melanie Dawson, Bianca Falbo, Brenda Glasgott, Gwen Gorzelsky, Linda Jordan, Joshua Kutney, Holly Middleton, April Sikorski, Chris Warnick, Kathleen Welsch, Jim Zukowski; and colleagues elsewhere—Pat Donahue, Joan Feinberg, Margie Ferguson,

Anne Ruggles Gere, Joe and Pat Harris, Nancy Metz, Susan Miller, Jacqueline Royster, Margaret Shaw, David Simpson.

For professional help, Lucy Schultz thanks Andrea B. Goldstein, Reference Specialist in the Harvard Archives; Cynthia Attwood, a specialist in digital reproduction and restoration; and at the University of Cincinnati: Rosemary Aud Franklin, English bibliographer; James W. Hart, Head of Instruction and Faculty Reference, Law Library; and Tom White, Head, Interlibrary Loan Borrowing. For conversation and good spirit, she is grateful to colleagues in the American Antiquarian Society's 2002 Summer Seminar in the History of the Book in American Culture; to colleagues and friends in the Department of English at the University of Cincinnati, especially Jonathan Alexander, Mary Beth Debs, Russel Durst, Lee Person, Kathy Rentz; and to colleagues and friends far and wide, Kathryn Adams, E. Jennifer Monaghan, Jane O'Brien, Marjorie Roemer, Amy Thomas, and Trudelle Thomas. Jean Carr and Lucy Schultz wish to thank Sue Carter for her contributions at an earlier stage of this project.

We are particularly grateful for the careful readings of the manuscript by John Brereton, Cinthia Gannett, and Jason McIntosh, whose queries and suggestions made this a better book. Robert Brooke, editor of the SWR series, has been with this project from its inception, and, at every turn, he has offered wise words. And Kathleen Kageff has been a superb project editor, both thoughtful and generous in her close reading of the text.

The making of a book relies on the nourishment (intellectual, emotional, and physical) provided by authors' families. We are grateful to ours—to David Smith, Mary Anne Ferguson, and Maggie and Julia Carr—to whom this book is dedicated.

A Note on the Cover Illustration

Images of Minerva, Roman goddess of wisdom, leading a youth to knowledge, were popular in late-eighteenth- and nineteenth-century school settings. Lucretia Champion, a student at Sarah Pierce's Litchfield Female Academy in the 1790s, is credited, for example, with both a watercolor and a silk embroidery in which Minerva leads a young woman to a site of learning (Sizer et al. 88–89).

The cover image here, an octagonal wood engraving of Minerva instructing a boy, is by American engraver Alexander Anderson (1775–1870) and appears as the frontispiece of an abridged version of Hugh Blair's *Lectures* (Brattleborough [VT]: Holbrook and Fessenden, 1824). This engraving also appears in Noah Webster's 1819 *The American Spelling Book* published in Brattleborough by Holbrook. An earlier slightly different version, a rectangular cut in which Minerva points to the "Temple of Virtue" and "Temple of Fame," appears in Increase Cooke's *The American Orator* (New Haven: Sidney's Press for John Babcock and Son, 1818). And a re-cut version appeared in Webster's 1829 *Elementary Spelling Book* (New York: George Cooledge) and was used repeatedly in later editions of the same book as well as in *Cobb's Spelling Book* by Lyman Cobb (St. Clairsville, OH: Horton J. Howard. Stereotyped by J. S. Redfield, New York [ca. 1843]).

Anderson's print derives from Francis Hayman's frontispiece design for the 1758 London edition of Robert Dodsley's influential instructional compendium, *The Preceptor.* The image functions as an emblem of the transmission of the old-world, classical knowledge to the young student in the United States; its history of publication marks the multiple exchanges and re-appropriations across different intellectual and textbook traditions.

For the publishing history of this engraving, we thank Jane R. Pomeroy, author of the forthcoming *Alexander Anderson (1775–*

1870), *Wood Engraver and Illustrator. An Annotated Bibliography,* to be published in three volumes by Oak Knoll Press, New Castle, Delaware. We thank the Serenus Press for scanning the graphic.

Archives of Instruction

An Introduction to Textbooks
and the Cultures of Literacy

This is a book about textbooks in rhetoric, reading, and composition published in the United States during the nineteenth century. Along the way, we talk about the disciplines and school subjects these books represent, the theoretical positions they disseminate, the teachers and students who wrote and used these books, and the varied cultures of literacy from which they emerge. But this is first and foremost a book about books.

We describe changing conditions of book production and offer bibliographic information about editions, printings, and circulation. We discuss steady sellers with national circulation and books printed a single time, often for local audiences. We examine textbooks with frequent reprintings, wide circulation, and important adaptations, such as Blair's *Lectures,* McGuffey's *Readers,* or Parker's *Progressive Exercises,* and books that mark points of emergence (Newman's *Practical System of Rhetoric*), or target particular student populations (the *Freedman's Reader*), or forge new directions for language instruction (Frost's *Easy Exercises*). Because the archive of nineteenth-century textbooks is so vast, fluid, scattered, fragmentary, and stratified, we cannot be fully comprehensive, but we represent a wide spectrum of the material diversity of the archive. In differing but related ways, each chapter examines the intellectual formation of these books, the traditions of literacy instruction from which they borrow or depart, and the education, career, and cultural location of their authors.

We hope our book fosters an understanding of nineteenth-century textbooks that is not dismissive, nostalgic, or antiquarian, but that recognizes the complexity and strangeness of past projects in order to excavate the sedimented histories of current disciplinary attitudes and practices. It has been our experience, and we invite others to share this with us, that reading textbooks from the past promotes critical attention to common dispositions toward language, teaching, and learning. As teachers and scholars, we have had the familiar experience of being so surrounded by textbooks—to quote Adrienne Rich, they are "the assumptions in which we are drenched" (35)—that we no longer see them clearly. We use what is at hand or what seems best for the occasion, copy a page from one book and an assignment from another, and do our work as best we can. Nineteenth-century textbooks often develop in broadly similar ways, appropriating diverse theoretical and pedagogical formations from earlier texts with little or no critical justification. Yet when practical, ad hoc, and casual adaptations are carried over into print, they lose their status as provisional tactics and appear as generalized procedures or rules. Our project offers ways of understanding the material and discursive practices that underwrite nineteenth-century instructional materials. We elaborate various traditions that current textbooks at times both draw on and resist. Our historical research has led us to a critical appreciation of textbooks as intriguingly peculiar and richly complex textual formations.

We also hope to suggest a sense of the pleasures of working with historical sources, not only as immediately useful prompts for pedagogical practice or critical reflection but also as occasions for dwelling on the eccentric, the distant, the humorous, the strange. Textbooks can be so embedded in another time and space as to seem other-worldly in their very worldliness, or they can be uncannily familiar in the persistence of topics, exercises, dispositions, and routines. While these qualities or effects may not always have a ready instrumental relationship to our professional work, they can restore a sense of openness and possibility, of alternative pasts and yet-to-be-realized futures for intellectual and pedagogical projects.

There is a rich tradition of scholarship on old schoolbooks,[1] including the work, for instance, of John Nietz, Clifton Johnson, Charles Carpenter, and Porter Perrin. Such studies embody an encyclopedic knowledge of the archive and usefully chart many of its most distinctive landmarks. As in any large-scale mapping of a complex field, however, there are inevitable simplifications or oversights. This earlier work does not describe some aspects of the archive that now seem especially relevant, and it sometimes comes to mistaken or misleading conclusions. But that said, our engagement with this material has helped us to clarify our own perspectives. We have also benefited greatly from the work of Ian Michael on British textbooks (with reference to the U.S. traditions): his work is exemplary for both its historical insights and its bibliographic care.[2]

There is likewise a long critical and bibliographic tradition of research on nineteenth-century U.S. textbooks more specifically oriented to rhetoric and composition studies that emerges decisively with often-cited contributions by Warren Guthrie and Albert Kitzhaber, whose influential 1953 dissertation became available in book form only in 1990. Kitzhaber's work serves as a reminder of other studies with limited circulation such as Janet Emig's survey of textbooks, "The Relation of Thought and Language Implicit in Some Early American Rhetoric and Composition Texts," originally written as her master's qualifying paper at Harvard's School of Education, or the photocopy publication of John Michael Wozniak's dissertation. In the 1980s, Jim Berlin's work revived an interest in the history of rhetoric and composition studies, an interest that was more fully realized by John Brereton, Sharon Crowley, Nan Johnson, and many others. We want especially to recall the contributions of our colleague Robert Connors, who persisted in valuing old books and articulating their usefulness for understanding present concerns. Our project builds upon, revises, and at times challenges this legacy of historical scholarship. We respond to a still common tendency to treat the period dismissively, to simplify its diversity, or to understand it primarily as a foil to current interests and practices. We seek to incorporate a larger array of texts and traditions into our historical understanding of literacy instruction: school readers, for instance, figure hardly at all in accounts of literacy materials or disciplinary formations, and the relationship between "first books" of composition and college texts is often ignored.[3]

Over the last decade or so, scholars have often focused on other nineteenth-century sites of literacy instruction, on groups or activities or institutions whose relationship to the cultures of literacy of the time is not defined by textbooks.[4] We believe that the study of textbooks continues to have much to offer to the concerns of this research on student work, teaching, attitudes about particular groups of learners, and engagement in a more widely defined culture of literacy. Textbooks offer different access to such interests: as materials used widely, for a long time, and by multiple and diverse teachers and students, they frame ways of reading student papers, of understanding teachers' choices and expectations, and of recognizing the relationships and spaces between school and extracurricular practices. Although a researcher can never know exactly how a textbook was used by either teacher or student, textbooks contain tantalizing traces of expected use and misuse, and of the pleasures and difficulties teachers and students are likely to face in entering literate culture.

Cultures of Literacy and Education

We are mindful that textbooks exist in a much larger institutional and educational matrix that includes teachers, students, institutions, and the broader public's investment in literacy and education.[5] Schools are, in Michael Katz's words, "culturally sensitive institutions" (*Reconstructing* 29), responding to shifts and changes in the political, economic, and cultural landscape, and textbooks, as Michael Apple reminds us, both reflect and act on such broad changes. Two aspects of nineteenth-century education seem to us especially relevant for understanding the development of textbooks from this time: first, that schooling generally became more inclusive, stratified, and systematic across the century, though earlier, more diversified and locally organized formations persisted in some areas and for some groups, and second, that the goals and forms of study, in both schools and colleges, substantively changed as the century came to its end, from the earlier focus on "mental discipline" toward an emphasis on being more "practical."

The nineteenth century in the United States witnessed the emergence and flourishing of public education and a shift in literacy instruction from a fairly restricted elite to a more democratic and varied audience. While the number of students attending school grew steadily, the opportunity for school varied among social groups. African Americans and Native Americans had far less access to public education than did whites; school was less available and less utilized by first-generation immigrants than by second-generation immigrants; among first and second generations of immigrants, Irish families in New York and New England used school less than did German families in the Midwest; and school options for girls and young women were far fewer than for boys and young men.[6]

Literacy often developed outside school, at work and at play, and at a range of other sites, including the family home, community settings, lyceums, and Sunday schools. Many of those excluded from formal schooling because of race, gender, or class became literate through what Lawrence Cremin calls "the ordinary business of living" (*Public* 28) or what Jacqueline Jones Royster calls association with a "literate environment"(136). Self-instruction was, indeed, a valued activity, cited in school readers as a response to circumstances—like travel, frontier life, seafaring, rural living, or illness—that made formal schooling difficult. Textbooks often advertised their usefulness "at home" as well as in "schools and academies." Any printed text, moreover, could be used for literacy instruction, just as many schoolbooks found a place on the family bookshelf. Especially early in the century, learners might practice their reading and writing with whatever printed material was at hand: a Bible or psalter, a hymnal, a copy of *Murray's Grammar,* an almanac or newspaper, an abridgment of Blair, or one of Peter Parley's collections of tales.

Formal schooling took diverse forms depending on the region and the family's economic circumstances. Children often attended school only when their labor was not needed at home, on the farm, or in the factory. Children of privilege often studied with private tutors until old enough to enter either a formal college-prep grammar school, where the emphasis was often on Latin grammar and Latin texts, or an academy, often a single-sex school with an academic emphasis as well as attention to "feminine arts," such as sewing, painting, and dance, or to "gentlemanly codes of conduct." And, while some form of high school existed almost from the beginning of the century, only at century's end were public high schools becoming widely available to middle-class families (more boys than girls attended) (Reese 166–81).[7] Many migrant or working-class families relied on children to supplement the family income, and these children might not have attended or completed high school. The most advanced instruction took different forms for different groups and could have occurred in a high school, an academy, a normal school, a divinity school, a college, or university.

The variety of instructional sites and purposes makes the determination of "elementary" and "advanced" textbooks a complicated issue.[8] Although some textbooks, especially readers, were produced in carefully graduated series marking stages of learning from beginning to advanced, others intermixed more "difficult" studies and selections with those that seem more preliminary. Even a very elementary book, like a primer, could include surprisingly advanced vocabulary and texts. A book could be designed for one audience but used (or reworked for use) at many different sites. Illustrations in a composition book, for example, might represent young learners, even when the book was used in high school. Students in smaller districts might share or reuse a limited stock of textbooks across age levels whereas students in metropolitan centers might use textbooks calibrated to grade level.

As the century advanced and with increasing urbanization and industrialization, schools and colleges grew in number, in size, and in the diversity of students.[9] New kinds of schools emerged, such as the land-grant institutions with agricultural and mechanical curricula funded under the 1862 Morrill Act; the normal schools (established from the 1820s on, with Hampton the first normal school for African Americans in 1868); technical institutes like M.I.T. (1865); coeducational schools (women were accepted to Oberlin in 1837 and to the University of Iowa in 1855); and women's colleges (Vassar 1861, Wellesley and Smith 1875). In high schools and normal schools, a more diverse and "practical" curriculum than the classical course of study developed: the so-called "English curriculum," which included scientific and technical fields, modern languages and literatures, and composition as fields of study. Even the more privileged institutions addressed calls for change, developing schools of applied sciences and engineering, and shifting from the long-standing required curriculum to an elective system.

This shift toward a more "practical" education has a complex relationship to ongoing, influential arguments in educational circles about "mental discipline," the theory that the mind had certain faculties in need of disciplined training.[10] In *Democracy and Education* (1916), John Dewey described mental or "formal" discipline as "a commonplace" derived from but "without explicit reference" to Lockean dualism (theorizing the outer world as presenting the material or content of knowledge on which the mind's faculties operate). Its value was that it "seemed to provide the educator with definite, instead of vague, tasks," and "made the elaboration of a technique of instruction relatively easy," focusing on "*repeated acts* of attending, observing, memorizing" sequenced in increasing levels of difficulty (72).

Theories of mental discipline shaped literacy instruction and textbooks by fostering memorization and recitation as common practices, encouraging a graduated course of study with repeated exercises, addressing students in terms of universal faculties rather than local abilities, and promoting certain subjects—typically Latin, Greek, mathematics, and moral philosophy, and later the study of grammar. The influential Yale Report of 1828 declared that "the two great points to be gained in intellectual culture, are the *discipline* and the *furniture* of the mind; expanding its powers, and storing it with knowledge." It also argued that such a focus would "throw the student upon the *resources of his own mind*. Without this, the whole apparatus of libraries, and instruments, and specimens, and lectures, and teachers, will be insufficient to secure distinguished excellence" (Hofstadter and Smith 1: 278, 279).[11]

Mental discipline had strong connections to a traditional classical curriculum, but it gained new associations and configurations across the century. It underwrote arguments about systematic or analytic instruction, visible in the textbooks' many exercises, sequenced lessons, selections for practice, even arguments about needing a "definite aim" in reading, and in the emphasis on memorization. It also framed quite varied discussions about the mind and learning. Ralph Waldo Emerson deployed the language of mental discipline in *Nature* (1836), whose fifth chapter ("Discipline") suggests the value of nature in disciplining the "understanding in intellectual truths" and forming the "organ" of the mind by creating a "constant exercise in the necessary lessons" that would counter that "tedious training" that forms "the common sense" (*Collected Works* 1: 23–24). Reform educator Friedrich Froebel might not have used the term "mental discipline" as a basis for his kindergarten pedagogy (he opened his first kindergarten in 1837), but he incorporated a similar idea in his staunch belief that children would play with the "gifts" he designed (*Fröbelgaben*, or geometrical manipulatives such as a ball, a cube, a block) not just as early tools for learning mathematics, but also, and perhaps more importantly, as a way of understanding and experiencing "order," "discovery," "insight" (Paul Klee and Frank Lloyd Wright are among the many artists and architects whose work was influenced by these "gifts").[12] By century's end, although the discourses of "mental discipline" often yielded to discourses that valorized "the practical" as an educational goal, the desire to exercise or cultivate the mental faculties never completely disappeared (we see traces today, for example, in arguments about "critical thinking").

Despite its initial promise to create resourceful students, mental discipline came to be associated with drill and rote learning. Student accounts of its pedagogical applications are grim, focusing on the tedium and repetition of recitation lessons. Here's what Quaker Elizabeth Buffum Chace wrote about memorizing in the 1820s:

> In grammar we were obliged to recite every word of Murray's large volume over and over, for a long time, before we were set to make practical application of it in the analysis or parsing of a sentence. We must repeat *of, to, for, by, with, in, into, within, without, over, under, through, above, below, before, behind, beneath, on* or *upon, among, after, about, against,* for months before we were permitted to tell what

should be done with the smallest preposition of them all.
(Chace and Lovell 23)

By the time she was twelve, Chace had recited *Murray's Grammar*
more than a dozen times, without any instruction in application of
the concepts. This kind of recitation persisted as a primary method
in elementary education and, as Laurence Veysey notes, "in nearly
every [college] classroom" well into the 1860s. Veysey cites a similarly disparaging comment by Lyman Bagg, a Yale student at the time:

> In a Latin or Greek recitation one [student] may be asked
> to read or scan a short passage, another to translate it, a
> third to answer questions as to its construction. . . . The
> reciter is expected simply to answer the questions which
> are put to him, but not to ask any of his instructor, or dis-
> pute his assertions. (37)

In reaction to criticism of such abstract and rote learning, new
subjects of study and pedagogies emphasized the "practical," promoting knowledge and skills that would assist students in their lives
and work. With younger students, changes from the abstract and
formal to the concrete and practical began, however slowly, in the
1830s; by the end of the Civil War, these changes also marked col-
lege-level study. The move toward the practical is evident on many
levels, encouraging changes in the aims and methods of education,
curriculum, and textbooks. Books on teaching, like John S. Hart's
In the School-Room (1868), promised "practical advantages" and
"practical inquiry," based on "professional experience" (v–vi). An
1868 report from Yale College's Sheffield Scientific School declared
that the "object of all education is to increase our capacity of happiness and usefulness," and urged that "discipline" be united with
"utility" (Hofstadter and Smith 2: 584–85).[13]
   A highly visible challenge to the classical curriculum and "abstract" studies came with Harvard's adoption of the elective system,
with attendant developments in "modern" studies in languages,
science, and social sciences and in more practical instruction. In his

1869 inaugural address as Harvard's president, Charles W. Eliot declared the intention to "establish, improve, and extend the elective system" (610), arguing that under the abstraction of mental discipline "the individual traits of different minds have not been sufficiently attended to" (608). He warned against the recitation system, and argued that "lectures alone are too often a useless expenditure of force. The lecturer pumps laboriously into sieves. The water may be wholesome, but it runs through. A mind must work to grow" (610).[14]

The move to the practical is evident in the textbooks' persistent effort to teach older subjects in context: teaching grammar through a series of questions keyed to specific reading lessons, as the 1857 McGuffey advanced readers advocate, or reframing Latin syntactic study with modern sentences and topics. It drives the many books that restructure the relationship between rhetoric and composition, or between spelling and reading. The inclusion of such topics as natural history and scientific experiment as composition assignments or reading selections shows how textbooks at many levels prefigured the expansion of disciplinary subjects in the colleges, and advocated such procedures as observation and recording to compete with emphasis on memorization and abstract learning.

The expansions—the kinds of schools, the school population, the range of subjects taught, and the pedagogical methods—signaled to some an exciting growth in democratic possibilities in education. To others, of course, such change marked the decline of earlier values and expectations. F. H. Stoddard addressed the extremes, writing in 1890, "The college has ceased to be a cloister and has become a workshop" (qtd. in Veysey 61). The textbooks reflect the mixture of responses, as older forms persist well beyond their "era," as late textbooks "return" to the values of earlier eras, and as "modern" textbooks apologize for offering a more limited or simplified course of study.

Textbooks as Material and Intellectual Property

In his 1869 inaugural address, Charles Eliot offered "some strong opinions about text-books and their use":

> Impatience with text-books and manuals is very natural in
> both teachers and taught. These books are indeed, for the
> most part, very imperfect, and stand in constant need of
> correction by the well-informed teacher. Stereotyping, in
> its present undeveloped condition, is in part to blame for
> their most exasperating defects. To make the metal plates
> keep pace with the progress of learning is costly. (610)

Yet despite his concerns about the "manifest deficiencies of textbooks," in particular of scientific manuals, he argued against a "too
sweeping condemnation of their use. It is a rare teacher who is su-
perior to all manuals in his subject." This articulation of the material means of book production with the quality and substance of an
educational program is a salutary reminder that textbooks are always simultaneously material and commercial artifacts and representations of intellectual and pedagogical projects.

Textbooks have a particular status in the history of the book.
They are unusual and difficult books in the variety of their parts,
the mode of their authoring, and their publication history. Like
cookbooks, children's books, and popular fiction, they often slide
beneath bibliographers' and historians' radar, mentioned as a total-
ity rather than in their particularity or difference. Virtually every
literate person encounters these books, yet their significance as
cultural texts is often ignored or devalued. They disrupt definitions
of the "popular" book, since although they may outsell even the
most celebrated bestseller, they are often not selected or even owned
by individuals. They are at once ubiquitous and rare. Often difficult to acquire, they are also objects that were battered and con-
sumed by successive generations of students. They can be encoun-
tered in the rare book room of a library or bought for a quarter at a
yard sale. They are preserved for the most part in only a very few
special collections, yet many copies are treasured for their deep
personal connections, as family heirlooms, sites of memory, evidence
of educational achievement or social distinction.

Nineteenth-century textbooks are often the outcome of practices of compilation involving the wholesale copying, redaction, and

transformation of earlier texts. They are thus sedimented artifacts, juxtaposing materials composed at different times and places with newer passages and organizations. Their innovation may be less in the "originality" of specific materials or conceptions, than in arrangement, emphasis, or forms of attention to student work. Reprinted over long stretches of time and by multiple publishing firms, they are remarkably durable and show the effects of local interests and variation. Their modes of production and reproduction challenge notions of authorship, composition, originality, and influence in ways that were—and still are—important to debates about copyright law or intellectual property.

Nineteenth-century textbooks are rarely "autonomous" or "original" works emerging from a single formative time and place. Rhetorics and composition books are commonly compiled by a single person drawing on other writers' texts. The multisectioned readers are often the production of a committee or sequence of people, offering materials "borrowed" from earlier books or adapted to different student populations, modes or levels of instruction. Even those most resembling the single-authored book may be "coauthored" by subsequent adapters, by those who transform text into topics or questions, who shape conjecture into rule, who construct exercises and select readings. They thus raise important questions about differing forms of authorship and labor—about such distributed authorial practices as adaptation, abridgment, or the writing of exercises and questions.[15] Although they are by convenience identified as the "creation" or "property" of a particular figure (e.g., named as "by" Blair or as "McGuffey's"), the facts of their composition and ownership are usually far more complex.

In many ways, the textbooks' complex juxtaposition of conserved texts and quotations with new materials reflects the most advanced textual theories of the day. Emerson's skepticism in "The American Scholar" (1837) about the value of books and the dependence on the past calls for a "creative reading" of those texts for the uses of the present (*Collected Works* 1: 58). In his 1859 lecture "Quotation and Originality," he gives a more explicit explanation of creative reading, discussing the practice of intellectual "borrowing" that so characterizes nineteenth-century textbook compilation. Using examples of the interdependency of old and new in the natural world ("Nature decomposes all her harvest for recomposition," 204), Emerson offers textual examples of interdependency that date to antiquity, arguing that our "mental indebtedness" (189) to what we have read and heard is so pervasive, so "massive," that "one would say there is no pure originality. All minds quote. Old and new mark the warp and woof of every moment" (178). He suggests that borrowing is valuable not only because it represents the thought of great minds ("and comes of magnanimity and stoutness" 183), but also because what a writer selects to borrow is as much a sign of his success as is his own work. "Every book," Emerson writes, "is a quotation; and every home is a quotation out of all forests and mines and stone-quarries; and every man is a quotation from all his ancestors" (176).

Such sentiments appear in more mundane terms in some of the apologies offered in nineteenth-century textbooks, where the practice of borrowing is acknowledged and even celebrated as a sign of responsible composition. Characteristic, perhaps, is this acknowledgment from the 1857 stereotyped edition of McGuffey's *Sixth Reader,* which addresses "free use" and adaptation as approved procedures rather than guilty secrets:

> In the preparation of this work, free use has been made of the writings of standard authors upon Elocution, such as Walker, McCulloch, Sheridan Knowles, Ewing, Pinnock, Scott, Bell, Graham, Mylins, Wood, Rush, and many others. . . . Considerable liberty has been taken with the articles selected, in order to adapt them to the especial purpose for which they are here designed. Much change and remodeling have been necessary. The lessons are therefore credited as taken '*from*' the author named. (8)

Other apologies evoke the language of "common property" or "public" discourse, which permeated nineteenth-century defenses against copyright infringement. The positive value of materials that circulated in and for the public benefit competes with the author's claim to private possession. The following passage, from a preface to an 1878 rhetoric, displays the range of attitudes toward textual "indebtedness," showing the material complications of citation in a culture where quotations circulated detached from their texts of origin.

> So many writers have been consulted in the preparation of this work that an acknowledgment of indebtedness would be little else than the catalogue of a good-sized library. Wherever special use has been made of any author, care has been taken to give full credit, and if this has not been done in any case, the omission has not been intentional. Some things will be found here which are jottings from memory, or newspaper clippings, the authorship of which could not be traced; but many others are the common property of writers on rhetoric, and for the use of these no acknowledgments are due. (De Mille vii)

Such prefatory comments suggest that nineteenth-century literacy textbooks are not simply derivative or unwitting instruments of dissemination. Or, we would argue, they derive and disseminate in complex and valuable ways.

Textbooks stretch the limits of copyright law and publishing agreements, in ways similar to Internet publication today.[16] The goal of disseminating knowledge to the public, articulated in early copyright law and court cases as crucial to the U.S. situation, offers a powerful rationale for these books' function as storehouses of valued cultural texts and practices. At the same time, their educational function demands that such materials be constantly revised, rethought, and reframed for new students, and that they address the changing literacy needs of the nation. Citing someone else's words or compiling texts that articulated multiply authored subtexts was at the time a sign of learning, of labor, and of participation in shared cultures of the past and present. Practices of reprinting became an important means of cultural exchange between the United States and Great Britain, Europe, and classical traditions.[17] Reprinting also circulated a wide array of U.S. authors, texts, and lore, borrowing from periodicals and treatises, or adapting philosophical, literary, psychological, or physiological works to the space constraints and educational level of the textbook.

Textbooks drew on periodical publications and adaptations, which eluded much copyright law, and they also reprinted materials beyond the term of copyright. Textbook writers and companies, as well as the books themselves, feature significantly in the history of U.S. copyright. The first book protected under the 1790 Copyright Act is a textbook, *The Philadelphia Spelling Book* by John Barry; and Noah Webster, the noted compiler of spellers, grammars, readers, and the dictionary, is referred to as "the Father of American copyright" for his vigorous efforts to advocate political and legal protection.[18] The Cincinnati firm that issued many volumes of McGuffey *Readers* was sued in 1838 for copyright infringement: its settlement called for a fine and slight changes of some entries ("Cat and Ball" becomes "Puss and Her Kittens"). The issue of copyright remained a contentious one throughout the century, the subject of innumerable suits, political challenges, and squabbles and resulted in several changes in copyright law.[19]

Nineteenth-century textbooks also complicate many of the shorthand conventions of descriptive bibliography and historiography. It can be surprisingly difficult to provide the simplest of bibliographical data about these books—their title, author, date, edition, place of publication, level of instruction—and it is always difficult to determine the extent of their distribution or circulation. Conventional ways of marking the "important" textbooks through numbers of editions or of copies sold rely on estimates or creative averaging rather than concrete publishing or distribution data. Textbooks that appeared over many decades, printed by various regional publishers, and issued in multiple formats are often addressed as if they were a single, unchanging book, a book whose revisions and variations can be dismissed as insignificant "noise," as accidents of marketing or dissemination, and books distributed under the conditions of mass publication are treated as if coequal with earlier regional printing practices. Complex collages of materials are often reduced to a single position or attitude, read from one or another part determined to be "the book" (e.g., the preface, the list of topics, the inclusion of a kind of selection, the level of instruction). These seemingly "basic" details about the reading of a book are not just "problems." They serve as interesting starting points for inquiry about the production and uses of a book, or of the textbook in its relationship to other books, other times, and other literacy practices.

Textbook Traditions

We understand rhetorics, readers, and composition books as comprising specific textbook traditions. Books within such traditions typically draw upon an ensemble of commonplace topics, examples, exercises, and arguments. They tend to have a range of broadly similar formats or organizations. Such shared features emerge in part from practices of compilation, from similar relationships of genealogical descent from the founding textbooks of each tradition. Especially in the second half of the nineteenth century, they may reflect as well developments in educational systems and the larger cultures of literacy that support an emerging consensus about the topics appropriate for different forms of literacy instruction or levels of schooling. Textbook traditions are also fairly conservative textual formations, with topics, arguments, organizational structures, and even formats persisting across the decades. Despite their persistence, however, they respond to innovations in educational theory and practice, to new technologies (such as the slate and blackboard) or student populations, and to social changes. Books from these different traditions are at times yoked—in their use, marketing, or theoretical implications. At other times, these traditions operate as if on different planes, tugging at the restraints or orthodoxies of the other fields. At certain periods, materials or theories cross from one tradition to another, although there is no necessary or overarching rationalization of their differing positions and approaches.

Studying textbooks within their tradition, as each of our individual chapters does, clarifies what various books have in common—the topics conventionally covered in each, the materials recycled or appropriated from earlier texts in the tradition—and it also makes visible how they differ—their idiosyncratic treatments of familiar materials, the occasional strategic reworking of normative practices. Placing these traditions in relationship to one another, as our collaborative authorship makes possible, has allowed us to trace the intermittent migrations of routines, practices, and principles from one tradition to another and to investigate the quite diverse relationships of each textbook tradition to various cultures of literacy and modes of textual production and reproduction.

Rhetorics, readers, and composition books at times share similar passages or exercises, pedagogical goals, and theoretical principles. But each tradition has a distinctive project, set of topics, and intellectual lineage; each has its characteristic conditions of authorship and modes of circulation; each typically addresses different ages and levels of education.

- *Rhetorics* typically propose theoretical ways of mapping the instructional field and articulate systematic principles about language, style, invention, and discourse as well as a varied list of other topics: pronunciation, grammar, genres of writing, prosody. They derive from classical rhetoric, as that tradition of inquiry was selectively adapted and reworked by later scholars and given a decisive inflection by eighteenth-century Scottish writers. Rhetorics were most often written by college professors, though teachers in high schools or academies published a fair sample across the century. They are often imagined as the most advanced form of literacy instruction, with some textbooks specifying a college or university audience. Sections of rhetorics are often redacted and disseminated through readers and composition books.
- *Readers* emerge from centuries-old compilations of classical or religious texts and from an eighteenth-century elocutionary tradition focused on oral performance of written texts. Drawing on rhetorical categories established through Sheridan, Walker, and Blair about articulation

and emphasis, readers instruct students in the analysis of texts and provide a storehouse of cultural materials on which to practice the art of reading. Compiled by educators, literacy experts, professional textbook writers, and publishers, they appear in enormous numbers and variety, adapted to different populations and educational levels, and revised to reflect changed cultural texts. Reading is a school subject from the lowest grades through high school; it is central to advanced study under the rubrics of rhetoric or literature and as a means of accumulating knowledge, and it is also a highly valued lifelong activity.

- Relative newcomers, *composition textbooks* organize and invigorate activities of writing that earlier operated primarily to support instruction in reading and grammar. While they are rooted in rhetorical traditions and borrow freely from the work of eighteenth-century rhetoricians, they are innovative in the ways they draw on emerging theories of child development, especially those of Pestalozzi, and in the new pedagogies they create. Their authors are, most often, teachers who write out of their classroom experience. As the curricula of advanced instruction begin more regularly to include composition as a subject, books appear for students in high schools and colleges. Thus the first composition books to appear are for children; the last are for college students.

Our work has made us acutely aware of the multiple exchanges of these traditions with other kinds of literacy instruction, particularly elocution and grammar. But the list of related traditions doesn't stop there. It also includes homiletics, oratorical books, punctuation guides, dictionaries, literary anthologies and surveys, school editions of standard authors, spellers, letter-writing guides, college periodicals, debate manuals, and Sunday school publications. We occasionally address some of these affiliated traditions as they interact with rhetorics, readers, and composition books, but our primary focus remains on what we believe were the most important traditions for instruction in reading and writing.

One of the foundational commitments of this project is its attempt to investigate rhetorics, readers, and composition books by locating them in larger fields of textual production, by reading them, that is, as members most immediately of what we call textbook traditions, but also of a yet larger and more amorphous class, the archive of nineteenth-century instructional texts. An archive is an official collection of written materials. Any particular archive is at once a *fragmentary* and an *interested* record of textual production, the consequence of innumerable local decisions and unforeseen contingencies about the production and preservation of a large array of texts.[20] Archival research has its own distinctive pleasures and difficulties. It entails wide reading at various repositories of materials, often systematically searching to work through a line of inquiry, compiling information from not fully reliable electronic and printed bibliographies, and also at times scanning piles of unfamiliar texts. Only after traversing an archive in several ways over some time is it possible to gain an informed sense of a textbook tradition, of its foundational texts, of its patterns of development, of its differences from affiliated traditions. And yet, the recognition of distinct textbook traditions does not resolve the larger archive into order; indeed, useful generalizations about one tradition need immediate qualifications and revisions when applied to another. There is no shortcut to mapping the archive, no synecdochal relation between any group of texts, whatever their historical importance, and the whole. We try in various ways to respect the open-ended complexity of the archive, to attend to the idiosyncratic and the obscure; but we seek also to chart some of the material features of the books that organize this archive and their contributions to the cultures of literacy in the nineteenth-century United States.

1 / Reproducing Rhetorics

> The author gives them to the world, neither as a work wholly
> original, nor as a compilation from the writings of others. On
> every subject contained in them, he has thought for himself.
> —Hugh Blair, *Lectures on Rhetoric and Belles Lettres*

Field, Book, Archive

Rhetoric can name both a discipline, or an entire field of study, and
a type of textbook, a single book used to instruct students. The relationship between the two is far from simple. The disciplinary field
often has diverse contending understandings of its scope, theoretical grounds, and articulations with other subjects. What might now
be recognized as an instructional text properly representing the
discipline depends significantly on how broadly or idiosyncratically
the larger field is construed. Old textbooks, conversely, can challenge current attitudes about the discipline. What rhetorics include
or exclude, what they highlight, or represent in peculiar ways, or
treat as commonplaces too familiar to need justification, are all
material traces of theoretical commitments or instructional practices
that can differ strangely from present-day dispositions to rhetorical study. The diversity of such texts, moreover, complicates the
history and self-understanding of the field, for archives of any size
or complexity support multiple and often contradictory representations of a field. I take it for granted that we always read from an
interested position, that there is no neutral recovery of the past, but
only selectively reconstructed versions of it. Yet archival research
that attends to the details of individual books and to the differences
across texts can keep the past a plural and contested resource. The
material diversity of the archive, that is, can prompt or support a
critical history that unsettles far more than it confirms present dispositions to the disciplinary field.

The archive of rhetorics that circulated in the United States during the nineteenth century is large, diverse, and complex. It includes celebrated rhetorical treatises and nearly anonymous textbooks. Rhetorics are significantly larger than most composition books and elementary school readers. Most range from 250 to 350 pages, though some early textbooks (Knox, Litch) and late rhetorical guides (Bancroft, Nichol) run less than a hundred pages, and several comprehensive studies approach five hundred or more pages (Blair, De Mille). Early in the century, many rhetorics advertised themselves without discriminating among use at schools, academies, or colleges or for private study. After the Civil War, rhetorics increasingly have a more stratified intended use, with some (Lockwood, Waddy) specifying a high school audience, a few (Bascom) addressing only college juniors and seniors, and others (A. S. Hill *Principles*, Genung *Practical*) primarily seeking collegiate underclassmen. Rhetorics generally adopt one of four modes of presentation. A few are written as *philosophical treatises* (Campbell or Bascom); they address or mention students only occasionally, if at all, and have no apparatus that identifies them as textbooks. Most rhetorics are more explicitly and sustainedly pedagogical. Several (Blair, Newman, Wendell) retain, or imitate, the form of *talking lectures*,[1] in which the writer directly addresses student readers in a conversational manner. A few (Knox, Andrews, Boyd) use *catechistic form:* like most catechisms, these books are not true dialogues, but an authoritarian form of question and answer that promotes rote learning. Finally, most rhetorics (e.g., G. P. Quackenbos, Kellogg, A. S. Hill, Genung) are *expository textbooks*. They use typographic features to mark the various uses, or relative importance, of different passages, usually printing illustrative examples in small type, and rules and definitions in large type or boldface. They often number paragraphs or sections for easy identification and cross reference, include "exercises" keyed to the exposition of various principles, and may have "lessons" instead of "chapters."

Within these broad categories of presentation, rhetorics rarely share a common protocol in their organization of study. The first few chapters of a rhetoric, for example, may enumerate the letters of the alphabet and the parts of speech (Boyd), or reflect on the difference between a science and an art (Bascom), or rehearse the history of the English language (G. P. Quackenbos, De Mille), or define an array of figures and tropes (Knox), or speculate about the origins of language (Jamieson) or its relationship to thought (D. Hill), or describe the parameters of proper usage (A. S. Hill). Rhetorics can also differ surprisingly from each other even when one text is a compilation of another: books that largely copy Hugh Blair's account of figurative language, for example, sometimes define many more figures and tropes (Knox, Andrews, Boyd), though Blair explicitly rejects the value of long catalogues of tropes (see XIV, 156).

Instabilities in the field of rhetoric match these large- and small-scale differences across individual books. The discipline has ill-defined and variable boundaries, as several writers of the time emphasize. Whately, for example, notes the many competing definitions of rhetoric, and warns against supposing "that a general term has some real object, properly corresponding to it" or that "some one definition is to be found which will comprehend every thing that is rightly designated by that term" (Introduction, London/Cambridge, Mass., edition). John Genung writes that fields as old as rhetoric "need from time to time to be newly defined and distributed, their perspective and emphasis need to be freshly determined, to suit changing conditions of thought" (*Practical,* xi). One fundamentally altered condition of thought across the nineteenth century is the growing importance of written media, which informs a sharpened pedagogical focus on writing, often to the exclusion of speech and oratory. Rhetoric reconfigures its inquiry in part because of emerging transformations of print culture—such complex social developments as increasing literacy rates, the growth of new genres and writing practices, and the inclusion of new groups, especially women, in advanced instruction in reading and writing and emerging arenas of public discourse.

Though nineteenth-century rhetorical instruction never quite abandons longstanding goals of preparing men for politics, the law, or the pulpit, its textbooks redistribute attention onto a range of new discursive skills and occasions in response to changing cultures of literacy. In the process, the organization of the rhetorical field—its canons, theoretical principles, and articulation with other practices—substantively changes. Nineteenth-century rhetorics do not treat some traditional topics—the topoi of classical invention, for example, or memory—while they address subjects that had been, or will become, the province of other forms of literacy instruction—of grammars, readers, philology, literary criticism, and literary history. Rhetorical instruction, moreover, is so distributed across an array of pedagogical genres that it is not always possible to identify cleanly or unproblematically a rhetoric from other texts on language use. The archive of nineteenth-century rhetoric, in short, has a messy architecture. As its edifice is reconstructed from decade to decade, barriers separate discursive arenas that had long shared theoretical and instructional programs; new networks of influence and investigation open passages between previously discrete areas; modules are replicated at different sites and gain new meanings, uses, or functions; and new additions are grafted onto existing structures.

Nineteenth-century rhetorics published in the United States only seem to constitute a field with clear chronological and national boundaries. Many distinctive features of these books emerge elsewhere, in classical rhetorics, Quintilian in particular, and in eighteenth-century Scottish writings by Hugh Blair, George Campbell, and Lord Kames. *Elements of Rhetoric* by Richard Whately, Archbishop of Dublin, is very influential from 1832, and the Scottish academic Alexander Bain contributes decisively, though on a smaller scale, to late-nineteenth-century rhetorics. Works by these (and other) British writers circulated long and widely in the States, and many of the commonplace concerns and principles of nineteenth-century U.S. rhetorics—a preeminent concern with style, for example, or a reliance on a psychology of separate faculties in which appeals to the will, or the understanding, or the passions call for different rhetorical strategies—are first formulated in these British texts.

Something more and something different than a shared epistemological or ideological investment is involved here. Intricate webs of influence, derivation, and repetition traverse the field of Anglo-American rhetoric. Throughout the century, most rhetorics selectively reproduce earlier texts more than they develop a substantively original perspective. They copy or redact long passages; freely adapt common topics, leading principles, and foundational arguments; and combine positions first articulated by diversely situated writers. This practice of *compilation* has received little attention, though it is a characteristic and noteworthy feature of the archive. Critics, to be sure, have long noted appropriations of Hugh Blair, though they rarely distinguish conceptual indebtedness from wholesale copying. The recycling of passages from other writers is less often remarked, and many rhetorics (e.g., Jamieson, Boyd, or Quackenbos) are treated as if they were independently authored books with some derivative ideas and not full-scale redactions of earlier texts. I understand compilation as a general *practice of writing* across the archive of nineteenth-century rhetorics. This mode of production significantly inflects the shape and development of its textbook tradition. It conserves certain topics or principles that are endlessly repeated: even at century's end, substantial sections of new rhetorics still rehearse arguments sometimes codified more than a hundred years earlier. It mixes and redistributes materials from disparate locations, bringing ideas and routines into new relationships with one another and isolating them from their originary emergence. Over time, frequently compiled materials become the common intellectual property of the tradition, the lore or common sense of the discipline.

When new ideas and instructional practices emerge, they are quickly taken up, reworked, and disseminated in other rhetorics. A distinctive tradition of rhetorical studies did indeed develop in the States across the nineteenth century, one that characteristically seeks to elaborate *practical* forms of inquiry and instruction. This national tradition, however, is always an appropriation and sometimes an active revision of earlier classical and British texts. Nineteenth-century U.S. rhetorics, that is, are always *hybrid texts,* their projects at least doubly inflected by an earlier articulation of a rhetorical principle or topic and its subsequent emergence in a new format, with varying degrees of revision, and with newly forged connections to affiliated discourses and instructional practices.

Adjacent Traditions

Nineteenth-century U.S. rhetorics develop primarily as a textbook tradition oriented toward instruction in written discourse. The characteristic concerns of rhetorics, however, are always inflected by changes in other affiliated theoretical and pedagogical practices, as functions or topics are redistributed throughout the century across different textbook traditions. *Readers,* for example, displace rhetorics as the primary textbooks for instruction not only in oral delivery but also in textual interpretation and analysis. At least in some venues, *composition books* supplant rhetorics as the instructional materials most immediately involved in training students to produce discourse. Such books pressure rhetorics to be "practical," to move from relatively abstract descriptive categories to readily applied precepts, and from the 1830s, many rhetorics include, with different degrees of sophistication, various writing exercises, topics for themes, and advice for student writers. Over time, categorical distinctions between the two fields become increasingly blurred. Other new or newly configured textbook traditions likewise have a tangled relationship with rhetoric. Developments in three affiliated areas—speech and oratory, letters (especially, but not exclusively, literature), and grammar—are especial important to the changing concerns of the textbook tradition in rhetoric.

Speech and Oratory. Over the course of the nineteenth century, speech and writing increasingly become discrete objects of study with separate textbook traditions. This is an intermittent and uneven development. Works by earlier writers like Blair and Campbell that attend to both speech and writing remain in instructional use through the 1880s. A few rhetorics retain oratory as their starting point and primary reference. Francis Theremin's *Eloquence a Virtue* (1850), translated from the German by W. G. T. Shedd, is an interesting philosophical treatise in which a focus on the figure of the orator informs an argument about the centrality of ethics to effective discourse, and Matthew Boyd Hope adapts Theremin in his expository textbook, *The Princeton Text Book in Rhetoric* (1859). A scattering of nineteenth-century rhetorics—by Whately, Henry Day, or John Bascom, for example—likewise imagine oratory as the paradigmatic occasion of discourse, but their arguments are ultimately as much addressed to writing as to speech. A few—Bardeen, Hepburn, De Mille—devote a long chapter or section to oratory. But most rhetorics, and especially the most widely circulating textbooks—those by Alexander Jamieson, Samuel Newman, James Boyd, G. P. Quackenbos, David Hill, John Hart, Alexander Bain, Adams Sherman Hill, Brainerd Kellogg, John Genung, Barrett Wendell, and others—ignore oratory entirely or treat it briefly as one of many genres of discourse.

Distinct textbook traditions develop around different aspects of speech and oratory. Homiletics, for example, or the eloquence of the pulpit, is a traditional topic of advanced rhetorics, and sermons are still studied through the early nineteenth century in Blair, Campbell, John Witherspoon, and John Quincy Adams. But with a few exceptions (Whately, Edward Channing, A. D. Hepburn), pulpit oratory increasingly became the sole concern of a discrete—and flourishing—textbook tradition. Widely circulating books on homiletics leave almost no citational track in more general rhetorics and have no direct effect on their theoretical programs. Such books, in turn, have only an occasional general indebtedness to other rhetorical traditions. The most frequently printed homiletic rhetoric in the United States, John Broadus's *A Treatise on the Preparation and Delivery of Sermons* (1870), analyzes style in terms of perspicuity, energy, and elegance, a conventional taxonomy derived from Whately, but otherwise does not directly borrow from the mainstream.[2] Like Broadus, Austin Phelps in *The Theory of Preaching* (1881) focuses so much on homiletic form—he devotes six lectures to the sacred text that begins a sermon—that he draws little from other kinds of rhetorics. Phelps's somewhat more generic rhetoric, *English Style in Public Discourse with Special Reference to the Usages of the Pulpit* (1883), does rehearse commonplace notions of purity, precision, and energy ultimately derived from Blair, Campbell, and Whately, but its specific arguments are very much tied to the circumstances of the sermon.

Elocution—understood as the theory and practice of oral performance[3]—may be even more isolated from rhetorics of written discourse. It was a distinct province of rhetoric in eighteenth-century Britain, and central works in this tradition by Thomas Sheridan or John Walker are reprinted into the nineteenth century in the States. Some early American elocutionary textbooks further elaborate concepts from British elocutionary theory. Ebenezer Porter's *Analysis of the Principles of Rhetorical Delivery* (1827), for example, addresses standard topics of articulation, accent, emphasis, and the like, in a familiar though not derivative manner. But American texts also develop new directions in the representation and analysis of speech, most importantly in James Rush's *The Philosophy of the Human Voice* (1827). Elocutionary texts flourish throughout the century, not only in enormous numbers of elocutionary readers but also in frequently printed analytical or theoretical accounts of oral performance. *Orthophony, or Vocal Culture* (1845), compiled by William Russell on the basis of Rush's theories, may be the most widely circulating of these texts, claiming an eighty-second edition by 1900.[4] But even such an oft-printed text receives no notice in rhetorics of written discourse. Indeed, very few nineteenth-century rhetorics discuss elocution. Blair is unusual in devoting an entire lecture (derived from Sheridan) to pronunciation. Three rhetorics issued a single time, by Samuel Willard, Ebenezer Porter (1836), and Matthew Hope, seek a fuller articulation of elocutionary and rhetorical concerns; three other rhetorics, by Henry Coppée, A. D. Hepburn, and E. O. Haven, more briefly rehearse some elocutionary commonplaces. Whately famously denounces artificial systems of elocutionary training, and most later rhetorics silently concur with this perspective.[5]

An indirect commerce across instructional fields may well exist without citations or cross-influences in textbook traditions. Most students probably studied both elocution and rhetoric in different classes or levels of instruction. Several rhetorics address stylistic qualities of harmony, or euphony, or the interplay of sound and sense, which can be closely allied with elocutionary concerns. Attention to the oral performance of written texts, moreover, can establish feedback loops that promote writing suitable to be read aloud. Yet whatever informal connections survive, the increasing isolation of various branches of rhetoric impoverishes them all.

Once the traditional rhetorical task of moving audiences to ethical action is redistributed specifically to homiletics, for example, other rhetorics need not attend to the civic goals of discourse. Similarly, privileging delivery over composition risks turning elocution into theatrics, while ignoring delivery diminishes an awareness of discourse as a performative action. I am struck by the way rhetorics from mid-century on explicitly define writing as single-mindedly oriented to the efficient communication of information, excluding from consideration the varied purposes and occasions of writing. (A student essay, for example, is always an act that fulfills an assignment, and this condition structures its discourse as much as its tactics of presentation.)[6]

Letters. The split within rhetorical study between oral and written discourse as the object of study responds in part to the increasing cultural value and social importance of written discourse of all types within an expanding print culture. Rhetorics are involved with letters in several ways. Throughout the century, most rhetorics use passages from leading British and American authors to illustrate various qualities of writing. Many rhetorics also discuss prosody or versification, often as part of a survey of discursive genres in the vernacular that may include poetry and novels as well as nonfiction prose. And on occasion, rhetorics may discuss taste, or the goals of criticism, or the relationship of aesthetics to rhetoric, or they may claim as part of their project fostering a critical appreciation of writing. These varied involvements with letters and literature are often characterized as "belletristic," though I do not think this a useful or accurate description of nineteenth-century rhetorics.

For one thing, the term is somewhat anachronistic. *Belles lettres* enters English from the French and was an accepted and useful term in the mid-eighteenth century. But by the early years of the nineteenth century, it was already a bit outmoded.[7] Some academic departments or professorships continue to use the term through mid-century, though it is always only one of several alternative ways of designating the field of study. Very few rhetorics use the term either in their title or as an important term of analysis. Indeed, only the extraordinary long-term popularity of Blair's *Lectures on Rhetoric and*

Belles Lettres underwrites the term within rhetorical study, and even in this case, most nineteenth-century abridgments of Blair drop "Belles Lettres" from their title.[8] *Belletristic,* moreover, is primarily a pejorative term, one used since the early nineteenth century to belittle a project and avoid acknowledging its ambitions. At times over the last few decades, it may have usefully served critical histories of the discipline of English as a polemical way of discrediting the past in order to contest the authority or prestige of literary study in the contemporary academy. But a tendentious term like *belletristic,* especially one with only limited authorization in historical usage, tends to obscure the complex actual uses of letters and literature in rhetorical instruction.

Consider, for example, what is often taken as a defining element of "belletristic" rhetoric, a preeminent concern with taste. Blair does indeed devote a single lecture to taste, offering a complex appreciation and synthesis of writing on the topic current when Blair first lectured at the University of Edinburgh in the mid-eighteenth century. At that time, taste was a commonplace topic of advanced critical discussion, but leading critical intellectuals had largely moved on to other issues even before the first publication of the *Lectures.* Blair preserves taste as a subject of rhetorical instruction in the academy, and several nineteenth-century rhetorics address the topic, usually by more or less close redactions of Blair's arguments, supplemented at times by passages compiled from other eighteenth-century writers. But it is not a topic that stimulates new thought. Moreover, only a smattering of frequently issued rhetorical textbooks—by Jamieson, Newman, Quackenbos, Coppée—address taste at any length, and only in Newman does it have an importance place in the overall argument.[9] It is, in effect, a minor and largely residual category of analysis across the archive.

Another feature attributed to belletristic rhetoric, the use of passages from leading British and American authors to illustrate rhetorical principles, has more complicated functions or effects than generally acknowledged. This practice, of course, has a long lineage—Quintilian describes the use of models drawn from the best writers in classical rhetorical instruction—and nineteenth-century rhetorics extend this tradition primarily by citing very recent writers. They use these passages as a pedagogical strategy to clarify general or abstract principles: as John Genung notes, "the best way to discern whether a rhetorical principle is true and practical is to study its effect in the concrete" (*Practical* xii). But rhetorics do not explicitly instruct students to imitate "literary" passages in their own writing. Indeed, passages from well-known authors are often used to demonstrate inappropriate or incorrect usage, a strategy popularized in Bishop Lowth's *A Short Introduction to Grammar* (1762) and deployed at length in influential rhetorics by Henry Day, Adams Sherman Hill, and others. Moreover, though poetry and, increasingly, novels are quoted frequently, many other genres—biographies, travel books, sermons, periodical essays, political speeches, natural philosophy, and so on—are also cited.[10] "Literature," that is, has a far more encompassing range of reference than it came to have in the twentieth century, as several writers of rhetorics clearly state. Samuel Newman, for example, distinguishes literature only from science and includes in this class "Poetry and Fictitious Prose, Historical, Epistolary, and Essay writing" (1835, 67). "Literature" emerges as both a category of high cultural value and an increasingly important object of study across all levels of the curriculum in the nineteenth century. Rhetorics that deploy numerous illustrative passages from leading British and American authors may well participate in some way in this large-scale transformation of the orders of discourse and its ideological effects. I see, however, no simple or single consequence to the varied uses of texts drawn from a broad construction of letters.

"Literary" concerns that appear as ancillary projects in some early rhetorics—the education of taste, the survey of various genres, prosody—do not entirely disappear from later ones but are rarely given prominent attention. But other textbook traditions, especially readers, are more consistently oriented toward literature. After 1840, there is a proliferation of anthologies and surveys of various national traditions, such as Rufus Griswold's *The Poets and Poetry of America* (1842), *The Prose Writers of America* (1846), and *The Female Poets of America* (1849), Thomas B. Shaw's *Outlines of English Literature*

(1849), and many others. Several writers of rhetorics also produce literary textbooks, such as Henry Day's *Introduction to the Study of Literature* (1866), John S. Hart's *Manual of English Literature* (1872) and *Manual of American Literature* (1872), and Henry Coppée's various anthologies. I take it as a sign of the redistribution and specialization of interest in "literary" matters that such books offer no explicit articulation with the arguments of their writers' rhetorics but pursue another kind of project.

Grammars. Rhetoric and grammar have long been understood as affiliated language arts, and Quintilian canonically establishes grammar as a necessary preliminary to rhetorical study. In the eighteenth and nineteenth centuries, the relationship becomes more tangled. Many widely used rhetorics discuss grammatical topics. Sometimes, this involves a principled discussion about the grounds of linguistic correctness: George Campbell's reflections in book 2 of *The Philosophy of Rhetoric* (1776) on proper usage and his canons or rules for deciding questions about proper usage are endlessly recycled in later rhetorics. Other times, even leading advanced rhetorics survey basic grammatical rules and definitions as well as examples of incorrect usage.

Many grammars, in turn, print substantive excerpts from leading rhetoricians. The American editions of John Walker's *Rhetorical Grammar,* for example, reprint selections from Ward and Priestly on invention and from Blair on style in an appendix. Lindley Murray's immensely popular *English Grammar* (1795), which had several hundred U.S. versions in various formats, usually ends with an appendix that combines a few precepts and examples drawn from Campbell with an extensive redaction of Blair on style and figurative language. Numerous other grammars across the century follow Murray's example and offer a highly abridged version of Blair and Campbell and sometimes other leading rhetorics. Such uses are of course derivative, and any single appropriation in itself is hardly significant. Yet collectively, across hundreds of issues of dozens of grammars, such adaptations forge links across genres of literacy instruction that make the association of grammar and rhetoric a normative expectation. These grammars are, for example, among the genealogical forebears of today's rhetorical handbooks, combining rules of correct usage with highly condensed advice on writing. Moreover, their condensed versions of leading rhetorics sometimes articulate significant new conceptual connections. Murray's incorporation of Campbell's arguments on usage with Blair's account of style is, I believe, the first time these two rhetoricians were presented as an integrated argument, and this synthesis is perhaps the most widespread and enduring component of nineteenth-century rhetorics.

These adjacent traditions establish a background against which developments in nineteenth-century rhetorics occur. This textbook tradition selectively appropriates and redeploys the writings of Hugh Blair, George Campbell, and Richard Whately through practices of compilation. Over time, other writers, both British and, increasingly, American, make substantive theoretical and pedagogical contributions and significantly redirect the leading concerns of the entire tradition. For several reasons, I divide the century roughly into thirds. I want, in part, to foreground changes in the publishing and marketing of books, especially the movement from a local production and use at the beginning of the century, to a national circulation at mid-century, and then to a market increasingly stratified into specialized niches after the Civil War. Several significant changes in rhetorics derive, I believe, from altered material circumstances of production and distribution, as such conditions interact with theoretical and pedagogical developments. I also seek to determine which rhetorics were in wide circulation at different times, based largely on the number of versions printed across a span of years. This is an inexact measure, since publication totals can vary greatly due to local and somewhat arbitrary publishing policies, such as, for example, the decision either to date each new printing of a stereotyped edition or to issue it silently. Yet if precise comparative judgments of circulation are difficult to attain, a more general sense of which books flourish, and when, can clarify the emerging historical trends in the discipline.[11]

Several of the best and most influential historical studies of the last twenty-five years have focused on the ways a particular topic has been treated across the field of nineteenth-century rhetoric.

Sharon Crowley, for example, studies invention (*Methodical*), while Robert Connors examines discourse taxonomies, or style, or grammatical correctness (*Comp-Rhet*). Alternatively, Nan Johnson elaborates underlying theoretical commitments and their persistence across the field of nineteenth-century rhetoric. Such studies inevitably pay less attention to the projects of individual textbooks, to the tactical importance of an argument or topic within a book, or to changes in normative practices at different times. In this chapter, I want to mark the differences that structure the intricacies of the archive. What books flourished, when, and in what formats? How are they organized? What topics do they treat? What gets special attention or prominence? What is ignored, or treated perfunctorily? What is distinctive, or conventional, or characteristic about rhetorics at different times?

Blair and His Echoes: 1800–1830

Hugh Blair massively dominates rhetorical theory and instruction in the early-nineteenth-century United States. The first U.S. edition of *Lectures on Rhetoric and Belles Lettres* comes out a year after the first London edition of 1783, and new editions appear at least every several years for the next century. It is the only rhetoric of the time to approach a national circulation, achieved through the local publication of many versions with small but overlapping systems of distribution. From 1802 through 1830, Blair's treatise appears in some twenty-six complete versions and fifty-one abridgements, far outpacing the combined printings of all other rhetorics then circulating in the States.[12] *Lectures on Rhetoric and Belles Lettres,* moreover, remained in wide use until the 1880s. It is also copied, redacted, quoted, and silently paraphrased in most later rhetorics and in the educational apparatus of many readers and composition books as well. Clearly, Blair substantively influences nineteenth-century rhetorical instruction in the States. Yet his influence is never monolithic. Various parts of the *Lectures* are selectively appropriated: some sections become, in effect, canonical formulations of a topic and are endlessly recycled; some leave little or no wake of citation and use.

Blair's *Lectures,* that is, may be ubiquitous, but its meanings vary depending on which of its aspects are subsequently redeployed.

Lectures on Rhetoric and Belles Lettres is a far more interesting and complex book than its generally dismissive critical reputation might suggest. Its introduction identifies five major divisions that examine in turn "the nature of taste," a "consideration of language," "style," "eloquence" (or "public speaking"), and "a critical examination of the most distinguished species of composition." Each section is remarkably self-contained: concepts or arguments developed in early lectures are not systematically deployed in later ones, nor does Blair explicitly develop any synthetic framework to integrate the varied topics he treats. He offers no master definition of either rhetoric or belles lettres, for example, and indeed these terms rarely even appear in the body of the text. His introduction often substitutes other terms—"writing and discourse," "language, style, and composition," "the arts of speech and writing," and "eloquence and composition"—to name his object of study, which reflects, I believe, a tacit understanding of the field as a set of allied arts, no one of which has any intrinsic privilege over the others. The book is composed, in effect, of relatively discrete modules, and when later rhetorics return to the *Lectures,* they can adopt a single module without regard for any larger ensemble of concerns.

Yet a recurrent set of strategies and attitudes unifies this book. Blair regularly moves from simple to more complex elements (e.g., from words, to sentences, to qualities of prose, to genres). He approaches topics historically, not only in surveying various oral and written genres from early to contemporary examples, but in conceptualizing the parts of speech, for example, or figurative language in relation to historical and developmental processes. Far more than later rhetorics, Blair regularly cites sources, analogues, influences, and alternative positions. Most importantly, the book retains its original format as spoken lectures, marking Blair's individual relationship to the argument in passages that foreground their emergence from a particular person at a certain occasion. Blair frequently uses the first-person pronoun, for example, or self-reflexively cites his prose in illustration of an argument (as in the opening paragraph on the pervasiveness of metaphor [XV, 158]), or pointedly treats a key concept as a provisional claim dependent on its contextual argument (as in his account of taste [II, 16–17] or definition of style [X, 101–2]). Most redactions of Blair abandon this strategy of presentation for a more dogmatic instruction oriented toward a decontextualized assertion of rules or principles.

The first section (II–V) investigates taste and affiliated concepts of criticism, genius, sublimity, and beauty. Its account of taste is more supple than is usually credited.[13] Blair identifies taste as an innate faculty or sensibility, for example, yet argues at length on the value of reason and critical reflection in clarifying, rectifying, and extending judgments of taste. He believes in a standard of taste but argues that "the tastes of men may differ very considerably as to their object, and yet none of them be wrong" (II, 22) and doubts that "there is any standard of taste, to which, in every circumstance, we can resort for clear and immediate determination" (II, 25). He suggests that critical appreciation can be a means of personal and ethical improvement but argues there is no necessary connection between "the improvement of taste and of virtue" (I, 15). Blair is clearly interested in taste, that is, but his complicated appreciation of its vagaries means that it offers him no readily specifiable consequences for the production or reception of any individual discourse.

Blair's account of language (VI–IX) addresses the origin of speech and writing and the emergence of parts of speech. His arguments are based not on philological research, but on what I would call an "imaginary anthropology": like many eighteenth-century philosophers of language, that is, he constructs a scenario of the state of primitive man and infers a plausible developmental process, drawing occasionally on classical languages to flesh out an argument. Thus, he imagines that a savage desiring fruit would start an utterance with a word designating the object of that desire, not the English order of "give me fruit," but "fruit give me," and links this with the structure of Latin and other supposedly ancient or primitive languages, including Greek, Russian, and Gaelic. Blair's orientation allows him to understand language as a historical human creation subject to change. Blair is noncommittal or equivocal about the supposed divine origin of language, which other rhetorics through mid-century piously advocate (see, for example, Boyd, Trench, Coppée, Haven). His historical focus provides a narrative framework to discuss the parts of speech, and not the unmotivated taxonomy found in the "Etymology" section of most eighteenth- and nineteenth-century grammars. Yet this section probably exerts the least influence on subsequent rhetorics: Blair's arguments quickly become outdated, and rhetorics that attend to the history of language draw on the new findings of comparative linguistics and philology.

The section on style (X–XXV) is the longest and most influential part of the book. Blair first analyses stylistic "perspicuity" at the level of diction via the alliterative trio of "purity, propriety, and precision": most nineteenth-century rhetorics adapt this analysis, often closely following Blair's language. He recognizes unity, strength, and harmony as sentence-level qualities of style, and again later textbooks frequently redact this analysis. Blair next focuses on figurative language or "ornament." Like other eighteenth-century writers—Anthony Blackwall in *An Introduction to the Classics* (1718), for example, or Lord Kames in *Elements of Criticism* (1762)—he avoids long catalogues of figures and tropes. He primarily discusses metaphor, allegory, hyperbole, personification, apostrophe, simile, antithesis, interrogation, exclamation, vision, and amplification and treats metonymy, metalepsis, and synecdoche more briefly. Blair's enumeration is the definitive analysis of figurative language for nineteenth-century rhetorics. Most later textbooks discuss the same figures with only minor additions or changes.

Blair characterizes prose through an elaborate series of critical terms, avoiding a coherent taxonomy in favor of several lines of analysis: "diffuse, concise, feeble, and nervous" refer to qualities of thought; "dry, plain, neat, elegant, and flowery" to degrees of ornament; "simple and affected" to authenticity; and "vehement" to vigor. This complex system may be unwieldy and abstract, but it is an innovative attempt to move beyond classical typologies of high, low, and mixed styles toward a more nuanced set of analytic descriptors. A few later rhetorics adopt some of these terms, but most propose a simpler, more uniform system of stylistic analysis.

The section ends with sentence-by-sentence critiques of four essays by Addison and one by Swift. These remarkable analyses are among Blair's most original contributions to rhetorical instruction. They focus on the perspicuous use of language at the level of diction and sentence structure: they seek, that is, to make language maximally transparent to thought by resolving any potential ambiguity of grammar or meaning. Blair's critique, then, is not so much aesthetic as epistemological. He avoids most issues of content or context and descends, at times, into fussy objections over grammatical minutiae, but he also enacts a sustained critical relationship to prose balanced between the emendation and the appreciation of two of England's most esteemed stylists. A few later rhetorics (Andrews, Lacey, Boyd) reprint Blair's analysis of a single Addison essay, and Alexander Bain analyzes sixteen shorter excerpts in a similar sentence-by-sentence reading, but no other rhetoric attempts such a detailed close critical reading.[14]

The account of "eloquence" (XXV–XXXIV) focuses on the traditional oratorical sites of popular assemblies, the bar, and the pulpit and includes a close analysis of a sermon by Bishop Atterbury, then a preacher of some renown. The lecture on pronunciation (XXXIII), compiled from Sheridan's *Course of Lectures on Elocution* (1762), was often abridged in grammars and elocutionary readers by Lindley Murray and many others and is undoubtedly the most widely circulating feature of the *Lectures*. Blair is unusual in addressing the history, occasions, and strategies of eloquence in significant detail. Yet he has received little recognition for this, even though Campbell recommends these lectures in his book on pulpit eloquence.[15]

Blair's survey in the *Lectures* of various "species of composition" (XXXV–XLVII) is a distinctive feature of the book, and a sign of rhetoric's turn from oral to written discourse. Blair offers a historical analysis of an array of genres, including history, philosophy, fiction, drama, poetry, and letter writing, discussing both classical authors as well as near contemporary writers in several European languages. No subsequent rhetorical textbook attempts such an expansive survey of the field of writing, though a few (Newman, Boyd, Hart) include more narrowly focused accounts of various genres or national traditions. This type of survey is increasingly redistributed to other branches of study, especially to literary histories of various national traditions of letters.

Just as subsequent rhetorics used only certain portions of Blair, the lectures themselves were often read selectively. Occasionally, student annotations in a book mark what was read: in the table of contents of a 1789 Irish edition of Blair at Williams College, for example, small stars are placed next to VI–XIX and XXXI–XXXII, with a notation that these chapters on language, style and the structure of a discourse were "Learned by the class of '78." Information about such partial use is not systematically available, though college catalogues occasionally specify the relevant section of required books. In Blair's case, however, a different form of selective use can be readily traced, since he circulates far more widely in the States in abridged than in complete versions. Abridgments of the *Lectures* have received scant notice, yet there are at least one hundred U.S. printings of five substantively different abridged editions between 1788 and 1911. The most successful of these books is slightly revised and extended from the earlier British *Essays on Rhetoric* (1784) by Eliphalet Pearson for use at Harvard:[16] *An Abridgment of Rhetoric* (1802) appears over sixty times under this title, as well as another twenty-three times as *Dr. Blair's Essays on Rhetoric*. This version alters the complete *Lectures* in a similar way as other abridgments. It pervasively rewrites Blair's prose, combining and simplifying sentences, and drops all footnotes, most Latin and Greek quotations, and many illustrative examples (see fig. 1). These revisions lose the format of spoken lectures, especially Blair's characteristic strategies of presentation—the use of the first person, self-reflective moments, expressions of uncertainty or qualified judgments. They become dogmatic accounts of rules and principles, a tendency exacerbated by the universal inclusion after 1820 of various sets of questions that ask for the rote recall of sentences from the abridged text. However impoverished their version of Blair, these abridgments contribute massively to the material transmission and reproduction of his arguments. They are, in effect, an intermediate formation between Blair's specific formulations and the transformation of his positions into abstract precepts in later textbooks.

The most substantive British competitor to Blair's *Lectures,* George Campbell's *The Philosophy of Rhetoric* (1776), circulates surprisingly little in the United States during the early nineteenth century. Its full argument was minimally available, since it did not go into a second British printing until 1800, and the first American edition appeared only circa 1813.[17] Indeed, Campbell's posthumously published *Lectures on Systematic Theology and Pulpit Eloquence* (1807) is printed in the States in 1810, several years before the larger and now more familiar rhetorical treatise. A few selected aspects of *Philosophy* did circulate earlier and more widely, however, in grammars by Murray and others and in compilations by David Irving, Alexander Jamieson and the first generation of American-produced rhetorics. These texts are the first of many to redact Campbell's criteria for determining proper usage. In book 2 of *The Philosophy,* Campbell argues that normative use should be *"National,"* as opposed to foreign imports or regional, dialects; *"Present,"* as opposed to obsolete, terms; and *"Reputable,"* as opposed to vulgar or low, idioms. He also proposes nine methodological canons or rules for resolving uncertain cases. Thus, for example, his second canon—"In doubtful cases regard ought to be had in our decisions to the analogy of the language" (156)—recommends word forms and idioms that follow standard patterns of construction over more idiosyncratic formations.

Campbell's arguments about pure and proper usage are the most frequently adapted parts of his treatise in nineteenth-century rhetorics. They have received little critical attention—the theories of argument Campbell proposes in book 1 are now more celebrated[18]— but they are an early and sophisticated proposal for determining a standardized national language that is not immediately defined, at least in principle, by the interests of any one group or region. Campbell emphasizes, that is, methodological principles for deciding normative use: he does not appeal to an academy of experts or to the language of the court, a metropolitan center, or a social elite. His principles codify and rationalize the linguistic grounds of national identity. As they are disseminated across the archive of instructional texts, they rectify and strengthen a discursive structure that

——Ille impiger hausit
Spumantem paterem, et pleno se proluit auro,

where it is obvious, that the cup and gold are put for
the liquor, contained in the golden cup. The name
of a country is often used to signify its inhabitants.
To pray for the assistance of Heaven is the same with
praying for the assistance of God, who is in heaven.
The relation between a sign and the thing signified
is another source of tropes. Thus,

Cedant arma togæ ; concedat laurea linguæ.

Here the " toga," which is the badge of the civil professions, and the "laurel," that of military honours,
are each of them put for the civil and military characters themselves. Tropes, founded on these several
relations of cause and effect, container and contained,
sign and thing signified, are called by the name of
metonymy.

When a trope is founded on the relation between
an antecedent and its consequent, it is called a metalepsis; as in the Roman phrase, "fuit" or "vixit," to
signify that one was dead. "Fuit Ilium et ingens
gloria Teucrum," expresses that the glory of Troy
is no more.

When the whole is put for a part, or a part for the
whole ; a genus for a species, or a species for a genus ;
the singular number for the plural, or the plural for
the singular ; in general, when any thing less, or any
thing more, is put for the precise object meant ; the
figure is then termed a synecdoche. We say, for instance, " A fleet of so many sail," instead of so many
" ships," we frequently use the " head" for the " person," the " pole" for the " earth," the " waves" for the
" sea." An attribute is often used for its subject ;
as, " youth and beauty," for the " young and beautiful ;" and sometimes a subject for its attribute. But
the relation by far the most fruitful of tropes, is simi-
litude, which is the sole foundation of metaphor.

What are figures ?
How are they divided ?
What are the former called ?

Fig. 1. Highly condensed version of the end of Blair's Lecture
XIV, with questions, and the beginning of Lecture XV. *An
Abridgement of Lectures on Rhetoric.* Philadelphia, 1856, 82–83.

Give an example.
What is the origin of tropes ?
On what are they founded ?
Give some examples.
What is metonymy ?
What is metalepsis ?
What is synecdoche ?
Give examples.

METAPHOR.

METAPHOR is founded entirely on the resemblance which one object bears to another. It is, therefore, nearly allied to simile or comparison; and is indeed a comparison in an abridged form. When we say of a great minister, "he upholds the state, like a pillar, which supports the weight of an edifice," we evidently make a comparison; but, when we say of him, he is "the pillar of the state," it becomes a metaphor.

Of all the figures of speech, none approaches so near to painting, as metaphor. It gives light and strength to description; makes intellectual ideas in some degree visible, by giving them colour, substance, and sensible qualities. To produce this effect, however, a delicate hand is requisite; for by a little inaccuracy we may introduce confusion, instead of promoting perspicuity. Several rules, therefore, must be given for the proper management of metaphors.

The first rule respecting metaphors is, they must be suited to the nature of the subject; neither too numerous, nor too gay, nor too elevated for it; we must neither attempt to force the subject by the use of them into a degree of elevation not congruous to it; nor, on the contrary, suffer it to fall below its proper dignity. Some metaphors are beautiful in poetry, which would be unnatural in prose; some are graceful in orations, which would be highly improper in historical or philosophical composition. Figures are the dress of sentiment. They should consequently be adapted to the ideas which they are intended to adorn.

The second rule respects the choice of objects,

fosters a self-conscious appreciation of participation in what Benedict Anderson calls the "imagined community" of the nation. Anderson argues that the proliferation of texts under print-capitalism promotes a tacit recognition of social relationship among differently located readerships of the same vernacular.[19] Campbell also locates in print culture the implicitly defined linguistic common ground of a national culture, when he locates "reputable" usages in the practices of writers who have long circulated to general esteem. Campbell seeks to remove language policy from immediate sectarian interests—indeed, he specifies that living writers not be included in determining proper use—and in seeking a (comparatively) impartial standard, he articulates a theoretical rationale for rhetoric's frequent use of esteemed writers in the vernacular to illustrate its principles. The attention to style in most nineteenth-century rhetorics certainly reflects a deep interest in the choices individual writers make, but the widely circulating accounts of "Reputable," "National," and "Present" usage indicate as well a political investment in style as a mark of a national language and identity.

David Irving's *Elements of English Composition* (1801) appears in two American editions (1803, 1825) and is the first rhetoric to combine Blair's strictures on purity and propriety with Campbell's account of reputable, national and present usage. It is primarily a catechistic redaction of Blair on style. Its question and answer format reduces Blair to a set of precepts and definitions to be memorized, and so, like abridgements of Blair, in simplifying the *Lectures,* it also increases their schematic and dogmatic qualities. Campbell is only briefly discussed in Irving, but he has a more important position in Alexander Jamieson's *A Grammar of Rhetoric and Polite Literature* (1818), which has four American printings from 1820 to 1826.

Jamieson has an interesting relationship to the field of rhetoric. Though he also prepared abridgments of Campbell and Kames, he is neither a teacher nor a theorist of rhetoric but something like a professional textbook writer—among his many other publications are such titles as *Mechanics for Practical Men, A Treatise on the Construction of Maps, Elements of Algebra,* and *A Celestial Atlas*—and I take it that his work embodies an efficient practice of producing books across a number of fields rather than a commitment to any rhetorical theory or system. In the little critical notice he has received, Jamieson is usually treated as indebted in one way or another to Blair, but his book is actually a compilation not only of Blair but also of Campbell, William Barron's *Lectures on Rhetoric and Belles Lettres* (1806), Murray's *English Grammar,* and Lord Kames's *Elements of Criticism.*

A Grammar is divided into seven books, which examine the origins of language, general grammar, the structure of sentences, figures, taste, style, and poetry. It is the first nineteenth-century rhetoric printed in the U.S. to number its sections, all 632 of them, and to use different type fonts for less important passages. Later rhetorics frequently use typography for pedagogical purposes, but something more is involved in Jamieson. Though he stays close to the prose of his source texts, he systematically organizes their several arguments into leading statements or definitions (with key words in different typefaces) at the beginning of a section followed by passages in small type headed by variously named logical categories—analysis, observation, illustration, example, corollary, or scholium—many of which are cross referenced to other numbered sections (see fig. 2). Jamieson takes different arguments and turns them, in effect, into a single coherent position. His account of grammar in book 2, for example, unifies Barron's epistemological account of the parts of speech, Campbell's arguments about national, present and reputable use and his various canons for deciding correct usage, and Blair's historical attitude toward language and his account of precision.[20] Organizing and cross-referencing these diverse positions into a systematic rhetoric is, in many ways, a remarkable intellectual contribution to the ongoing consolidation of rhetoric as a systematic discipline.

The First American-Authored Rhetorics

The earliest nineteenth-century rhetorics published initially in the States are all written by teachers and emerge from local institutional use. I identify three types of rhetorics defined by conditions of authorship and modes of circulation. The first is a *commemorative rec-*

264. Of all the figures of speech, *none comes so near to painting as metaphor.* Its peculiar effect is to give light and strength to description ; to make intellectual ideas, in some sort, visible to the eye, by giving them colour, and substance, and sensible qualities. In order, however, to produce this effect, a delicate hand is required ; for, by a very little inaccuracy, we are in hazard of introducing confusion, in place of promoting perspicuity. *(Art.* 257.)

Illus. Several rules, therefore, are necessary to be given for the proper management of metaphor. But, before entering on these, we shall give one instance of a very beautiful metaphor, that we may shew the figure to full advantage. We shall take our instance from Lord Bolingbroke's Remarks on the History of England. Just at the conclusion of his work, he is speaking of the behaviour of Charles I. to his last parliament : " In a word," says he, " about a month after their meeting, he dissolved them ; and, as soon as he had dissolved them, he repented ; but he repented too late of his rashness. Well might he repent, for the vessel was now full, and this last drop made the waters of bitterness overflow."—" Here," he adds, " we draw the curtain, and put an end to our remarks."

Analysis. Nothing could be more happily thrown off. The metaphor, we see, is continued through several expressions. The *vessel is* put for the state or temper of the nation already *full,* that is, provoked to the highest by former oppressions and wrongs ; this *last drop,* stands for the provocation recently received by the abrupt dissolution of the parliament ; and the *overflowing of the waters of bitterness,* beautifully expresses all the effects of resentment let loose by an exasperated people.

Scholia. Nothing forms a more spirited and dignified conclusion of a subject, than a figure of this kind happily placed at the close. We see the effect of it in this instance. The author goes off with a good grace ; and leaves a strong and full impression of his subject on the reader's mind. A metaphor has frequently an advantage above a formal comparison. How much would the sentiment here have been enfeebled, if it had been expressed in the style of a regular simile, thus : " Well might he repent ; for the state of the nation, loaded with grievances and provocation, resembled a vessel that was now full, and this superadded provocation, like the last drop infused, made their rage and resentment, as waters of bitterness, overflow." It has infinitely more spirit and force as it now stands, in the form of a metaphor. " Well might he repent ; for the vessel was now full ; and this last drop made the waters of bitterness overflow."

265. The first rule to be observed in the conduct of metaphors, is, that they *be suited* to the *nature* of the subject of which we treat : *neither too many, nor too gay ; nor too elevated* for it ; that we neither attempt to *force the subject,* by means of them, into a degree of *elevation* which is not congruous to it ; nor, on the other hand, *allow it to sink* below its proper dignity. *(Art.* 258. *Illus.* 3.)

Illus. 1. This is a direction which belongs to all figurative language,

Fig. 2. Redacted version of the beginning of Blair's Lecture XV, "Metaphor," organized with subheadings. Alexander Jamieson, *A Grammar of Rhetoric and Polite Literature.* New Haven, 1826, 144.

ognition of influential teachers: such rhetorics are typically published posthumously, are issued infrequently, usually in a single edition, and are rarely cited in subsequent textbooks. The earliest example is John Witherspoon's *Lectures on Eloquence,* edited by Ashbel Green from the notes Witherspoon used to deliver his lectures at Princeton. It is issued posthumously in his collected writings (1800–1801) and as a single volume joined with his *Lectures on Moral Philosophy* in 1810. These lectures address many of the same topics as do Blair's— some reflections on the origins and structure of language; the sublime; the use and abuse of figures; the pulpit, the bar, and the senate; taste—though Witherspoon is somewhat more engaged with the civic purposes of oratory.[21] John Q. Adams's *Lectures on Rhetoric and Oratory* (1810) comes out some years after he resigned the Boylston Chair at Harvard. It largely reviews various classical positions on rhetoric, in accord with the statutes that established his professorship. Neither book has an appreciable effect on later rhetorics, though Adams is very occasionally cited.

A second type of early U.S. rhetorics is the *compilation,* which redacts earlier British texts for local use in instruction. Redactions of Blair, such as *Abridgment of Lectures on Rhetoric* (1802) or *A Compend of Rhetoric in Question and Answer* (1808), a catechistic textbook printed for use at the Schenectady Female Academy, could be taken as prototypical examples. But the first compiled rhetoric not primarily an abridgment of a single text is *A Compendious System of Rhetoric* (1809) by Samuel Knox, prepared "chiefly for the use of the students in Baltimore College" (iii) where he was the principal. It reworks Blair's sections on taste, genius, style, and figurative language and is more distantly indebted to Blair on the origins of language. Knox also includes several passages from John Holmes's *The Art of Rhetoric Made Easy* (1739), most notably his enumeration of the seven parts of a theme, and he reprints ninety-four rhymed couplets defining various figures from John Stirling's *A System of Rhetoric* (1733). *A Concise Treatise of Retoric* (1813) by Samuel Litch is also prepared for use at a specific institution. It provides a highly abridged redaction of Blair's introduction and his account of figures and tropes. The rest of the text is a grab-bag of assorted materials: it reprints a poem, "On Death, The Resurrection, and the Judgment;" a short section on punctuation (from various grammars); a brief catechism on language, the alphabet, and accent, emphasis, and cadence (common elocutionary topics); some "Necessary Grammatical Rules and Remarks"; and two poems by Litch, one addressed to his students in Jaffrey, New Hampshire.

Elements of Rhetorick and Belles Lettres (1813) by John Andrews, provost of the University of Pennsylvania, is a more substantial text, closer in ambition to the compilations by Irving and Jamieson than those of Knox and Litch. It is based on twenty years of teaching at Penn, but it is the first U.S. rhetoric that avowedly seeks an audience beyond its local institution. Andrews notes "that the quotations which are introduced from the Latin classicks, are followed by English translations; that the work may be as well adopted to English Schools, including Female Academies, as to Latin Schools, and those of a higher order" (vii). Appearing only in a single edition, the book evidently did not achieve a wider circulation, but its eclectic use of sources anticipates the strategy of more successful later rhetorics. The book is written in catechistic style and draws largely from Blair; Andrews also acknowledges debts to James Beattie, Irving, and Kames. The first of its four parts, "Elements of Style," reprises Blair on style and perspicuity and draws on his account of figurative language, though Andrews discusses more tropes and figures. "Of the Different Kinds of Style" restates Blair's taxonomy of prose style, adding "sublime" as another characteristic. "Of the Different Kinds of Prose Composition" reviews the same genres Blair does (in XXXV–XXXVII), adds a new chapter on the "popular essay," and discusses the parts of a discourse (from Blair, XXXI–XXXII). "Of Poetry" cites Blair's definition of poetry but replaces Blair's historical and generic survey for a moral and epistemological inquiry into the ends of poetry, based on James Beattie's *Elements of Moral Science* (1790). Appendices reprint material from Irving on grammatical mistakes (itself derived from Lowth's *Grammar*), Blair's analysis of Addison's first essay on the pleasures of the imagination, and some definitions of additional figures, again from Beattie.

It is easy to ignore or to disparage the work of compilation, but we should hesitate before dismissing such a widespread practice. Andrews, like Irving and Jamieson, selectively appropriates the work of earlier rhetoricians and rearticulates their theories in the interests of a new pedagogical project. Such compilers integrate distinct theoretical positions and concerns into a single system. Jamieson does this most fully and coherently, but even idiosyncratic texts like those of Knox or Litch contribute to the systematization of rhetorical thought by dispersing the particular location from which a specific formulation emerges. Nineteenth-century compilations, that is, are more than mechanical repetitions of their eighteenth-century sources; they actively rework that tradition, selectively reappropriating and refashioning older texts. They at once *amplify* and *narrow* the effects and influence of earlier rhetorics, transforming more fully and diversely elaborated arguments into a few memorable positions. Thus, Knox, Litch, and Andrews all mainly reproduce Blair on style, largely to the exclusion of his other concerns. They also *dispossess* arguments from earlier authors, diminishing the distinctive stylistic or conceptual qualities that might identify them with a specific historical and theoretical position. They thereby facilitate the production of doxa, or received opinion, of what has been said so often and at so many diverse locations that it hardly needs saying at all.

The third type of early U.S. rhetorics emerges in the late 1820s. Like the elocutionary texts that Porter and Rush published at this time, these rhetorics are individually authored texts that propose their own project, even though they remain indebted to British rhetorical thought. In *Rhetoric, or the Principles of Elocution and Rhetorical Composition* (1830), Samuel Willard refers readers to "Quinctillian, Lawson, Ward, Blair, Kaims, Campbell, and J. Q. Adams, from whom I have freely borrowed" (127), yet he subordinates these borrowings to his distinctive and unusual attempt to blend rhetoric and elocution. The first part of his book explains elocutionary strategies and principles in a similar manner to Porter's *Analysis of the Principles of Rhetorical Delivery* (1827); the second part reviews rhetorical principles, drawn more from Blair than other sources, but relates them innovatively to issues of "euphony" and "rhetorical intonation."

Samuel P. Newman's *A Practical System of Rhetoric* is the most consequential example of these rhetorics. Its earliest editions (especially 1827 and 1829) are substantively different from the better-known stereotyped edition of 1835,[22] and like other rhetorics of the time, they clearly emerge from use in the author's local institution, in Newman's case Bowdoin College. His 1827 preface, for example, refers to passages from "Pierpont's *American First Class Book,* which is in use in the Seminary with which he is connected" instead of printing a full range of illustrative examples. Again, like other early works, this book adopts Blair and Campbell in its major concepts as well as its treatment of several specific topics. Yet Newman writes very much in his own manner and departs from his sources in the organization, the phrasing, and, at times, the substance of his arguments. The first of five chapters, "On Thought as a Foundation of Good Writing," foregrounds thought over style for the first time in a U.S. rhetoric. "Taste" covers much the same ground as Blair did, though Newman specifically disagrees with Blair and defines taste as an act of judgment, not a condition of sensibility. "Of Literary Taste" proposes that good writing appeals to the primary laws of our nature, to familiar associations, and to qualities of fitness or adaptation. Newman draws on this analysis to discuss figurative language, starting not with the usual list of definitions but with elaborated critiques of numerous passages with more or less successful uses of figures. "On Skill in the Use of Language" adopts Campbell's account of grounds of proper usage and the canons for deciding questions of use. It also draws from Campbell's account of perspicuity in sentences (book 2, vi) and his analysis of connective words and phrases (3, iv and v). The final chapter, "On Style," follows Blair in discussing perspicuity, some qualities of style, and various genres of writing.

Even in these early editions, Newman adopts Blair and Campbell very selectively and departs at times from their formulations. His account of figurative language, for example, discusses only four of Blair's tropes—"Simile," "Metaphor," "Personification," and "Apostrophe"—and treats for the first time in a U.S. rhetoric "Allusion" as a figurative strategy. Newman, that is, has a critical relation to his sources, at times borrowing their positions and other times developing his own. He consistently reorients their arguments, moreover, by newly deriving familiar principles through the close reading of illustrative examples. His critical appropriation of British theory marks the emergence of a new disposition to the study of rhetoric in the States.

Contesting the Field: 1831–1865

The circulation of rhetorics in the middle years of the nineteenth century is far more complicated and competitive than earlier. Blair's *Lectures* remains the most widely circulating rhetoric, with over forty abridged and two dozen complete versions appearing in the States in these years. Yet it no longer solely defines the field: at least eight other rhetorics—by Jamieson, Campbell, Whately, Newman, Boyd, G. P. Quackenbos, Day, and Coppée—have ten or more issues in these years (or for those published after 1850, within two decades of their first edition). In this flourishing market, new rhetorics are produced less for immediate use at a local institution than for wide adoption across the nation. In the process, idiosyncratic textbooks, such as Knox's or Litch's rhetorics, are supplanted by books that systematically cover familiar topics of the field. Eighteenth-century Scottish rhetorical theory still largely informs the grounds of instruction, but there are significant conceptual developments, such as Whately's innovations in the theory of argument and a new attention to invention in the work of Henry Day and others. Textbooks also develop a more sophisticated pedagogical presentation. Catechistic formats nearly disappear, and most new rhetorics adopt a typographical layout that highlights leading rules and definitions and include various exercises, questions for review, or lists of writing assignments. Even Blair appears in a "stereotyped university, college, and school edition" prepared by Abraham Mills, which has extensive questions and outlines after most lectures, an unusual feature for an advanced rhetoric though common in elementary textbooks.

British Rhetorics in the States

Several British books are among those that contest Blair's preeminence in rhetorical instruction. New printings of the stereotyped fourth edition (1826) of Jamieson's *Grammar of Rhetoric* appear almost yearly from 1830 to the mid-1850s, as this textbook becomes one of the most widely circulating nineteenth-century rhetorics in the States. From the mid-1830s, Campbell's *The Philosophy of Rhetoric* is issued nearly as often in the States as Blair's complete *Lectures*. Its more frequent publication coincides with greater use in other rhetorics of Campbell's theories of argument in book 1 and his analysis in book 3 of qualities of diction, figurative language, and grammar that contribute to vivacity, or stylistic liveliness. Whately's *Elements of Rhetoric* (1828) reworks many of these topics and may have fostered an interest in other aspects of the *Philosophy* beyond its account of pure and proper usage.

Kames's *Elements of Criticism* circulates widely in school editions edited by Abraham Mills (1833) and James Boyd (1855) as well as in John Frost's abridgment (1831). Kames's book is difficult to classify. Some of its topics—its account of tropes, for example, or discussion of wit and humor—often appear in nineteenth-century rhetorics. It is sometimes included in a course of rhetorical study, or cited as an influential source. Yet it primarily focuses on the mental processes associated with aesthetic response and critical judgment. Its peculiar reemergence as a steady seller seventy years after its initial publication may well be tied to the proliferation of other instructional texts in literature and suggests that by the 1840s, what may be broadly construed as "literary" topics were redistributed away from a specifically rhetorical instruction.

In 1832, the first American edition of Whately's *Elements of Rhetoric* appears to immediate success: *Elements* roughly matches the circulation of all versions of Blair over the rest of the century. Whately focuses on "Argumentative Composition," though he touches upon other uses or qualities of discourse. Virtually all treatments of argument in later rhetorics derive from Whately's theories. Part 1, "Of the Invention, Arrangement, and Introduction of Propositions and Arguments," surveys various methods of producing rational conviction. Whately discusses various logical processes and topics, but he is especially astute about strategies that appeal to the understanding without requiring demonstrative certainty. His account of "Testimony" (1, ii, 4), for instance, discusses the effect of a witness's character on whether a claim will be accepted, and the special value of information given without apparent understanding or belief. Similarly, part 2, "Of Persuasion," examines appeals to the will that cannot be reduced to logical compulsion, giving special attention to the character and modes of self-presentation of a speaker in relation to various audiences. Whately's paradigmatic model of discourse is oratory, especially as performed at the traditional locations of public assemblies, the bar and the pulpit. A section on "Presumption and Burden of Proof" (1, iii, 2) is affiliated with legal argument, for example, and an analysis of "Exhortation" (2, ii, 1) refers to the delivery of sermons. His attention to the extralogical components of argument may reflect an awareness of the social contexts of oratorical performance. It distinguishes his theory of argument from Campbell's, which also discriminates between the conviction of the understanding and the persuasion of the will, and which similarly examines the evidentiary uses of experience, testimony, analogy, and the calculation of chances. Whately often cites Campbell, but his ideas on argument do not derive from the *Philosophy of Rhetoric* so much as they are in dialogue with that text.

Part 3 analyses style in terms of perspicuity, energy, and elegance, a simple taxonomy that many later rhetorics adopt, even though much of this section is not particularly original. Whately's account of perspicuity and energy, for example, depends significantly on Campbell's treatment of vivacity; he has little to say, or to recommend, about elegance. Yet there are interesting qualities in this section. Whately proposes the innovative idea that there are discourses in which "some *different* End is proposed" than convincing or persuading (3, i, 4). Whately draws upon Campbell's account of sophistry (*Philosophy*, 2, vii, 1) but quickly goes beyond specious attempts to persuade, and discusses speech or writing that merely displays eloquence or, even more surprisingly, seeks only to occupy time. It is a very rare, and perhaps unique, recognition in nineteenth-century rhetorics of nonserious discourse, of performances that do not just fail to communicate effectively but that refuse the goal of communication. Whately's reflections on this topic mark, I believe, a lost opportunity in nineteenth-century rhetoric, one to which we might now usefully return to consider anew the obsessive concern in most school rhetorics to the present day with functional discourse oriented only toward a unified and practical goal. Part 4, "Of Elocution," recognizes the importance of oral performance but skeptically questions the validity of artificial systems of elocution whose elaborate instructions vitiate the unselfconsciousness Whately recommends.

Elements of Rhetoric expands considerably over the years, and there are significant differences between the two most frequently printed American editions, one deriving from the third London edition (1830), the other from the considerably larger seventh London (1846). Many of the additions extend the substance of Whately's ideas on argument or style, by further elaborating a topic like "Analogy" (1, ii, vii) or by treating a new component such as "Deference" (1, iii, 2). An appendix printed for the first time in the third edition extends Whately's treatment of various topics by reprinting extracts from other writers, including Campbell; it doubles in size by the seventh edition. Other changes reflect, I believe, a developing appreciation of the book's use in rhetorical education. U.S. printings derived from the seventh London edition translate classical quotations, generally moving Latin and Greek passages to footnotes; this revision implies an awareness of a differently educated and larger audience, including women. A new section on "Debating-Societies" responds ambivalently to a popular collegiate activity that functioned alongside the official curriculum; in conjunction with an existing section on the problems and possibilities of "Composition Exercises," Whately's reflections on debating show some self-consciousness about his book's status as a staple of college instruction. His *Elements* lacks the pedagogical apparatus of most rhetorical textbooks but also departs from the presumption of most treatises that they primarily address other advanced thinkers. In this respect, it is a transitional text between an older, elite culture of rhetorical instruction and rhetoric's emerging location as a subject of study in a larger-scale educational system.

Another British import, Richard Chenivix Trench's *On the Study of Words* (1851) is, like Kames's *Elements,* not strictly a rhetoric, though this steady seller was often included in the collegiate study of rhetoric from the 1850s through 1910.[23] In six lectures, this peculiar and critically neglected book ruminates on the history of words, their derivations and changes. Trench represents an alternative tradition, one derived from the etymological speculations of Horne Tooke's *Diversions of Purley* (1786), but clarified by ongoing research in the history of the language. It is an interesting attempt to use philology to expand the terms of discussion about diction beyond restrictive notions of purity and propriety.

U.S. Rhetorics at Mid-Century

The number of American-authored rhetorics vastly expanded over these years, and many went into multiple printings. It is still possible to discern the three types of rhetorics from earlier in the century, though developments in rhetorical theory and instruction and changing material conditions of book production prompt some substantive transformations. Two commemorative rhetorics recognize significant teaching at influential institutions. *Lectures on Eloquence and Style* (1836) by Ebenezer Porter of the Andover Theological Seminary focuses on elocution and style. Edward Channing's *Lectures Read to the Seniors in Harvard College* (1856) appears posthumously years after his 1851 retirement from the Boylston Chair of Rhetoric and Oratory. This text does not propose a coherent course of studies but prints a selection of lectures on various oratorical, literary, and rhetorical topics. Porter's elocutionary textbooks had an enormous circulation; Channing taught many influential writers and orators who acknowledge his influence. Their commemorative rhetorics, however, like those of Witherspoon and Adams, have little or no impact on the rhetorical textbook tradition.

Compilations remained an important segment of the American market. Some were still linked to local institutions and teachers and had only a limited circulation. William B. Lacey's *Illustrations of the*

Principles of Rhetorick (1834) derives from his teaching at the Western Female Collegiate Institute in Western Pennsylvania. Though he claims his work is not a compilation, its substance is almost entirely taken from the rhetorics of Blair and Jamieson and from Murray's *English Grammar.* The five chapters of the first part of his book treat "Perspicuity," "Precision," "Propriety," "Harmony," and "Figures of Speech." Lacey transforms his sources into rules, adds questions at the bottom of the page, and offers some illustrative examples. The second part is mostly a close redaction of Blair's opening lectures. Another single-issued textbook is Eustace Ansley's *Elements of Literature* (1849), which is compiled from two French rhetorics; its section on figures may also derive in part from Blair, at least as a source for illustrative examples.

James A. Getty's *Elements of Rhetoric* (1831) is perhaps the most peculiar and interesting compilation produced in the nineteenth-century States. The body of its text is largely drawn from Holmes's *Art of Rhetoric Made Easy* and Stirling's *A System of Rhetoric* and incorporates Holmes's catechistic form and Stirling's rhymed couplets. But Getty adds lengthy footnotes to parallel passages in Greek and Roman rhetoricians and in a few modern writers, including two in Blair. A second edition, retitled *The Art of Rhetoric* (1849), represents itself as an edition of Holmes, though Getty prints even more long selections from classical rhetoricians, especially Quintilian, Cicero, and Aristotle, as footnotes or stand-alone excerpts. Many passages and some whole sections of text or exercises are in Latin or Greek. The book ends with a lengthy selection of the first book of Quintilian's *Institutes,* which is, I believe, the only nineteenth-century translation from that work published in the States. Getty's compilations are at once entirely derivative and immensely learned. They provide an unusually extensive and still useful identification of the classical sources of eighteenth-century British rhetoric and its nineteenth-century uses in the States. Getty's innovative grafting of Anglo-American rhetoric back onto its classical roots did not influence subsequent rhetorics, but it strikingly exemplifies both the diversity of the textbook tradition in rhetoric and the range of intellectual work possible to accomplish through practices of compilation.

Two far more successful compilations—they are among the most frequently printed nineteenth-century U.S. rhetorics—are far more pedestrian. These books, one by James R. Boyd, the other by George Payn Quackenbos, mark the culmination—and exhaustion—of compilation as a practice of textbook production. Boyd redacts virtually his entire text from various earlier books. I suspect the same is true for Quackenbos's rhetoric; I have not traced the source of every passage, that is, but every section I have studied either freely paraphrases or copies fairly closely several sources. Both writers acknowledge a general indebtedness to many others, moreover, and Boyd in particular fairly regularly gives an attribution for a section.[24]

Boyd's *Elements of Rhetoric and Literary Criticism* (1844) is a steady seller, with twenty-one printings into the 1870s. It has seven sections: "Practical Exercises in the Use of Words"; "Style and Figurative Language"; "Of Different Kinds of Composition"; "Of Original Composition"; "History of the English Language"; "British Literature"; and "American Literature." An eighth section of appendices is added in 1846. Boyd's *Elements* is the last advanced rhetoric to use a catechistic format. It is also among the first rhetorics to compile selections from periodical literature and instructional texts designed for a popular or general audience: Boyd's section on letter writing, for example, comes from the *Young Ladies' Own Book* (1838). It is also the first widely circulating rhetoric in the States to include extensive writing exercises, some tied to grammatical drills, but others asking for student essays, especially in part 4, "Of Original Composition." Here, Boyd silently borrows from earlier rhetorics—he takes the analysis of a theme into seven parts from Holmes's *The Art of Rhetoric Made Easy*—but also from composition books like John Walker's *The Teacher's Assistant in English Composition* (1801), from which he takes a five-part plan of invention.

G. P. Quackenbos's *Advanced Course of Composition and Rhetoric* (1855) may be with thirty-two printings the most often issued U.S. rhetoric. The book is intended at least in part for college use but also circulates at the secondary level.[25] Its five parts—"History of the English Language," "Punctuation," "Rhetoric," "Prose Composition," and "Poetical Composition"—are divided into lessons of numbered paragraphs, with exercises at the end of most lessons and questions at the bottom of each page, which both largely ask for the rote recall of the topics just covered. It ends with a list of 566 topics for theme writing, the first such list in an advanced rhetoric, though some earlier composition books (e.g., Parker) print them.[26] This textbook is a hodgepodge of borrowings. Its account of taste and style, for example, adopts passages from Whately, Newman, Edmund Burke, Alison, and especially Blair. It rehearses Campbell on "Reputable," "National" and "Present Use," and its treatment of invention reduces Newman's meditative reflections on preparing to write (1835, 18–27) into a schematic series of stages.

Like Jamieson, Boyd and Quackenbos are not so much rhetorical theorists as textbook writers. Unlike Jamieson, however, they do not integrate their sources into a coherent argument. They offer no rationale for why they include what they include, nor do they cross reference arguments developed in one section in another. Their compilations exhibit a *shallow comprehensiveness:* they offer, that is, a wide array of definitions, principles, and analytic distinctions gleaned from diverse sources and connected only by the scaffolding of the textbook apparatus. In successive lessons on style (LVIII–LXIV), for example, Quackenbos discusses "Precision," which Blair (Lecture X) treats as a quality of diction; "Clearness or Perspicuity," which Campbell (2, vi) understands as a general discursive quality; and "Strength, Harmony, and Unity," all features of sentences for Blair (XII, XIII, and XI). Quackenbos does not explain why he selects only these terms for his stylistic taxonomy, and not, say, vivacity or propriety. He redacts his sources, moreover, without overt recognition that Blair and Campbell analyze different levels of stylistic qualities. His book not only develops no new conceptual linkages, that is, but earlier distinctions are lost in the *drift of compilation,* in which local decisions to abbreviate or reorganize a source text introduce changes for no apparent purpose.

The third type of rhetoric, those advancing a relatively independent project even though still indebted to British theory, undergoes the most influential and interesting development over these years.

I return here to Samuel Newman's *A Practical System of Rhetoric,* which is substantively revised and extended over several editions in the early 1830s, until it achieves its definitive form in an 1835 stereotyped edition. In this format, it becomes the first American-authored rhetoric to gain a national audience through frequent reprinting.[27] The substantive changes between the 1827 and 1835 versions embody some key differences between early and mid-century textbooks. The stereotype version, for example, is no longer directly linked with a local institution. Newman drops references to other books available at his college and includes instead forty-one pages of self-contained exercises to demonstrate the principles of each chapter. He removes some illustrative passages that might seem to have only a personal or regional value, such as a reference to a biography of Amos Fisher by Harvard president Kirkland. He adds several passages from writers, like Irving, with a national reputation, as well as two anecdotes about George Washington (1835, 44 and 50). His original two-page preface moves to the beginning of the first chapter, and a longer introduction, extracted from an 1830 address, explicitly elaborates the programmatic goals of rhetorical education and offers for the first time in a U.S. rhetoric some practical advice about writing instruction.

The stereotyped edition, moreover, is more ambitious than the 1827 edition, as seems fitting for a book that moves beyond its initial local or regional use. It now includes, for example, a lengthy historical dissertation on English style. Newman continues to revise and extend positions initially derived from Blair and Campbell: to the discussion of perspicuity, for example, he adds paragraphs that urge adapting writing to its audience (162–63) or that warn against the obscurity produced by too much familiarity with a topic (164). Newman is the first to incorporate ideas from Whately's *Elements* into a U.S. rhetoric, and he often revises even as he uses this British source.[28] Perhaps the most significant section of the stereotype edition is its new advice on composing writing (see 1835, 18–30). Newman counsels, first, patient reflection; next, the methodical arrangement of one's thoughts; and then, their amplification according to a range of strategies. This process is allied with one suggested in Richard Green Parker's *Progressive Exercises in Composition* (1832), which also has subheadings on method and amplification (indeed, Parker cites Newman approvingly in a footnote added in 1833). Newman also adapts Whately's methods of "Induction," "Testimony," and "Analogy" into strategies for enlarging the substance of an argument. The result is an innovative inventional method that recurs in most later rhetorics, which similarly treat "Invention" as the methodical amplification of a basic outline of an argument. A final interesting development in the stereotyped edition is its brief taxonomy of the different kinds of composition as "didactic, persuasive, argumentative, descriptive and narrative" (28), which, as several critics have noted, is the first emergence of what will become the familiar modes of writing.[29] The first edition of *A Practical System* is, as I have suggested, a remarkable break from the common practice of re-presenting British writers; the revisions culminating in the 1835 stereotyped edition produce the first substantively original U.S. rhetoric.

Henry Noble Day's *Elements of the Art of Rhetoric* (1850) is the most theoretically innovative rhetoric of the nineteenth century. It is also dogmatic, obsessively systematic, and at times reductive about writing. Encountering Day's *Elements,* so different from earlier rhetorics in its construction of the field, so peculiarly distant from most current dispositions toward writing, is one of the pleasures of archival research. Day polemically disputes the preeminent concern with style in other textbooks, focusing for the first time in nineteenth-century U.S. rhetorics on "Invention," which he understands as entailing both the development of ideas and their arrangement in discourse. He develops his own idiosyncratic terms of analysis and states his ideas briefly and with little qualification or elaboration, in numbered sections with the leading idea in larger type, the sign in most textbooks of a rule or definition. When novel ideas are so starkly and dogmatically presented, it is difficult to appreciate their potential—the textbook format, in effect, works against the intellectual project—yet Day is a thoughtful writer who repays careful attention to his work.

Day binds invention to specific discursive processes, collapsing inventional practices into discrete strategies for developing or expanding passages of writing. This is an innovative and influential development, one followed in all subsequent nineteenth-century rhetorics that address invention. Yet it depends on a restrictive notion of writing as singly focused on efficient communication. Day claims that the "possible immediate objects of all proper discourse are but four in number, viz. EXPLANATION, CONVICTION, EXCITATION, and PERSUASION" (no. 54), and he specifies that they must always proceed in the sequence in which he lists them (no. 57). He argues, moreover, that discursive unity requires that "there be one leading object proposed to be effected, and that this object be steadily pursued throughout the discourse" (no. 55). Day here explicitly asserts a common presumption of nineteenth-century rhetoric: in the interest of providing a practical and systematic account of discourse, that is, he precludes attention to the performative aspects of discourse, and especially to playful, parodic, digressive or metacritical writing practices. This exclusion is understandable, a reasonable response even today given the pressures of teaching writing in a limited time. But it promotes a monologic or homogeneous writing as the all-too-familiar product of school rhetoric.

Day describes a limited number of discursive options for achieving each of the four appropriate objects of discourse. He identifies, for example, five possible processes for the development of an explanation: "Narration," "Description," "Analysis," "Exemplification," and "Comparison and Contrast" (no. 77). As Robert Connors notes (*Comp-Rhet* 228–29), this is the first systematic elaboration of what will become the "modes of exposition." Yet Day's processes are not yet generic classes of writing, but the possible logical relations of a topic. Thus, "Narration" treats an object in time, "Description" in space, "Analysis" as parts related in time or space, and so on. Day provides a similar menu of possible strategies for amplifying a discourse for each of his four categories. In his account of "Conviction," for example, Day includes many of the topics in the theory of argument that Campbell and Whately previously discussed ("Testimony," "Presumption," "Refutation") but treats them as methods of developing an argument.

The book's second division, "Style," also offers a distinctive conceptual scaffolding: Day analyzes the topic under three general headings—"Absolute," "Subjective," and "Objective"—each in turn subdivided into three qualities. Yet the substance of this tidy systematization is fairly conventional. He likens "Absolute" properties, those founded in the nature of language itself, to Campbell's "essential properties of elocution" and describes the "grammatical" subdivision of this category by rehearsing Campbell on "Purity and Propriety," on "National, Present and Reputable Use," and on the canons of usage. Similarly, "Objective" properties, or those determined in relation to one's audience, largely derive from Whately's terms of "Clearness," "Energy," and "Elegance."

Despite its idiosyncratic nomenclature and argument, *Elements of the Art of Rhetoric* was a steady seller for over twenty-five years, appearing in at least a dozen printings. Like Newman, Day produces a hybrid rhetoric that reworks earlier positions toward a new mode of rhetorical instruction and inquiry. Newman inaugurates the treatment of characteristic elements in most later rhetorics—some form of modal organization of the field of writing, for example, or strategies of amplification as invention—but Day probably had more direct immediate influence on the discipline, with numerous textbooks (Coppée, Bancroft, D. J. Hill, Gilmore, McElroy, and others) explicitly acknowledging or silently appropriating his work. After Day, moreover, most U.S. rhetorics discuss invention, though few approach his innovative account of the topic. Neither author has received much critical appreciation, though they wrote thoughtful, successful, and surprisingly original books at a time when most U.S. rhetorics are compilations of British texts.[30] A national disciplinary tradition of rhetorical inquiry starts with their work.

Matthew Boyd Hope's *The Princeton Text Book in Rhetoric* (1859) is among the first rhetorics to note Day's influence, though Hope also acknowledges indebtedness to Theremin, Rush, and Whately. It is one of the few nineteenth-century U.S. rhetorics to keep oratory as its central topic and conceptual focus. It also harkens back to earlier formations of study in another way, for it is the last rhetoric to be tied to use at a single institution without seeking a larger circulation. Hope intends it solely "for the use of the author's own pupils," and describes it as "*printed—*but not *published*." It appears in a single issue the same year as Hope's death and leaves no citational track in later rhetorics.

Henry Coppée's *Elements of Rhetoric* (1859) is a frequently published, but very derivative, textbook. Coppée follows Day in understanding rhetoric as centrally defined by "Invention," "Arrangement," and "Style." Day organizes his book as a systematic exposition of these topics, however, while Coppée digresses repeatedly on topics unrelated to the rhetorical theory he professes. He writes, that is, more in the manner of Boyd or Quackenbos, providing a shallowly comprehensive account of familiar topics—the history of rhetoric, its relationship to aesthetics, a survey of the various genres of discourse—without integrating them into his central argument. And when he finally turns to invention, halfway through the book, he merely calls upon a writer "to ponder upon that general and perhaps vague *subject,* until it resolve itself into distinct shape." He offers no strategies to foster such a resolution but imagines that "by a strong but invariable process, the mind, on thus dwelling upon a general subject, finds the nebulous particles of thought aggregating themselves into symmetrical forms, and shaping themselves into beautiful and instructive discourse" (183). Such a claim, however grandly phrased, loses the substance of Day's turn to invention.

Coppée's textbook is a new, more diffuse kind of compilation, for he typically adapts the general concepts and not the phrasing of source texts. Coppée silently borrows from Day in his treatment of "Invention," from Campbell and Whately on theories of argument, and from Blair for his accounts of taste, language, and style. Coppée pretends to an independent project, yet unlike Newman or Day, he proposes little if anything that is new. His *Elements of Rhetoric* represents, I believe, an emerging formation of textbooks, one in which a rhetoric seeks to find its niche in the rapidly growing national market through a slightly varied presentation of conventional topics. The *shallow comprehensiveness* of Coppée's rhetoric, like that of Boyd's or Quackenbos's texts, might well be seen as an unfortunate consequence of the increasingly disciplined field of rhetorical study at mid-century, in which intellectual discovery or argument is displaced by the normative exposition of standard topics.

Being Practical: 1866–1900

The number of rhetorics circulating in the States increases enormously in the last third of the century, and many of them are printed multiple times. At least sixteen rhetorics have ten or more issues in these years: those by Whately and Quackenbos from earlier in the century, and new titles by Edwin Abbott, Abbott and John Robert Seeley, George Pierce Baker, Alexander Bain, J. Scott Clark, Henry Day (*Art*), John Hart, Brainerd Kellogg, A. S. Hill (*Principles*), Sarah Lockwood, John Genung (*Practical*), Herbert Spencer, Barrett Wendell, and William Williams. This proliferation of books reflects not only a larger educational market but also an increasingly stratified one. Rhetorics now often specify a narrow range of grade levels as their intended audience: they address the lower or the upper classes in high schools, or span the school-college divide, or seek a segment of the collegiate curriculum. The field gains a few theoretical or conceptual innovations, mostly around the paragraph as a unit of discourse, and some rhetorics offer new scientific, philosophic, or historical descriptions of the subject. But probably the most striking development is the insistently expressed concern with being "practical," with articulating rhetorical principles with local or immediate occasions of writing.[31] This concern is not new—recall the title of Newman's 1827 text, *A Practical System of Rhetoric*, or Quackenbos's 1854 subtitle, "a series of practical lessons"—but it is insistently claimed in the title and prefaces of new books and clearly inflects their projects. As various strategic responses to the desire for the "practical" emerge, the textbook tradition of rhetorics breaks into two discrete branches with distinctive ambitions, pedagogical strategies, and theoretical positions.

British Rhetorics

In the last third of the century, the long dominion of British rhetoricians in the United States at last begins to fade. Blair is still issued from old stereotypes through the 1870s but increasingly becomes a residual feature in the curriculum. Campbell too declines from his previous circulation and use, though in the 1870s and 1880s his *Philosophy* outpaces Blair's *Lectures* for the first time in both the frequency of reprints and the number of adoptions in college courses. Whately remains an active presence a bit longer, with reprints of *Elements* appearing into the 1890s, but loses his preeminent position by the late 1870s. By the 1880s, several American-authored texts displace the writings of Blair, Campbell, and Whately as the most frequently published and widely studied rhetorics in the States.

Several new British rhetorics become steady sellers in the States, though even the most substantive—Alexander Bain's *English Composition and Rhetoric* (1866)—never approaches the influence of earlier rhetorics. Much of this text derives from Campbell, Blair, and Whately—Bain admits that his text is "more closely affiliated" to these writers than most new rhetorics (4)—though he often inflects their positions with psychological arguments. He defines the same figures as Blair does and in a similar manner, for example, but reorganizes them according to basic operations of the mind as figures of similarity, contiguity, and contrast.

Yet Bain does make two decisive contributions to late nineteenth-century rhetorics. He organizes the second part of his book, "Kinds of Composition," not by genres or occasions of writing but by what will later become the "modes of discourse." He lists five "kinds": description, narrative, exposition, persuasion, and poetry. Newman and Day anticipate modal models of discourse, and Bain's inclusion of poetry distinguishes his taxonomy from the later standard of four modes. But here for the first time, Bain both uses the modal structure as a major structural unit of a nineteenth-century rhetoric and elaborates in detail the writing strategies appropriate to each mode. Bain's book is also the first rhetoric to treat the paragraph as a major structure of discourse. Previously, paragraphs were discussed as a matter of punctuation, the heading under which Murray's *English Grammar*, for example, describes its protocols. Bain defines the paragraph unexceptionably as "a collection of sentences with unity of purpose" (no. 158) but then advances six principles that narrowly and dogmatically specify the structural qualities of such unity. He asserts, with minimal elaboration or explanation, that "the bearing of each sentence upon what precedes shall be explicit and unmistakable" (no. 159); that sentences with similar topics should have a similar syntax (no. 175); that the opening sentence should usually "indicate with prominence" the subject of the paragraph (no. 176); that paragraphs should be "consecutive, or free from dislocation" (no. 177); that unity "implies a definite purpose, and forbids digressions and irrelevant matter" (no. 178); and "as in the sentence, so in the paragraph, a due proportion should obtain" (no. 179). Though Bain offers no rationale for these precepts, they are adopted by most subsequent rhetorics and quickly enter the orthodoxy of writing instruction. They articulate a readily taught technology of writing that makes possible the single-mindedly monologic writing that Day earlier proposed as a compositional ideal.

English Lessons for English People (1871) by Edwin Abbott and J. R. Seeley is a basic or simplified rhetoric, designed initially for English schoolboys, with sections on "Vocabulary," "Diction," "Meter," "Styles of Composition," and "Errors in Reasoning." This rhetoric does not specifically derive from leading earlier textbooks, but neither does it propose new concepts or instructional strategies. Abbott's *How to Write Clearly* (1874) is often used in colleges. It transforms familiar precepts into brief rules on "Clearness and Force" and "Brevity," and it prints exercises illustrating stylistic errors and their revision, though it never prompts students to compose. Its format of a short handbook with clear injunctions about usage is innovative and influential. Herbert Spencer's "Philosophy of Style," an essay initially published in 1852, appears as a separate rhetoric in several editions from 1871 on. Several late-nineteenth-century U.S. rhetorics adapt Spencer's psychologistic reduction of desirable style to the principle of economy; some—Hepburn, D. J. Hill, Genung—cite Spencer positively, while others— A. S. Hill, Cairns, J. Quackenbos—question if economy sufficiently explains the range of stylistic effects. A remarkable critical edition by Fred Newton Scott in 1892 provides a biographical and intellectual context for Spencer's arguments and challenges several aspects of the theory; it epitomizes the more sustainedly critical relation to British thought of the new U.S. rhetorics.

U.S. Rhetorics to Century's End

There is a substantial shift across the archive of American-authored rhetorics after the Civil War. No more commemorative rhetorics are published; perhaps the growing market prompts teachers at leading institutions to publish textbooks early in their careers. Compilation, meanwhile, becomes a more diffuse and generalized practice. Frequent redaction has so thoroughly dispossessed accounts of language, style, argument, and figurative language from the moment of their original emergence that they appear, in effect, as the common property of the field. Austin Phelps admits without embarrassment that he has freely "appropriated principles of which no one knows the origin" (*English Style,* iii); since the foundational texts of the field are still widely studied, it is surely less a matter of knowing the origin of leading rhetorical principles than of willfully forgetting the history of the discipline and one's intellectual debts. Materials codified by earlier writers, especially Blair, Campbell, and Whately, but also increasingly Bain, Day, and other American authors, are freely recycled, sometimes with a nod toward attribution, but more usually as silently appropriated tenets of the discipline.

The new rhetorics share a common concern with the "practical," which is named in many titles (Coppens, Clark, Genung, Raub, Williams, J. Quackenbos) and often discussed in prefaces. The term has a complex range of meanings and is neither simply opposed to the theoretical nor always articulated with specific practices of writing. Several rhetorics claim their practical orientation is an innovative break from the dominant textbook tradition. J. Scott Clark notes, for example, "the only reason to add to the already long list of textbooks on English Composition, is the desire to aid in giving to the rhetorical training in our schools a more practical character" (iii). John McElroy writes:

> I have tried to fill what seemed to me an empty place among
> books on Rhetoric. None of them, I thought, aimed at prac-

tical results, without sacrificing too far the principles of the art; none of them taught these principles in their fullness, without sacrificing in part or in whole the practical side of the work. (3)

Such anxious attempts to differentiate one's work from the ever more densely populated field of textbooks are peculiar since so many competitors also claim the practical as their mark of distinction. Yet the value placed on "the practical" in quite varied educational discourses and practices of the time made it a popular appeal, and rhetorics in particular sought "the practical" as a way both to accommodate and to contain the challenge the emerging field of composition poses to the older discipline.

The textbook tradition of U.S. rhetorics divides into two major branches in response to the increased interest in "the practical." Books in one branch retain as their primary focus the traditional project of elaborating the general theoretical principles of the field. They may modulate their articulation of principles by considering their application, by illustrating a topic with numerous examples, or by formulating rules that govern usage or structure, but their emphasis remains on the systematic presentation of the knowledge of the field. Rhetorics in the other branch orient their account of rhetorical principles toward a direct intervention in student writing. They selectively adopt some practices of composition books and are, in effect, an intermediate formation between the textbook traditions of rhetorics and composition books. I call this branch of the tradition "composition-rhetoric." I adapt the name, the title of an 1897 textbook by Fred Newton Scott and Joseph Denny, from Robert Connors, who uses it to designate successive stages of rhetorical study in the States between 1800 and 1960. I think it more useful and accurate to restrict the term to a single late-nineteenth-century branch of the field.[32]

Because arguments and strategies migrate readily across textbook traditions through processes of compilation, this taxonomy inevitably has some blurred boundaries, but there are significant differences in the projects of composition books, composition-rhetorics, and general rhetorics. Late-nineteenth-century composition books typically concentrate on exercises and grant little importance to the presentation of rhetorical principles. In Simon Kerl's *Elements of Composition and Rhetoric* (1869), for example, most of the text is given over to elaborate exercises that ask students to work on various practices of writing, while schematic or attenuated accounts of rhetorical principles appear only occasionally among the exercises. Lucy Chittenden, in *The Elements of English Composition* (1884), claims to offer directions and exercises "with as little theory as possible" (iii), and Alphonso Newcomer notes that "there is not a formal rule" in his *Practical Course in English Composition* (1893). Composition-rhetorics, however, argue for the union of theory and practice: as Sarah Lockwood notes in *Lessons in English* (1887), "it is almost universally conceded that the best teaching of English is that in which precept and example are most happily combined" (v). As a result, they offer a more integrated and equitable presentation of rhetorical principles alongside exercises. Albert Raub's *Practical Rhetoric and Composition* (1887), for example, begins each chapter with several pages of exposition about the relevant principles or rules of the field before moving to exercises in their practical application. General rhetorics, meanwhile, have few or no exercises, emphasizing instead the discursive elaboration and illustration of underlying principles.

The distinctions I am drawing among textbook traditions are similar to those made by textbook writers of the day in describing different instructional projects. James De Mille, for example, characterizes composition as "concerned with practical exercises by which the student acquires skill in writing," while rhetoric "embraces that wide field of survey by which he makes himself familiar with the qualities of literature" (iii). Similarly, when David J. Hill differentiates *The Science of Rhetoric* (1877), whose "aim is to present the laws of discourse as a scientific system," from *Elements of Rhetoric and Composition* (1878), whose "aim is to transmit a compendium of rules for guidance in the art of writing" (iii), he marks a boundary between types of rhetorics and not just these two textbooks.

Composition-Rhetorics. One of the most frequently published of all American-authored rhetorics, John S. Hart's *A Manual of*

Composition and Rhetoric (1870), is the earliest example of a composition-rhetoric. Like many later rhetorics of this type, it does not pretend to develop new rhetorical theory: "It has been written for learners, not for the learned. Its object is, not to extend the boundaries of the science by excursion into debatable ground, but to present its admitted truths in a form easily apprehended" (iii). *A Manual's* first and longest section, on "Style," reviews "Punctuation" and "Capitalization," before rehearsing familiar positions on diction (from Campbell on "Reputable, Present, and National" use and the grounds of pure and proper usage), sentences and figures (largely from Blair), and other assorted topics. Its second section mentions "Invention" (mainly to place it beyond rhetoric's scope), briefly describes various organizational plans of composition, and ends with an essay on the study of the English language (redacted from Whitney's *Language and the Study of Language*). Hart offers numerous exercises in which students correct grammar or diction, or develop outlines for possible themes, but though he lists possible essay topics, his book does not guide students through the actual practice of composing their own work.

From the mid 1870s to the mid 1880s, at least eight more composition-rhetorics are published. All of them address either a college audience or a combination of advanced high school and lower college classes.[33] They differ little in the rhetorical principles they espouse, though they adopt a range of pedagogical strategies. Brainerd Kellogg's *A Text-book on Rhetoric* (1880), the next most frequently published rhetoric of this type after Hart's *Manual,* stays closest to that text's combination of exercise drills and brief accounts of familiar rhetorical principles. Charles Coppens's *Practical Introduction to English Rhetoric* (1880) offers a fuller survey of rhetorical principles and rules, with exercises that regularly ask for student writing. Following in the wake of Abbott's *How to Write Clearly* are three brief rhetorical handbooks offering highly condensed expositions of rhetorical definitions, rules, and procedures. Henry Jameson's *Rhetorical Method* (1879) is the most comprehensive guide, encapsulating in 301 sections advice on topics ranging from punctuation, diction, and sentence structure to the characteristics of poetry, the types of composition, and questions appropriate to criticism. It contains numerous exercises and a list of 360 topics for composition. John Nichol's *English Composition* (1879) and Timothy Bancroft's *A Method of English Composition* (1884) have no exercises and fewer salient definitions and principles, with Nichol oriented to grammar and diction, and Bancroft more to argument. Like these manuals, several longer texts recast rhetorical principles into rules that specify the correct format or appropriate procedure for every aspect of writing. David J. Hill's *Elements of Rhetoric and Composition* (1878), the most thorough of these textbooks, offers rules for "Invention" as well as for "Style" and "Punctuation," before moving to a more general consideration of criticism and the common forms of writing, and ending with extensive exercises. Charles Bardeen's *System of Rhetoric* (1884) focuses more narrowly on issues of correctness, beginning, for example, with rules for the grammatical construction of sentences. J. Scott Clark's *Practical Rhetoric for Instruction in English Composition* (1886) is the most insistent lawgiver, enumerating 310 rules that govern details of style, grammar, organization, and diction. Hill tries to help writers find things to say; Clark usually teaches what not to say. Nineteen of his thirty-five rules that formalize Campbell's views of good usage begin with *"Avoid."*

In the late 1880s, several textbooks offer a fuller and more sophisticated integration of compositional exercises with their elaborations of rhetorical principles. They combine exercises that involve students in the correction and production of writing with abridged accounts of familiar rhetorical principles and definitions. Some of these texts, such as Sarah Lockwood's *Lessons in English* (1887) or Virginia Waddy's *Elements of Composition and Rhetoric* (1888), are designed for high school.[34] William Williams's *Composition and Rhetoric by Practice* (1888) is intended for either advanced high school or beginning college classes, and Albert Raub's *Practical Rhetoric and Composition* (1887) is primarily for college. These books have more imaginative compositional exercises than Hart, but they typically rehearse very much the same set of well-established rhetorical ideas. Like Hart, that is, they all describe "Purity,"

"Propriety," and "Precision" as principles of diction and cover Campbell's dictates about "Reputable, National and Present" use. They all describe pretty much the same tropes and figures that Blair long ago codified, though Williams and Raub also adopt Bain's classificatory scheme of figures of "Resemblance," "Contiguity," and "Contrast." Waddy, Williams, and Raub have similar treatments of letter writing that may derive from Hart (or from Hart's source). Lockwood begins her text with an account of the history of the English language that, like Hart's, is redacted from Whitney's linguistic study. Williams and Raub redact Bain's rules on paragraphing in similar fashion. As the extent of overlap in these accounts of rhetorical principles suggests, this new branch of the textbook tradition fairly quickly settled into a comfortable orthodoxy.

In the 1890s, however, several college professors published remarkable textbooks that challenge this orthodoxy. Rather than defining rule-based treatments of individual elements, they foreground the immediate purposes and contexts of writing. Fred Newton Scott and Joseph Denny, from Michigan and Ohio State, produced a series of books designed for high schools that propose a different object of inquiry and instruction, one primarily focused on the paragraph. Bain's rules for the paragraph had become orthodox precepts in composition-rhetorics from the mid-1870s. Scott and Denny are broadly indebted to Bain in the importance they accord the topic sentence as the unifying essential idea of a paragraph. Instead of listing rules that specify the formal features of a well-written paragraph, however, they stress that paragraphs emerge out of a generative idea. In *Paragraph-Writing* (1893), they discuss the topic sentence as a "germ-idea" that "contains, potentially, all that may be said on the subject in hand" (2). In *Composition-Rhetoric* (1897), an extension of the earlier book, they propose a model of "organic form" and the metaphor of "growth" in order to describe discursive organization not as a predetermined structure but as a form that evolves from the treatment of a germinal idea.

Two of these rhetorics are second-generation textbooks out of the Harvard composition curriculum. George Pierce Baker's *The Principles of Argumentation* (1893) derives from a course taught at

Harvard and is dedicated to the founder of that curriculum, Adams Sherman Hill. Like Whately, Baker focuses on argument, and like Whately, his views are informed by a consideration of the forensic oratory of the bar. By this time, Whately's ideas had been endlessly redacted and often reduced to an aridly formalistic account of testimony, refutation, and the calculation of chances. Baker's return to the model of legal argument revivifies the theory of argument. He claims argument can be reduced neither to logic nor to abstract strategies of persuasion but needs to be understand as a practice responsive to its immediate situation. Henry Pearson's *Principles of Composition* (1898) describes a course taught at Massachusetts Institute of Technology, but developed at Harvard. Pearson dedicates his book to his Harvard teacher and colleague Barrett Wendell. He reverses Wendell's conventional sequence of moving from words, to sentences, to paragraphs and then to themes, and focuses first on the whole composition. This inversion allows him to attend more fully and directly with the purposes or goals of writing, and to consider its component elements as subordinated to such purposes.

Four textbooks from the 1890s are remarkable as much for their engaging manner as for their departures from a rule-bound orthodoxy. They are, in effect, updates of the older format of the talking lecture, written in an informal manner, referring to their writers' personal attitudes and beliefs and often directly addressing their student readers. *Constructive Rhetoric* (1896), by Edward Everett Hale Jr. of Union College, has a distant relationship to an earlier Harvard curriculum: Hale's dedication recalls the debt his father professed to Edward Channing. The first part of his book covers the modes of narration, description, exposition, and argument; the second part focuses on the paragraph. Hale typically phrases his advice as rules of thumb, not universal laws.

Elements of Rhetoric (1898), by Alphonso Newcomer of Stanford University, is an expository textbook with numbered sections and different type fonts for different passages, yet he writes in a conversational style, offering guidance from his own interested position and not as a series of decontextualized rules. Like Pearson, he reverses the conventional sequence of topics and begins with the whole composition, moving then to paragraphs, sentences, and diction. He refuses to treat some familiar topics, breaking from the standard rehearsal of Campbell's laws of usage, since "discussion of obsolete words, for example, is in a rhetoric, only dead matter. No student ever writes obsolete words" (iv).

Gertrude Buck's *A Course in Expository Writing* (1899), co-authored with Elisabeth Woodbridge, and *A Course in Argumentative Writing* (1899) emerge from the Vassar College curriculum. Both rhetorics are meditative inquiries interested in the psychology of perception, conviction, and communication. They offer no rules but pose problems or questions about the topics they discuss. They invite students, that is, to reflect on what makes for effective exposition or argument and prompt them to investigate the relevant processes and qualities through imaginative reading and writing assignments in the extensive lessons that accompany each chapter. These thoughtful and innovative textbooks, together with the other composition-rhetorics published in the 1890s, suggest how vibrant this branch of the textbook tradition had become; in two decades, it moved from a simplified rehearsal of familiar rhetorical principles toward a nondogmatic inquiry into the context and situations of writing.

General Rhetorics. Throughout this time, a steady stream of textbooks continues the longstanding rhetorical project of describing the general principles of the field. These rhetorics are almost all written by college professors and intended for college use, though a few (Haven, Hepburn, Gilmore) also seek a high school market. They address similar subjects as earlier rhetorics—diction, figurative language, style, modes of discourse, and invention—but typically propose new ways of organizing the field or of describing specific topics. These books have less immediate interest in monitoring student writing than composition-rhetorics; they have, that is, comparatively few or no exercises, and they embed any rules of composition in discursive explanations of principles.

Philosophy of Rhetoric (1866) by John Bascom of Williams College self-consciously announces a new conceptual map of the rhetorical field. He distinguishes his book from a "simple rhetoric of rules," and proposes a "more extensive and philosophical discussion" of rhetorical principles for advanced undergraduates (3–4). Its first two sections, "Ends" and "Means," divide the field into three parts, "Argument," "Poetry," and "Oratory," drawing upon an eighteenth-century psychology of separate faculties to classify rhetorical aims by their appeal to thought, emotions, or will. Bascom also reverts to an earlier formation by naming poetry as a subdivision of rhetoric and retaining an emphasis on oratory, and his attention to these fields allows him to discuss the aesthetic and ethical dimensions largely neglected in composition-rhetorics. Yet in his final section on "Methods," Bascom too slights these qualities and describes features of style in familiar terms derived from Blair and Whately.

Henry Day of Western Reserve University calls *The Art of Discourse* (1867) a "reconstruction" of his *Elements of the Art of Rhetoric*. Over half the new book reprints sections from *Elements* and continues its project of elaborating a scientific theory of rhetoric. Yet Day revises his earlier position, moving to fuller accounts of both logic and, interestingly, aesthetics in relation to invention. He argues, for example, that the mind "to be properly and effectively moved, must be addressed in accordance with its aesthetic nature" (10). Day also softens his assertively dogmatic manner in order to involve his audience in his arguments and adds exercises for the various discursive processes he enumerates: like so many other writers of textbooks at this time, that is, he seeks "not merely to present a collection of doctrines and observations for acquisition as bare knowledge, but to make practical thinkers and writers" (iv).

Rhetorics over the next decade or so typically propose a systematic way of understanding rhetorical inquiry and practice, sometimes, like Bascom, pursuing some broadly "philosophical" distinctions, and sometimes, like Day, advancing universal "scientific" laws. In *Rhetoric: A Text-book* (1869), Erastus Haven, president of the University of Michigan, begins with reflections on the nature of language. He rejects the usefulness of "abstruse arguments about style and oratory" and other familiar rhetorical topics while also condemning "mere exercises in composition" as "too superficial to produce the desired result" (vii). His book is an orderly review of rhetorical principles with illustrations of their application and use.

Haven covers conventional topics but often departs from received wisdom. His opening section on words, for example, is one of the very few contemporary discussions of diction that does not foreground Campbell's strictures on usage; indeed, Haven implicitly challenges this tradition by approving at least the occasional use of technical or foreign terms (nos. 27 and 34). James De Mille, from Dalhousie University, reflects at length on the psychology of the emotions in part 5 of *Elements of Rhetoric* (1878), though he usually ends up elaborating a familiar set of rhetorical topics, with occasional intelligent, if fairly minor, variations in treatment of specific topics.

In *The Science of Rhetoric,* David J. Hill of the University at Lewisburg (Bucknell) follows Day in claiming "a systematic presentation of the laws of discourse, for advanced classes" (3). Hill elaborates an idiosyncratic superstructure of various laws, based on Spencer's principle of economy and dogmatically stated as universal laws of mind, but his system largely restates familiar positions of Whately on argument, Blair on figurative language (with an overlay of Bain's classification of figures), Campbell on diction and usage, and Bain on the modes of discourse. A. D. Hepburn, from Davidson College, understands rhetoric as "the Science of the Laws and Forms of Prose. It investigates the method and general principles to which every discourse must conform that is designed to instruct, convince, or persuade" (13). His *Manual of English Rhetoric* (1875) refers to first principles a lot but generally covers the usual array of topics, sometimes departing slightly from familiar treatments, as when, for example, he substitutes for Campbell's "Reputable Use" his own category of "Moral Dignity" (83–86). John McElroy of the University of Pennsylvania stays close to Day's *Elements* in *The Structure of English Prose* (1885) in, for example, dividing style into "Subjective" and "Objective Qualities" (247–80) or in identifying the four possible modes of discussion as "Explanation," "Argument," "Excitation," and "Persuasion" (290–328). McElroy draws heavily on Bain as well, especially in his treatment of the paragraph, and he quarrels with many other rhetorics in notes or asides. He thinks his book is distinctive in its balanced articulation of theoretical principles and practical application, but there is little substantively new in either its argument or format.

In *Outlines of Rhetoric* (1877, 1891), J. H. Gilmore of the University of Rochester seeks to put generally accepted rhetorical precepts into systematic relation to one another. The book evolved over four substantively revised and extended editions into a comprehensive mapping of advanced thought on common rhetorical topics, complete with appropriate citations to most leading rhetoricians. This project, in effect, repeats on a larger scale and as a conceptual outline what Jamieson did in compiling the leading British rhetoricians at the beginning of the century; it organizes diversely articulated principles into a coherent system.

Three rhetorics—by Adams Sherman Hill, John Genung, and Barrett Wendell—dominate this segment of the market into the twentieth century. Hill's *The Principles of Rhetoric and Their Application* (1878) is the most widely circulating, though it breaks almost no new conceptual ground, with the exception, perhaps, of its brief analysis of narration and description in terms of movement and method. Its account of diction derives entirely from Campbell, and of sentence structure mainly from Blair; its taxonomy of style—clearness, force, and elegance—slightly revises Whately's terms of perspicuity, energy, and elegance; and its position on argument is taken wholesale from Whately. Hill's textbook probably benefits from his institutional location at Harvard's influential composition program.[35] Yet Hill also makes familiar rhetorical positions readily accessible and memorable through the enormous number of sources he quotes to illustrate these ideas—a special index to the passages Hill cites lists well over two hundred authors, many of whom are quoted several times and at length.

Over time, the substance of the 1878 *Principles* is redistributed across several other books. In 1892, Hill published *The Foundations of Rhetoric* for younger students, covering much the same ground as his earlier book, though with revisions that respond to developments in the field as well as to its different audience. This text, for example, pays more attention to the paragraph, a topic regularly treated in composition-rhetorics by the 1880s. Hill also redefines his master terms for style, substituting "ease" for "elegance," perhaps to clarify the application of his analysis to practical, everyday writing. The 1895 revision of *Principles of Rhetoric* also uses "ease" and extends its treatment of this stylistic quality. This edition adds illustrative examples; treats each level of discourse more systematically in terms of clearness, force, and ease; organizes its survey of the kinds of composition by the four modes of description, narration, exposition and argument; and drops an appendix on punctuation and capitalization. This appendix reappears in Hill's *Beginnings of Composition and Rhetoric* (1902), a yet more elementary text that includes compositional exercises taken from Huber Buehler's *Practical Exercises in English* (1895), which had originally supplemented Hill's *Foundations*. As this quick publication history suggests, at century's end, the field of rhetorical instruction was becoming ever more stratified by audience and by purpose, with substantive content being rearranged or recast more than rethought in order to suit new occasions.

The *Practical Elements of Rhetoric* (1886) by John Genung of Amherst College is an exceptionally thoughtful elaboration and reformulation of many characteristic arguments of late-nineteenth-century U.S. rhetorics. Genung's most important contribution is to stress the rhetorical importance of adaptation to audience and situation. A few earlier rhetorics touch occasionally upon this topic; Genung makes it central to his work, defining rhetoric as "the art of adapting discourse, in harmony with its subject and occasion, to the requirements of a reader or hearer" (1), and regularly examining the ways context inflects the application of rhetorical principles.[36] He insists on being practical. He is willing, on occasion, to specify unambiguous rules for aspiring writers to follow (he lists fifteen rules in boldface concerning diction; 30–37). More usually, however, he analyzes passages from contemporary American and English authors (his index of quotations lists over 150 authors) to illustrate how rhetorical elements function. The first part of his book treats style and addresses familiar topics of diction, figurative language, grammar, and the structure of sentences and paragraphs; the second part discusses invention, developed in relation to five modes—description, narration, exposition, argument, and persuasion. Some aspects of Genung's views on most topics can be traced back to earlier rhetorics. And yet on every topic, he develops new analytic distinctions or innovative ways of understanding or applying rhetorical principles. He adopts Campbell's account of "Present Use," for example, but Genung's other categories of usage are "Accurate," "Intelligible," and "Scholarly Use." He describes the same figures that Blair did and notes similar problems and values in their use, but he classifies them newly into those that promote clearness and those that foster emphasis. Like Newman, Genung recommends reading and personal reflection as prompts to invention, planning and outlining as intermediate steps, and amplification as its primary method of articulation, but to what Newman sketches in a single chapter, Genung devotes over 250 pages of elaboration, refinement, and revisionary suggestions.

Genung, like Hill, subsequently redistributes the arguments of his treatise across a series of more elementary or "practical" texts. *Handbook of Rhetorical Analysis* (1888) supplements *The Practical Elements* with an anthology of passages and questions that illustrate the application of its rhetorical principles. *Outlines of Rhetoric* (1893) simplifies his theoretical arguments into a series of numbered rules printed in the margin, accompanied by a brief paragraph of exposition and illustrative examples. Genung also adds exercises indebted, in part, to Abbott's *How to Write Clearly. The Working Principles of Rhetoric* (1900) is a "re-studied and re-proportioned" version of *Practical Elements* with interesting minor changes, including greater attention to grammar and a shuffling of its treatment of modes from five to four (persuasion joins argument, which is in turn subdivided into debate and oratory). Yet this revision does not substantively develop Genung's basic theoretical position; indeed, like Hill, Genung rearranges more than rethinks his rhetorical arguments across his subsequent publications.

In a way, *English Composition* (1891), by Hill's Harvard colleague Barrett Wendell, is yet another redistribution of *The Principles of Rhetoric*, where most of its major ideas can be found. Wendell acknowledges a debt to Hill among others, which is perhaps most visible in his use of "Clearness," "Force," and "Elegance" as terms of stylistic analysis. The book emerges from Wendell's teaching at Harvard, but it was initially delivered to a nonacademic audience at the Lowell Institute, and it preserves the format of the talking lecture. Its witty and informal manner of presentation distinguishes it from most rhetorics and almost allows its paucity of original material to be overlooked. Wendell's main contribution is his notion that sentences, paragraphs, and compositions should all be approached in terms of "Unity," "Mass" and "Coherence": "Unity" specifies the grouping of parts under one leading idea; "Mass" designates (somewhat misleadingly) their emphatic placement or arrangement; and "Coherence" identifies the clear relationship of parts to one another. This may be a readily teachable approach, but it further homogenizes the writing students are supposed to produce. Wendell proceeds by anecdote and illustration and consistently reduces rhetorical principles into simple definitions and procedures. He transforms, for example, "Clearness," "Force," and "Elegance," the stylistic taxonomy he takes from Adams Sherman Hill, into denotation, connotation, and adaptation.

Few general rhetorics new in the late nineteenth century compete with Hill, Genung, and Wendell, and most that do largely recast their arguments. Arlo Bates's *Talks on Writing English* (1896), like Wendell's text, reprints a series of lectures delivered at the Lowell Institute. It is substantively indebted to Wendell in its account of structure, diction, and style, and its account of "Exposition," "Argument," "Description," and "Narration" rehearses commonplace observations on the modes. William Cairns's *The Forms of Discourse* (1896) follows Genung, with a first chapter on "Style" and subsequent chapters on invention in the modes of "Narration," "Description," "Exposition," "Argument," and "Persuasion." John Quackenbos, a Lecturer at Columbia, who had previously updated his father's rhetoric, produces a peculiar mixture of old and new in *Practical Rhetoric* (1896). The first rhetoric since Coppée's to include a substantial discussion of taste, it is a less sophisticated attempt than Day's *Art of Rhetoric* to have aesthetic concerns inform practical writing. As the derivative qualities of these and other late-century general rhetorics suggest, after Genung's *Practical Elements,* this branch of the textbook traditions becomes increasingly orthodox in striking contrast to the innovative composition-rhetorics that flourished through the 1890s.

Reprise: Archive and Field

The earliest archives were official repositories or sites of institutional memory. Archives of the recent past are often more eclectic collections of texts, and those, like the archive of nineteenth-century textbooks, reflect the complexity of cataloguing materials relevant to disciplinary fields that are both pervasive and dispersed formations. Archival research on nineteenth-century U.S. rhetorics makes it possible to understand the field as a dynamic system. Its texts are ordered, through practices of compilation, as a series of reproductions, redistributions, and critical appropriations and in some cases appear only as the tedious monotony of simple repetition. Yet the field as a whole is never static. Authors with quite different projects come momentarily into preeminence and then fade; diverse types of textbooks emerge or flourish across the century. A few eighteenth-century formulations—on perspicuous style, appropriate diction, and figurative language—persist surprisingly intact across the archive, but most disappear or are substantively reworked. New issues—amplification, invention, modal categories of discourse, the practical uses of rhetoric—enter the textbook tradition, and there is often little consensus on how they are understood: the number and identity of the modes fluctuates across rhetorics, for example, and antithetical approaches to "the practical" coexist in different kinds of textbooks. Such diversity makes it hard to credit large-scale generalizations about the discursive field of nineteenth-century rhetoric with much explanatory power or accuracy.

Attending to rhetorics as books with distinctive histories of publication and circulation does allow us to trace some broad regularities across the archive. British texts, for example, dominate the textbook tradition. Blair and then Whately are by far the most frequently issued rhetorics, and Campbell, Spencer, and Jamieson are reprinted about as often as the most widely circulating American-authored texts. British texts, moreover, are the most often redacted, and so it seems appropriate to understand nineteenth-century rhetoric in the States as not only emerging from a British heritage but also continually reincorporating and revising it. Yet British influence is never monolithic: British rhetorics circulate at different rates and at different times across the century, and only certain sections or passages get taken up in later compilations. The British component of Anglo-American rhetoric, that is, requires a fairly precise determination of its material forms of circulation to be understood.

Questions of influence or historical importance are raised in a different way by the list of the most often printed U.S. rhetorics—in descending order, G. P. Quackenbos, Hart, A. S. Hill *(Principles)*, Boyd, Newman, Kellogg, Wendell, Genung *(Practical)*—since there appears to be little correlation between circulation and rhetorical sophistication. Publication totals, of course, are always interested calculations, but this list usefully suggests that what is important in a field of study—then as now—is not only what is most innovative or advanced but also what inculcates normative expectations and procedures, what transforms arguments into rehearsals of commonplace principles and integrates them as a practice of writing instruction.

I have sought to describe the general tendencies of the field, its normative ideas and routine procedures as they change over the century, but I have also discussed some books and ideas that were lost in the subsequent evolution of the textbook tradition—Getty's mapping of British theory back onto classical sources, for example, or Whately's speculations about nonserious discourse, or Day's concern with the aesthetics of effective communication—and the complexity and diversity of this archive insures that any interested reading will uncover others. What had little discernable historical effect can still, I hope, unsettle present dispositions and may lead us to rethink the practices we inhabit.

2 / Reading School Readers

But why is [reading] so important? . . . It is not enough to say
that it enables a person to transact business, to read his own
accounts and letters from other people, to know what is going
on at New York or Washington, to pore over newspapers, to
gape over a few tales of blood and murder, or now and then to
extract a thought from a good book on Sunday. If this were all,
it were indeed worth all the cost, as the experience and the
common sense of the world shows. The transactions and
intercourse of civilized life depend on this acquisition; and the
unconscious discipline of civilized man that comes from the
process, even in the limited and careless uses to which it is
applied, reward the pains-taking a thousand-fold.

—Noah Porter, *Books and Reading*

R*eaders* are textbooks designed to teach reading, which, as a school
subject in the nineteenth century, primarily meant reading aloud,
or elocutionary performance. The more privatized, silent textual practice now called reading was figured in the school context as preparatory, as study or analysis of a text to be delivered. As Noah Porter,
professor and president of Yale University, suggested, reading enabled
the "transactions and intercourse of civilized life," even as it shaped
civilized persons. Reading was a powerful school discipline—allowing a student access to the knowledge, thoughts, and expressions
of others and representing an acquired habit of focus and understanding. It comprised the most elementary moment of instruction—the letters taught at a mother's knee, the memorized psalm,
or the pictured alphabet—and it extended through grammar and high
schools, university, and into lifelong practices of self-culture and adult
learning. Learning to read was a *textual* practice: learning to recognize and recite an alphabet, syllables, words, sentences, and texts;
to read graphic symbols; and to understand the organization of

81

printed texts. And in the nineteenth century, it was an *oral* practice: learning to pronounce, enunciate, and articulate sounds and sentences; to emphasize and pause; to adjust the body to speech; to declaim and recite. Learning to read also meant entering a complex cultural system for monitoring the texts, activities, and uses of reading. It meant learning how to care for and select books, to organize them into what Noah Porter called "a definite aim in reading,"[1] and to cultivate the many uses of reading admired in the century.

This diverse valuation of reading is reflected in the multitude of textbooks that propose reading as a subject. An advertisement inserted in an 1821 Blair's *Lectures* illustrates the range of books addressing what Porter called the "acquisition" of reading. Offering "a handsome discount" for "Preceptors of Academies, Schoolmasters, &c. who may purchase in quantities for schools" (i), the catalogue lists books and equipment for all the branches of study. Reading was to be taught as it had been for centuries through the classics (Latin and Greek readers, as well as translations), although "English Reading Books" confirm the flourishing of a vernacular tradition, in English rather than Latin or Greek. The "English" in the list refers to reading in English—although the titles also reflect national competition with books signaling their "American" concerns. Many books suggest the British elocutionary tradition; others recall traditional linkages of religion and literacy, dominant in the American colonies as well as in the history of literacy books in Europe; and still others suggest attention to children's interests. Books of logic, and on "useful" topics like surveying and bookkeeping suggest the harnessing of reading as a delivery system for other subjects, as does a historical reader proposed to "store the minds of young persons with knowledge of the most interesting and useful portions of history, while they are learning to read" (xiii). The list addresses literary reading, offering an eclectic collection of "miniature editions" (xii), including a concordance, quotation books, volumes of poetry, and John Mason's *Treatise on Self-Knowledge*. But most of the titles are school readers: single volumes, like Bingham's *The Columbian Orator* or Picket's *The Juvenile Mentor,* or sequential volumes, like Lindley Murray's *English Reader* and *Sequel,* or *The New York Readers*.[2]

This 1821 advertising circular suggests the range and complexity of books dedicated to reading, as well as the overdetermined importance of reading as a school subject. Nineteenth-century reading books carry out older rhetorical and elocutionary traditions and extend their influence to a broader student population. Long after the rhetorics shift focus from oral to written discourse, the school readers redact and disseminate scholarly arguments about oratory, management of the voice, pronunciation, and articulation. Readers provide occasions for grammatical practice as well, connecting the more abstract lessons in grammar with textual interpretation and emphasis. They collect "beauties" or "choice sentences" for memorization, and they facilitate the transition to print culture, with an emphasis on book parts and features, on spelling, and on the graphic differences between print and handwriting. Lower-level readers in particular model the kinds of compositions students were being asked to prepare, offering poems, brief essays, and children's letters reproduced in handwriting for slate work or copying.

Reading was identified with long-established and valued traditions, with the maintenance of the classical curriculum and the transmission of religious texts. The earliest readers published in the United States look back, drawing on—or even reprinting—earlier British textbooks or treatises. Readers are, in many ways, conservative books, serving as repositories for the treasured texts and routines of an educational culture, yet they are also particularly responsive to change and difference. They appear in startling numbers and variety, printed in every region of the country and across the century, addressed to every level and class of learner, and regularly revised or "made new" to account for cultural shifts and moods. One effect of this publishing practice is that readers continually refigure traditions to address the needs of emerging classes of learners and to operate in the nation's diverse geographic, political, economic, and social contexts. They articulate the more abstract art of reading to the needs of many a "common reader," and they press against the boundaries of school by promoting self-education, reflective reading, and an ongoing practice of reading outside the academy. By the 1860s, readers adapt aims and methods to address "modern" concerns about efficiency, "practical" education, and the production of "American" culture and values, and thus assist in reshaping the aims of schooling in the U.S.[3]

The following pages address the proliferation and changing nature of school readers in the nineteenth century. The chapter begins by situating readers in the larger cultural context of a growth in readership and textual materials, and in shifts in the economic, social, and ideological value of reading. It then focuses on how readers extend interests developed in other kinds of textbooks, such as spellers and primers, and examines them as a textbook tradition, a medium for representing reading and learning, and a material artifact. How do these books represent diverse ways of reading, and how do the sections of these books address these differences? How do they develop over time and to address different populations? How are they produced and distributed? What can such texts contribute to modern discussions about reading and learning?

Cultural Investment in Reading

School readers are part of a broad cultural investment in the nineteenth century in reading as a lifelong activity, one guided by the institutions of school, church, library, and literary culture, as well as by individual attention to learning and improvement. Reading is proposed as a crucial national project, one that will shape citizens, unite a diffuse geographical space, and help negotiate differences in language, background, and class. The project of forming a "reading public" is powerful in both national and sectarian ways: it postulates a people unified through shared notions of taste and desired knowledge, and it divides people according to local interests and practices.[4] Reading was important preparation for the nineteenth-century's three most valued professions—religion, politics, and the law—and it was understood as a way to demonstrate individual worth to the public.

Reading as performance, as an activity that linked the private to the public, was an important religious and moral activity. Close analysis and the pursuit of a course of reading offered valued lessons in

mental discipline. Reading occupied students' time (and thus preserved them from more dangerous temptations of idleness or imagination) and taught them the habits of time management (how to
process, recall, and report on a text, how to read widely and closely).
School reading carried out important socializing functions: it delin-
eated prescribed relationships to family, community, and nation; it
promoted moral habits, civic virtue, and industry; and it articulated
the lines of class and status. It was also a valuable personal resource,
offering a way of guarding against despair or ennui, of marshalling
strength and resolve in times of need.

Reading was one of the few school subjects characterized as
both discipline and pleasure. The memoir of Warren Burton, *The
District School as It Was* (1833), illustrates this doubled perception.
Describing his first days at school as a three-year-old "abecedarian,"
Burton contrasts the "tedious process" of learning his letters with
the rich, almost physical pleasure he took in his own, more acci-
dental encounters with the letters:

> I had . . . learned the name of capital A, because it stood at
> the head of the column, and was the similitude of a harrow
> frame; of O, also, from its resemblance to a hoop. Its sono-
> rous name, moreover, was a frequent passenger through my
> mouth. (6)

Reading provided more advanced students with a language with
which to locate themselves (in Nature, in landscape, in a nation)
and offered them a diversity of models (through history and legend,
through geographical stories about different lands and customs or
about different social locations in the U.S.). School readers helped
create a vocabulary and syntax for feelings, beliefs, and values, and
the activity populated the imagination with biographies, narratives,
dialogues, and poetic expression, with what would become literary
culture. An excerpt by Thomas Bigland, printed in the 1844
McGuffey's *Rhetorical Guide*, argues for the centrality of reading and
of experience of the wide variety of genres figured as "literature":

A man of letters, when compared with one that is illiterate, exhibits nearly the same contrast as that which exists between a blind man, and one that can see. . . . It affords pleasures which wealth can not procure, and which poverty can not entirely take away. (380–83)

Given such a range of cultural values, it is not surprising that the ability to read was one of the first projects of missionaries or reformers endeavoring to assist targeted populations—the poor, slaves and freedmen, Native Americans, and immigrants. Charitable organizations like New York's Children's Aid Society (founded 1853) assisted vagrant and poor children in their education (Nye 44), and settlement houses like Jane Addams's Hull House (founded in Chicago, 1889) offered literacy instruction and organized reading circles.[5] The British Society for the Propagation of the Gospel organized slave schools in South Carolina as early as 1740, providing British reading books (Cornelius 13–15). Despite legal prohibitions against teaching slaves to read, Charles C. Jones, a southern, white plantation owner and Presbyterian assigned to "home missions," prepared a catechism for slaves and published *The Religious Instruction of the Negroes* (1842), an argument for oral instruction in scripture. The Freedman's Bureau, established in 1865 to aid freed slaves in their acculturation from slavery to a northern work force, did so partially through the publication of reading books—speller, primer, readers, and literary magazine. English readers were reconfigured, with translated text interlined (smaller type inserted in the white space between printed lines) or printed on facing pages, for use by Native Americans such as the Mohawk or Dakota tribes. Many bilingual readers were printed for immigrants and were used by missionaries, the military, and commercial travelers to disseminate "American" culture to foreign lands, like the Philippines or Japan. As Judge Joseph Story announced in his 1826 Phi Beta Kappa address at Harvard, the time was "emphatically the age of reading," in which what used to be "the accomplishment of those in the higher orders" or "the privilege of the few" had become "the possession of the many": "With such a demand for books, with such facilities of intercourse, it is no wonder that reading should cease to be a mere luxury, and should be classed among the necessaries of life."[6]

Reading was too important to be left to the schools alone; it was a topic that circulated widely in other public forums—in religious and political circles, in periodicals and fiction, in the lyceum and college literary society, in the growing number of public libraries,[7] and as a lynchpin in the self-culture movement. Every children's and ladies' magazine had something to say on the topic, from advice about how to take care of books (making bookcases or book covers, avoiding smudged pages) to counsel on how to select appropriate titles for a course of reading. And reading was a central topic for the leading intellectual magazines of the day, showing up in book reviews, articles on libraries and literary activities, debates about dictionaries and authorship, and editorials on the reading public. Free blacks in the North established literary and library societies from the 1820s, and newspapers like *Freedom's Journal* (1827–29) or periodicals like the *Anglo-African Magazine* (1859–65) widely disseminated reading materials and instruction.[8] Churches and divinity schools were active in the teaching of reading, initially to improve pulpit oratory, but also to facilitate congregations' ability to line hymns and read the Bible and, through the considerable outreach of the Sunday School Union and the American Tract Society, to extend literacy as a way of life to a broad population.[9]

Literacy activities in the extracurriculum and in the many venues outside the academy thus competed with the school's investment in reading and were in turn appropriated by school readers that reprinted periodical literature, Sabbath school tracts, and excerpts from popular authors.[10] Many readers were designated for multiple uses (for school and home, for example, or for public schools and private academies), and the material history of their use suggests their value across institutional lines, as situations and literacy needs changed. The school readers were not isolated from the swirling cultural attention to reading: rather school and the broader culture coexisted in a complicated system of citation and exchange.

Reading was inflected by its uses across regions of the United States and across class and gender lines, and the explosion of reading materials made uniform practices an impossible ideal. As periodicals grew exponentially in number in the nineteenth century to reach new readers with diverse interests, they circulated advice about reading, from the academic essay on biblical exegesis to practical advice on participating in book clubs. Cheap editions of literary texts, often with instructional notes and questions, were offered to factory workers and sold on the frontier through the Sears catalogue. Sailors broke up the monotony of voyages from the east coast to California by reading editions borrowed from the Boston Mercantile Library Association or tracts donated by Father Taylor's Seaman's Bethel. Civil War soldiers from both the North and South reported reading as an activity and desire. "Any printed matter is eagerly perused by the men," wrote one soldier. "I wish I had some books," wrote a Michigan soldier. "The best I can do now is repeat over and over such pieces of poetry as I have committed to memory" (Kaser 14).[11] Publishing firms developed from small, entrepreneurial, local establishments printing materials for a limited readership to large national houses, distributing materials by train and boat across the growing nation. The growth and spread of reading matter pressured publishers' advertising strategies and informed calls for the regulation of the "popular taste."

The methods and materials of reading became significant class markers. Rich young gentlemen in New England and South Carolina were taught using Latin readers, while rural midwesterners read the classics in translation or as selections of famous quotations. In 1822, Ralph Waldo Emerson rejoiced that French reprints of the classics made such books affordable,[12] and U.S. publishing firms issued both American and European authors in variable-priced editions, to suit the resources of a wide range of customers.[13] Middle-class families purchased elaborately bound "libraries" of selected texts, while working girls read fiction serialized in the urban story papers. In the 1840s, brightly colored paper "extras" were sold at half the price of their leather-bound cousins, and firms like Harper's sold off-copyright British fiction for far less than books by U.S. authors. The notion of a "cheap" library was popularized in the 1870s by such series as Beadle and Adams's "Half-Dime Library," DeWitt's "Ten-Cent Romances,"

and the Lakeside Library (which advertised that "the great, popular want today is for Cheap, Good Literature"), and the term "cheap"
began to shift from describing cost to naming value.[14]

Readers were instrumental both in segmenting the readership
and in circulating materials across social lines and literacy functions.
Their publishing history underscores complex acts of trespass and
changing status, as people borrowed books designed for others, read
adapted versions, or turned with renewed interest to texts cast off
by those already in power. Perhaps the most telling example is that
of the classics, which gave way to a more modern and practical
canon for young gentlemen as newcomers to literacy sought out its
associated value.[15]

British writer Frances Trollope made fun of such differently
classed experiences of texts, as in the case of the Cincinnati "gentleman" who knew Dryden "only by quotations" (92). Her *Domestic
Manners of the Americans* (1832) mocked the literacy pretensions
of American citizens, noting that "throughout all ranks of society,
from the successful merchant, which is the highest, to the domestic serving man, which is the lowest," they were "too actively employed to read, except at such broken moments as may suffice for a
peep at a newspaper" (92–93). Indeed, many at the time associated
reading with leisure time and clean hands, the privilege of quiet libraries and private moments, and a respite from manual labor or
daily duties. Reading materials were, as a consequence, adapted to
confront concerns about those who had only "broken moments."
The surge in reading instruction can be seen in part as a response
to such economic pressures and to a need to broaden the reading
public. Similarly, such concerns helped create a market for textual
materials that made reading more "efficient" and accessible to those
with little leisure or strained financial resources. Collections of short
passages, periodicals reprinting gathered materials, abridged and
redacted volumes, and the growing numbers of textbooks served to
make reading materials available to people of different education and
economic status.[16]

Despite a shared belief in reading's importance, there were
strongly competing notions of what made a "good" reader. A "good"

reader was a dutiful student, who received instruction in appropriate language use, but a "good" reader also understood how to use language in fluid social situations to address specific audiences. "The Good Reader," a selection in McGuffey's *Fifth Eclectic Reader* (1857) depicts the competition between well-to-do boys and a working-class girl, who reads "with so much feeling, and with an articulation so just" as to bring a tear to the king's eye. In an irony often repeated in readers, the unschooled girl bests the badly trained boys, by selflessly recognizing how to use literacy to serve the community (326–29). An antithetical selection on "Tact and Talent" in McGuffey's *Sixth* similarly challenges received school values of reading, promoting the active, entrepreneurial student over one with weightier learning (113–15). Such debates about competing styles of reading appeared frequently in school readers and also framed the experience of reading outside school. Novelists like Susan Warner and Harriet Beecher Stowe often place the responsibility for negotiating conflicting attitudes about reading on children, or on socially constrained characters like the poor or slaves. Ellen, the orphaned heroine of Warner's *The Wide, Wide World* (1850), agonizes over the implications of purchasing the appropriate Bible, writing desk, and implements. The object of numerous lessons about reading, she engages in scenes of reading letters, scripture, and hymns and applying such textual experience to read the landscape and people's emotions. In Stowe's *Uncle Tom's Cabin* (1851), a novel replete with commentary about diverse reading practices, children like Little Eva and Topsy—and slaves like Tom and Eliza—challenge authoritative uses of reading.

School scenes and literacy lessons abound in nineteenth-century fictions, with depictions of early learning, reading practices, and such activities as spelling bees, recitations, or declamation contests.[17] But reading also figures significantly in the antischool story, in the story that promotes reading as pleasure, as an escape from public performance or narrow disciplinary knowledge, or as "stolen reading."[18] Fictions often feature a character shut out of school—by illness, disciplinary issues, or poverty—whose alternative modes of learning compete with school learning (such is the case in Alcott's

Jack and Jill, Hawthorne's *The Scarlet Letter,* Elizabeth Stoddard's *The Morgesons,* and the emblematic story of literacy outside school, Horatio Alger's *Ragged Dick*). Books figure in such narratives as texts "owned" by school and, in competing ways, as texts made their "own" by boys and girls. Publishing firms capitalized on this complication, developing narrative series and publishing "libraries" for targeted audiences, and offering instructional books for home use like Lydia Maria Child's *Girl's Own Book* (1831), which contained lessons on games, singing, crafts, and physical exercise, as well as a selection of reading materials.[19] Books and reading were thus understood as a mechanism of educational and social control and as a method of self-development. Nineteenth-century reading books were built on these contradictions and tensions, working across the divide between school and "nature," between discipline and play, between public and personal forms of culture.

Learning to read was regularly held up as a matter of national and professional concern, depicted as a subject needing constant improvement in its theory, pedagogy, and practice. Indeed, much of what modern critics deplore about nineteenth-century reading instruction was amply articulated at the time, and textbooks advertised competing methods that would rescue students from outmoded instruction. *The Franklin Primer* (Willard 1802) promoted itself as a "substitute" for *The New-England Primer,* "which has of late become almost obsolete" (qtd. in C. Johnson 233), Leavitt's *Easy Lessons in Reading* (1823) expressed concern over using scripture as a reading text (Nietz, *Old Textbooks* 236), and Cobb's *Juvenile Reader, No. 3* (1831) decried the "practice of giving children dialogues between wolves and sheep, cats and mice, &c. &c., often met with in elementary Reading-Books, containing statements and details of things which never did, and which never can take place" (v). Many books promised efficiency or reduced cost. Stickney promised in *Word by Word* (1890) to "secure the best results at the least expense of time and effort" (156), and William Alcott (1842) promoted the "new" educational technology of his age, slate and blackboard:

There is hardly a pupil in our common schools who will not learn to read more, by spending half an hour or an hour daily on one or two or three short sentences, which he prepares for himself, than in reading over, in haste, as many pages of that which he neither understands nor cares any thing at all about. (148–49).

By the 1870s, pedagogical materials were offered separately, as a teacher's manual, or referenced to normal school manuals, periodical debates, or specific how-to books on teaching. Experts like Samuel Hall (1829), Baynard Hall (1848), and Horace Mann (*Lectures* 1855) debated the efficacy of literacy instruction, and the growing number of educational periodicals, such as William Russell's *American Journal of Education* (1826–30) and *American Annals of Education* (1830–39) and Henry Barnard's later *Journal of Education* (1855–82), circulated debates about elocution and reading, reviews of textbooks, sample classroom dialogues, and teacher tips. The normal schools and local institutes like the Cincinnati group, in which McGuffey was active, made professional concerns available to a wider audience of teachers and interested adults. A book like W. H. Cole's *Institute Reader and Normal Class-Book* (1870) combined an array of reading selections with teacher training, articulated with the structure and content of the graduated readers (part 2, for example, addresses "the teacher of the third, fourth, and fifth readers").[20]

The teaching of reading was gradually professionalized in the nineteenth century, as exemplified by the inclusion of educational apparatus in readers. But there was a tradeoff: rising pressure from commercial publishers, national standards, and mass markets made school readers of the last third of the century more uniform, more conservative about new methods, and more isolated from alternative traditions and literacy practices. Although late readers are often remarkably innovative in terms of reading selections, many lack the theoretical richness and complexity of those composed in the heady literacy debates of the 1830s and 1840s. The teaching of reading was caught up, as Mariolina Salvatori has argued and docu-

mented in *Pedagogy* (1996), in debates about the value and expertise of teaching more generally, in concerns about whether teaching—and the compiling of teaching aids—was a hobby, a vocation,
or a profession.

Teaching Reading by Letters, Words, Sentences, and Primers

Nineteenth-century textbooks organize the study of reading as attention to letters and words—initially in terms of alphabets, syllabification, spelling, and pronunciation, then in terms of etymology
and vocabulary, and later in terms of style and diction. They focus
attention on syntax and rhythm of sentences, and on sentences articulated by narrative, opposition, or dramatic sequence. All levels
stress oral performance of text, teaching students to pronounce; to
read with rising and falling action, with pauses and emphasis; and
to accompany text with appropriate gestures and postures. The more
advanced teaching of reading was carried out through books offering substantial passages, poems, and exercises—through books
called "readers." Reading was also the object of elocutionary treatises on the "art of reading" and of other instructional books—including hornbooks, alphabet books, battledores, spellers, word
books, and primers—that focused on smaller units of text, on letters, words, and sentences.

The earliest reading "books" in the United States were not actually material books at all. Eighteenth-century hornbooks were
single pieces of horn or wood covered in cloth or paper and printed
on one or both sides; they typically offered alphabets in capital and
small letters, vowels, syllables, sometimes Roman numerals, and a
prayer such as a benediction or the Lord's Prayer. Battledores (a page
or card folded once or twice) were more popular in England than
in the colonies and offered four to six pages of instruction. Embroidered samplers marked off the alphabet, numbers, and a simple text.
Many of the early reading books were what John Nietz, in *Old Textbooks* (10), calls "omnibus textbooks," that is, they offer pieces of
an entire curriculum— spelling, reading, grammar, catechism, history, geography, and sometimes even arithmetic—all in one book.

Noah Webster's *An American Selection of Lessons in Reading and Speaking* (1785), for example, was "Calculated to improve the Minds and refine the Taste of Youth" but was "also to instruct them in the Geography, History, and Politicks of the United States" (title page). Even more specialized reading books retained the variety of subject matter, printing excerpts on natural history, religion, politics, and geography, along with more literary selections in biography, prose, and poetry. Marcius Willson's *Third Reader* of the *School and Family* series (1860), for example, organized its selections into four parts: "Stories from the Bible," "Moral Lessons," "Zoology," and "Miscellaneous," which included the poem "The Nine Parts of Speech" (262). Charles Barnes's *New National Fifth Reader* (1884) included excerpts on natural history (ants, elephant hunting, bamboo, hurricanes, typhoons) and history (burning of Moscow, discovery of America, battle of Thermopylæ) with more literary passages. Geography was early on proposed as an interesting new subject that would encourage reading, and students used maps to study the plan for a classroom as well as the shape of a nation. William Swinton, who compiled readers for Harper's as well as a composition book, included a perspectival elevation and ground plan of a "schoolroom" in an initial map-making lesson in his two geographies (1876, 1882). Readers offered both young and old lessons in natural history—from caring for pets and livestock, negotiating moral terrain by reading fables about industrious ants or bees, to learning about exotic plants and animals, or reading "God's Book" of Nature.[21]

Topical books, like Jacob Abbott's Rollo stories (1855–70) or Samuel Goodrich's Peter Parley tales (1827–54), were promoted as teaching subject knowledge and making reading more interesting. In the preface to *Tales of Peter Parley about America* (1827), the first of over a hundred small reading books published under the Parley pseudonym, Goodrich announced his plan "to convey to children under the guise of amusement, the first ideas" of such subjects as geography, history, and science (3). Goodrich drew on his experience as an editor of periodicals to design richly illustrated informational books presented in story-telling form.[22] The books were also attentive to their potential as school readers: the first edition of *Tales about America* has numbered paragraphs and annotated chapter heads, and a note to the second edition announces reading questions and chapter breaks, "arranged with a view to its introduction into schools" (4). Jacob Abbott's Rollo series of twenty-eight novels (in print 1830s–70s) similarly encouraged children to reflect on their education, with volumes like *Rollo at School* (1838) or *Rollo Learning to Read* (1835). Abbott's didactic fictions are small-sized books of 150 to 200 pages focusing on some aspect of children's education, including what they learn at play and through travel. The book on reading includes selections from Rollo's school reader, interspersed with instructional passages on punctuation, letters, paragraphing, fonts, formatting, and the care of books: "What do you suppose is the reason why we left off in the middle of the line and began again in the next line, leaving a little blank space? . . . Should you like to know what such a place is called? It is called a new paragraph" (67–68).

Reading thus traveled to and borrowed from other school subjects, but at the same time reading itself became a more specialized topic, and its instruction was dispersed across different aspects of reading and learning. These reading books differ in approach, level, and method, but they often show overlapping or multiple interests. Hornbooks focus on the alphabet but may also include the full text of the Lord's Prayer. Alphabet books, distributed both as "popular" children's books and for school use, print a pictured alphabet but also include short verses or definitions. "Word" books and spellers are recognizable physically by their columns of single words but often include sentences, prose passages, and short poems. Readers include alphabet pages, vocabulary lists, and tables of words "often misspelled." To further complicate matters, what looks like comparable attention—to lists of words, for example—may well signal radically different concerns (with syllabification, vocabulary, or etymology rather than spelling).

Letters

Learning to read began in nineteenth-century books with attention to the alphabet and syllables. Letters were printed in the first pages of elementary books, usually in both small and capital forms, often in "italicks," in the "double" printing forms common in the 1700s, and in multiple fonts. The alphabet appears thus as a graphic or print form, and, in columns of "Easie Syllables for Children" (ab, eb, ib, ob, ub), as a procedure to teach pronunciation. Syllables are usually organized by initial vowels and consonants, but they sometimes form short words (ox, go, no, us, up), or stress an ending sound (bri*ck*, toa*st*, tru*dge*). In McGuffey's *Fourth Eclectic Reader* (1879), letters and syllables are organized as elaborate tables of vocals, subvocals, and aspirates, and students are offered exercises in the "more common errors in articulation and pronunciation."[23] Letters are also printed in script forms, as are numbers and longer samples of writing, showing these books' potential use for dictation, blackboard, or copying exercises.

The alphabet is reprinted with both texts and images as mnemonics to aid in learning, or, one could argue, alphabetical order is a useful device for organizing and giving interest to a series of "choice sentences," lessons, or bits of cultural knowledge. Nineteenth-century primers usually offer a *pictured* or *emblematical alphabet*, composed of words, sentences, or short rhymed couplets accompanying a small image for each letter. Appearing as early in Britain as John Hart's *A Methode, or Comfortable Beginning for All Unlearned* (1570) or *Visible World* (a 1659 translation of John Comenius's 1658 Latin reader),[24] these pictured alphabets were a staple of children's book publication from the eighteenth century on (many appeared in chapbook form, i.e. in small inexpensive books usually of sixteen pages, folded from a single sheet). The version made famous through multiple printings of *The New-England Primer* (1697–1830) organizes the alphabet through twenty-four small woodcut images (omitting *j* and *u*)[25] and a rhymed verse, covering multiple interests, from the expected religious or moral concerns and history to more secular observations about animals, death, politics, and idle schoolboys. Some verses make specific references to history (Xerxes, the British king) or the Bible (such figures as Peter, Job, and Queen Esther). Others organize the moral and natural world in a brief rhyme:

A	In *Adam's* Fall	K	Our *King* the good
	We Sinned all.		No man of blood.
B	Thy Life to Mend	I	The *Idle* fool
	This *Book* Attend		Is whipt at School.
C	The *Cat* doth play	Y	*Youth* forward slips
	And after slay.		Death soonest nips.

The New-England Primer also offers an "Alphabet of Lessons for Youth" that arranges in acrostic fashion a series of longer statements, many of them quotations from the Bible: "A Wise Son makes a glad Father, but a foolish Son is the heaviness of his Mother," or "Foolishness is bound up in the heart of a Child, but the rod of Correction shall drive it far from him."

Later primers continue to associate images with verses or words in alphabetical order, although they draw content from different domains: natural history, exotic plants, household objects, or American politics. Osgood's *American Primer* (1870) prints the twenty-six letters of the alphabet in elaborate illustrated form, but rearranged as phonetic lessons. One page uses the letter *x* (*ax, ox, fox, box*), and another gives words with a short *a* (*bat, cat, hat, rat, fan*). Such inattention to alphabetic order moves away from recitation and memory towards spelling and writing. The arrangement of letters suggests that children are being taught to spell, to recognize print conventions, and ultimately to write. In one copy of this primer, for example, a child has printed the word *DO* following Lesson 26 ("Do we go at it? Do we go up to it? We do go up to it? Oh! so we do") and next to Lesson 27 ("Up we go. So we go. I am up. Is he up? No."). *Do* is spelled similarly but pronounced differently from *go, so,* and *no,* whereas, in the next lesson, *Oh* is pronounced similarly but spelled differently. In an earlier primer, such a lesson would have been marked for its potential to produce error in reading aloud. This primer offers, instead, the very confusions of English orthography facing students as they learn to write.

Words
Reading was also taught by presenting lists of words, arranged by length of syllable, associative category, etymology, or first letter. The

practice of *syllabification* taught readers to divide potentially difficult words into units to facilitate pronunciation. This system allowed them to parse any word, however long, making it possible for students to sound out new words and study them without a teacher's help. Such a practice refigured, in part, the instruction in Latin readers, in which students were taught to recognize roots and endings and thereby to decipher unknown words by analysis. *The New-England Primer* (1727), for example, divides important texts like the Lord's Prayer and the Apostles' Creed. As the more modern sense of spelling emerged, syllabification became a method of producing the correct spelling of a word *(ab— a-b— sence— s-e-n-c-e —absence),* a practice that persists in spelling bees.

Spelling was an early aim for such lists of words and considered a necessary stage in learning to read. In the eighteenth and early nineteenth century, *spelling* meant dividing words into syllables, what Ian Michael calls an "analytic process," although, as Michael explains, students were taught in "synthetic" ways, adding consonants to vowels in increasing complexity (*Teaching* 90–92). *The New-England Primer* (1727) indicates spelling's place in a chain of instruction, marking in a note to the teacher, "Now the Child being entred in his Letters and Spelling, let him learn these and such like Sentences by Heart." By the 1830s, however, spelling was under challenge, and textbooks rushed to redefine its value as literacy instruction. Salem Town's *Spelling and Defining Book* (1838) insisted that "a child being taught, both to read and to spell, *should* be taught, at the same time, to *understand* what he reads and spells" (3); his book was to counter "the mere mechanical exercise of spelling, and storing the memory with words which, as yet, convey no sense." J. H. Stickney's "advanced" speller, *Word by Word* (1890), argued that spelling focused words so that "the pupil has them, as it were, unstrung, or released from their temporary thought connection, that his undivided attention may be given to their form" (4).

By the end of the century, through the popularity of spelling bees, spelling was a visible performance of school literacy; like grammar, it captured the public imagination as a measure of "good" students. Spelling was valued, claims *Sheldon's Word Studies* (1886), as "daily exercise" because of the difficulty of English orthography, "together with the fact that correct spelling is considered a test of scholarship" (3). As Richard Bailey argues, it became "enshrined as an evidence of education and gentility" (64).[26] Yet even as spelling's public value rose, it was critiqued in educational circles as a study of "doubtful profit," as Sheldon's *Word Studies* acknowledged, "which has only escaped banishment from the schoolroom because no fitting substitute could be found for the work it aimed to do" (7). Arthur Applebee argues that modern attention to spelling transforms English studies into "a set of mechanical skills in language use" in which "students have been tested and drilled" (253). Yet despite its position as a test subject and public performance, spelling and its atomistic attention to letters and words were never simply mechanical drill in the nineteenth century. Spelling remained throughout the century a much-debated topic, a subject for reform and arguments about national and regional language. It reflected the fascination with words as sounds and graphic representations evident in the circulation of games such as anagrams, acrostics, conundrums, enigmas, and charades. Its persistence in the schools represented nationalistic concerns about "Americanisms," dialect, and slang that engaged such writers as Noah Webster, James Fenimore Cooper, Emerson, Walt Whitman, and Mark Twain.[27]

The most famous American spelling book was Noah Webster's "blue-backed speller," as *The Elementary Spelling Book* was popularly called. The speller derived from part 1 of Webster's 1783 *Grammatical Institute of the English Language,* which included a "standard" of pronunciation, a grammar, and *An American Selection of Lessons in Reading and Speaking* (issued as a separate reader in 1785). Part 1 was reissued in 1787 as *The American Spelling Book,* although it also included brief reading selections and "A Moral Catechism." By 1829, a revised version focused on spelling—printing lists of words with phonetic, syllable, and accent markings, followed by sentences containing the words. Organized from two-letter syllables to words of seven syllables, the 151 numbered lessons also cluster words by short and long vowels, by accented and unaccented syllables, and by consonant sounds. Former slaves testified about working their way through its syllable and word lessons, marking the achievement of learning to "spell to baker" (the first of the two-syllable words).[28] Webster's *Speller* looks like a long list of words, but it was also a radical argument about language. His *Dictionary* (1828) and the reissuing of the *Speller* (1829) challenged the hold on American language by English dictionaries, definitions, spelling, and pronunciation. Webster invited students to study words as they were being used in the United States—often in distinction from their use in Great Britain.[29]

Sentences

Early eighteenth-century British and American readers were compilations of "choice" or "select" sentences, organized by increasing length and complexity or by sentence structure. Occasionally the author of a particularly important sentence is identified, but often sentences appear out of context, listed without author or source. Many are the quasi-anonymous sayings of an era, like "Prosperity gains friends, and adversity tries them," but others are famous quotations, like Shakespeare's "What a piece of work is man!" (Enfield's *Speaker* 26, 32). Murray's *English Reader* (1799) begins both its prose and poetry selections with chapters of closely printed "select sentences." So does Webster's *American Selection* (1785), although the entire section is copied without attribution from Enfield's *Speaker* (1774). Pierpont's *Introduction to the National Reader* (1835) prints sentences from Psalms and Ecclesiasticus, followed by several lessons of "select moral sentences," and Cobb's *Juvenile Reader, No. 3* (1831) opens with a page of numbered "select sentences" ("It costs more to revenge injuries than to bear them," and "Deliberate with caution, but act with decision"). An advanced reader like McGuffey's *Rhetorical Guide* (1844) incorporates select sentences into its introductory exercises. Many readers number sentences throughout their volume, even in longer reading lessons.

Noted Unitarian preacher Orville Dewey proposed, in an 1829 essay, "Principles of Elocution," that "*the making of good sentences*" is "the first business of a public speaker." He complained that in most public speeches "violations of sense, of the structure of sentences, nay, and of grammar, too, are constantly witnessed. It is really perilous to listen. We are in perpetual terror lest the speaker should make shipwreck of all reason and sense" (50). Spellers and readers exposed prospective orators and speakers to a wide variety of sentences: short informational or dramatic sentences, loose and periodic sentences, complex sentences with embedded clauses and parentheses. Sometimes these were typeset on a slant to indicate rising and falling action, sometimes marked with symbols to indicate emphasis, pause, or monotone. Many of these sentences would become extremely familiar across the nation, as they appear over many printings, in multiple textbooks, and to illustrate varying principles. Sentences that particularly suit elocutionary analysis appeared repeatedly, lasting well beyond their initial time and importance because of their instructional value. Antithetical sentences, for example, like those about Homer and Virgil drawn from Blair's *Lectures,* Dr. Johnson's contrast of Dryden and Pope, or self-referential sentences like "Did you read it correctly, or incorrectly?" appear in many readers over the century, serving advanced as well as elementary students (see fig. 3). Texts became widely known as "reading texts," not because of their literary value per se, but because of their use by an educational system. Nevertheless, they were often read with unexpected pleasure in ways different from their exercise function. Emerson remarked in a letter to his brother William (July 23, 1818; *Letters* 1: 68) that he was excited by one of "Tacitus' elliptical sentences" he came across in his Latin reader. And the working-class poet Lucy Larcom reported her pleasure in metric examples: "A tattered copy of Johnson's large Dictionary was a great delight to me, on account of the specimens of English versification which I found in the Introduction. I learned them as if there were so many poems" (127).

Sentences from different sources and genres were juxtaposed in elocutionary exercises, organized by form or length rather than by belletristic qualities. Murray's poetry lines, for example, are organized topically, by length, and by the challenge they pose readers: "short and easy" (182) sentences are followed by those "containing exclamations, interrogations, parentheses" (185). A practice

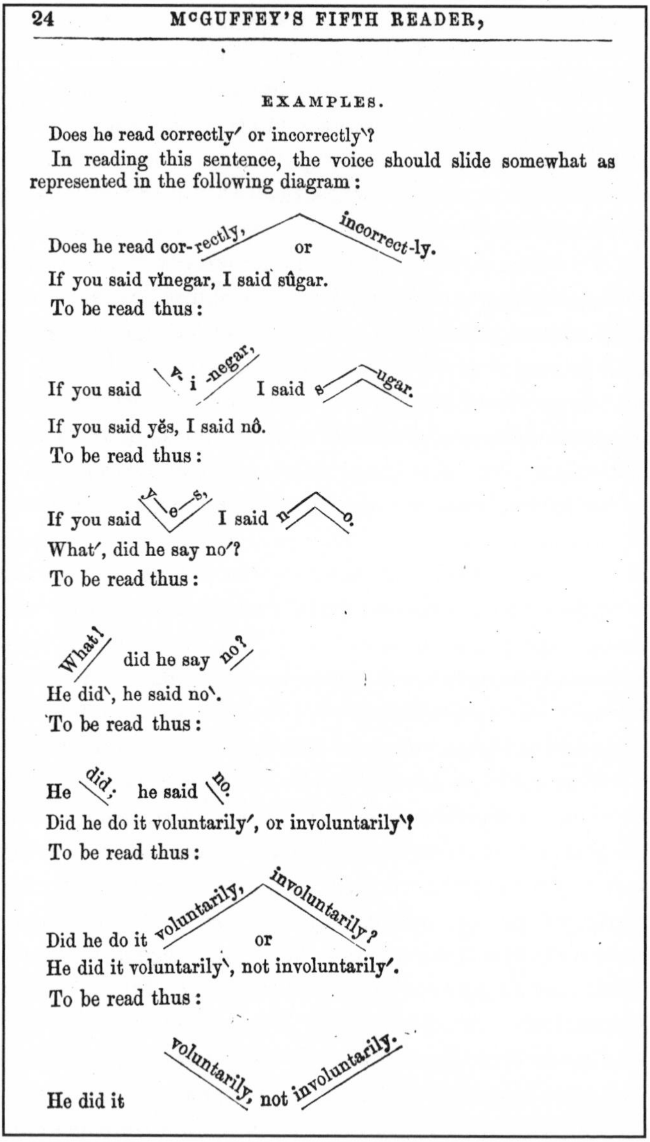

24 McGUFFEY'S FIFTH READER,

EXAMPLES.

Does he read correctly′ or incorrectly‵?

In reading this sentence, the voice should slide somewhat as represented in the following diagram:

Does he read cor-rectly, or incorrect-ly.

If you said vĭnegar, I said sûgar.

To be read thus:

If you said vi-negar, I said sugar.

If you said yĕs, I said nô.

To be read thus:

If you said yes, I said no.

What′, did he say no′?

To be read thus:

What! did he say no?

He did‵, he said no‵.

To be read thus:

He did; he said no.

Did he do it voluntarily′, or involuntarily‵?

To be read thus:

Did he do it voluntarily, or involuntarily?

He did it voluntarily‵, not involuntarily′.

To be read thus:

He did it voluntarily, not involuntarily.

Fig. 3. Exercise examples of rising and falling action. *McGuffey's Rhetorical Guide; or Fifth Reader of the Eclectic Series,* Cincinnati, 1853, 24.

sequence in McGuffey's *Rhetorical Guide* (1844) shows a startling mix of discourses: "She mil*k*ed six cows. Give me a ya*r*d and *th*ree eigh*th*s. Ha! laug*h'*st thou, Lochiel, my vision to *s*co*r*n?" (22). A note to Southey's poem "The Cataract of Lodore" in McGuffey's *Rhetorical Guide* (63) makes clear such functional attention: "this lesson is inserted on account of its very peculiar adaptation for practice on the difficult sound *ing*" (the poem describes a cataract of water: "Here it comes sparkling/ And there it lies darkling/. . . Collecting, projecting/ Receding and speeding . . ."). Byron's poetic sentence "Roll on, thou deep and dark blue Ocean—roll!" ("Childe Harold" 4.179.1) appears in many readers to illustrate everything from monotone to emphasis. Such a sentence was so valuable that it appeared even in a textbook explicitly warning against the infamous poet's "poison": the 1871 Catholic *Metropolitan Fifth Reader* includes the sentence (Gillespie 48) despite its qualms about Byron's reputation (iv).

Even when readers announce themselves as "new and enlarged" or "improved," they often repeat the exemplary sentences of earlier textbooks. Perhaps the most famous of such sentences is "Shall you ride to Town to-day?" which appeared in various guises in British rhetorics as early as John Mason (1748) and Thomas Sheridan (1762) and then with remarkable persistence in American readers from 1790–1870.[30] Noah Webster (*American Selection* 1785) and Caleb Bingham (*Columbian Orator* 1797) cite the example in almost identical ways, indicating that "this short question, 'Will you ride to town to-day?'" can be asked and answered in four different ways, "according to the placing of the emphasis" (Webster 4, Bingham 11). McGuffey's *Fourth Reader* (1837) calls attention to the tradition, crediting Blair as its source: "There is no better illustration of the nature and importance of emphasis, than the following example . . . which has often been quoted" (25). Versions also appear in Ebenezer Porter's 1832 *Rhetorical Reader* ("Will you go today—or tomorrow?" "Will you ride—or walk?" appear as examples of rising and falling inflection); in Parker's *Progressive Exercises in Rhetorical Reading* (1835); and in the *American Educational Fifth Reader* (1873). Murray's *English Reader* (1799) cites the famous four-fold sentence

(8–9) but shifts its analysis to the opening line of Milton's *Paradise Lost* ("Of man's first disobedience . . .").

Nineteenth-century readers provide an anthology of important cultural texts, often eclectic in genre and style, drawn from English writers as well as from those writing in the United States. Many of these passages were the staples of public performances, declamation contests, and parlor gatherings and circulated as quotations in literary and literate culture of the day. Critics of modern cultural literacy claim, with nostalgia, that ordinary citizens used to be able to call up lines from Shakespeare, or that they were widely read in a set of shared cultural texts.[31] Certainly, nineteenth-century students were familiar with an impressive range of sentences and syntactic rhythms, and with certain kinds of high styles (oratory, sermon, literary). Yet much of their textual knowledge was derived from readers rather than from whole texts. Indeed, the most familiar lines were probably not even from the anthology of longer excerpts, but from the exercise examples, lines like Longfellow's "Footprints on the sands of time" ("Psalm of Life") or Shakespeare's "Alas! poor Yorick!" (*Hamlet*). The sentences provide a manageable canon of texts to master, and they may have had broader effects as well, such as promoting a taste for the epigrammatic practice favored by such writers as Benjamin Franklin and Emerson.

Primers

These multiple forms of reading instruction could be found in curtailed ways in reading books called primers. In the nineteenth century, *primer* refers to the first in a series of readers, but, in an older sense, it may derive from the "prime" hour for prayers, signaling a book of prayers that includes reading instruction. Early primers collect the central religious documents of a culture, translated into the vernacular for each parishioner's daily use. The pictured alphabets and reading lessons associated with nineteenth-century primers were added to help teach individuals to read these documents without the help of clergy. As Samuel Johnson's *Dictionary* defined it in 1755, a primer was "a small prayer-book in which children are taught to read." Such primers are often characterized as slipping moral lessons into a pedagogical textbook; historically, the drive for literacy came second, as a condition of the book's use as a privately owned volume to be read at home. A 1727 version of *The New-England Primer* marks this doubled function by a note to teachers suggesting the child should be "both instructed in his Duty, and encouraged in his Learning." Such primers were valuable cultural texts because they isolated a set of readings out of the multiplicity of the Bible and disseminated those texts in specific translation and form, framed with a pedagogical apparatus. Students were taught set responses to questions; they memorized catechisms, prayers, and biblical passages.

Primers in the 1700s were "small" books: sometimes only two or three inches tall, they contained few and relatively brief texts. Although primers look like children's books, the texts they reprint are hardly childish or simplified for a beginning reader. *The New-England Primer* (1727) offers the complex vocabulary of Old and New Testament (words such as *Beelzebub, Ecclesiastes, crucifixion,* and *fornication*), reproduces commandments, and selects from the Bible sentences proclaiming the "duty of children towards their parents" and articulating proper attitudes toward death, learning, and work. Many of its lessons can be seen as aids to help readers make their way through the Bible, the longest and most complex of reading books, a sufficient text for a life's worth of learning. It lists the books of the Bible, complicated biblical names, geographical terms, and the numbers needed to locate chapter and verse. The New Testament or a psalm book often served as the accompanying reader for eighteenth-century students, and, as E. Jennifer Monaghan has argued, since the selected texts were basic cultural documents, "comprehension of the text was assumed" ("Literacy Instruction" 58). *The New-England Primer's* texts are thus referential of a broader reading experience rather than complete in themselves.

The primers of the 1800s, like Lindley Murray's *First Book for Children* (1805) and McGuffey's *Primer* (1838), were more explicitly books for children, teaching the first lessons in reading to students who would then proceed to graduated levels of readers. Later editions of *The New-England Primer* substitute "children's" texts (rhymes like "A was an apple pie" or Watt's "Cradle Song") for the earlier somber catechism and moral sentences. By 1879, McGuffey's *Primer* insisted it took care to "insure a gradation suited to the youngest children" by limiting the number of new words for each lesson to six (iii). With ample illustrations and large type, it begins its sixty-four pages with a printed alphabet (in capital and small letters), ends with script slate exercises and alphabet, and in between offers fifty-two brief lessons, with words marked for phonetic sounds. Unlike the earlier vocabulary of sin and repentance, this primer offers a child's diction developed through sound and rhyme ("A cat and a rat. A rat and a cat. The rat ran at Ann. Nat has a fan."). Lessons are typically five sentences long, developing by the end of the book into brief verses—"I love my dear puss/ Her fur is so warm" (56).

What Is a "Reader"?

Even this brief account of competing kinds of reading books—alphabets, spellers, word books, and primers—suggests how difficult it is to characterize "a reader." Although in some sense, readers succeed or displace these books, in another sense, they continue many of the activities these books represent, and these specialized books continue to be produced and used in the schools. The choice sentence or brief exercise recurs in the readers, often as a longer text, or as an exercise with more context provided. Advanced lessons may mark spelling words or compile glossaries of words to define. The smaller unit is not necessarily more or less "complex" as an object of study; indeed, procedures like antithesis or emphasis that students tried out on smaller texts return to structure their experience of other, longer texts.

Readers are also an internally diverse tradition. They share many features and concerns, recycling excerpts, examples, structures, and topics; they also differ widely, in size (both of the physical book and number of entries), in design, in audience and level of address, in educational apparatus and helps. A reader issued in the early part of the century, like Cobb's *Juvenile Reader, No. 3* (1831), is as small as a primer (pocket-sized or 4" x 6"), yet it may contain over two hundred pages of closely printed text. By the 1850s and on, advanced readers are substantial books: four hundred to six hundred pages of text measuring 5" x 7 ¾", although the font size is usually more readable than the earlier volumes, and it is rare to see the double-columned style prevalent in some readers before the 1830s. Even the most elementary volumes, the primer and first reader, are long books (sixty to one hundred pages) in comparison with other literacy books (e.g., spellers, composition books) aimed at young children, and advanced readers compete with rhetorics for size and scale.

Size is, of course, a difficult feature to correlate with educational level or cultural use. Shorter books often redact more complex, fuller books—for less advanced students or for those with fewer resources in time or income. But size—both physical and textual—was also determined by use. Early reading books were designed to be easily held or carried, as were much later vest or pocket books designed for adults. Early in the century, many advanced books are physically small, with impossibly small type; by the 1830s, following a profusion of articles about the strain reading causes on eyes, readers begin to appear in larger type, especially for younger readers.[32] The shape and design of reading books were inflected by technological developments in lighting and eyewear; as well as by the material conditions of book production, changes in paper making, printing, binding, and image reproduction; the economies of marketing and distributing books; and the aesthetics of illustration, design, and layout.

As material books, readers also suggest their affiliation with literary culture. Designed to blend into a literary collection, upper-level readers are often elegant books, with tooled leather bindings, marbled end pages, illustrations, and graphic embellishments, whereas lower level readers reflect the design of children's books—in shape, size, and quantity of illustration. Advanced readers contain many of the paratextual materials of nineteenth-century periodicals and literary publications: lists of authors and illustrators, biographical introductions of authors, tables of contents and plates, recommended readings, and prefaces.[33]

Readers are often rich in educational apparatus, with pedagogical introductions, appendices, vocabulary lists, punctuation tables, reading questions, and footnoted reminders about texts posing particular difficulties. Early in the century, most readers include a letter or preface directed to teachers, advertising the special features of the book and characterizing how it addresses the "needs" of students. Even an elementary reader can print a surprising array of texts aimed at teachers, suggesting how the teaching of reading should be understood, valued, and delivered. Cobb's *Juvenile Reader, No. 3* (1831) begins with two notes (v–vi), one to students (reminding them to "pay great attention to the manner in which their teacher, and other persons of approved skill, perform the business of reading" and "to imitate them as nearly as possible") and one to teachers (clarifying reading pedagogy, sequence of learning, choice of a system of pronunciation, and value of enunciation to prevent the "embarrassments" of "a confirmed habit of stammering"). The fourteen-page introduction, offering a familiar disquisition on reading, is addressed to teachers and to a broader public concerned about the efficacy of reading instruction. A punctuation table that looks initially like a modern handbook's corrections page presents "the stops or points, and other characters used in writing and printing" (xxiii); these are marked as a rhetorical code (assisting a student "to discern the grammatical construction, and next, to regulate his pronunciation") and a set of printer's conventions indicating subtle relationships of text.

More advanced elocutionary readers reproduce a set of topics on the art of reading, often including complicated tables of rhetorical symbols (which they contrast to punctuation as a more effective system of indicating delivery). Others print lessons in phonetic representations, so that on quick glance, a page looks like a foreign language. Lindley Murray's *English Reader* (1799) titles its thirteen pages of advice "Observations on the Principles of Good Reading." A note indicates its debt to "Dr. Blair and to the Encyclopedia Britannica" (v), although Murray does not indicate the full extent of the debt, nor does he mention (or recognize?) that Blair's *Lectures* (1783) borrow from Thomas Sheridan's *Course of Lectures on Elocution* (1762). He composes his introduction by copying word for word large sections of Blair's Lecture XXXIII, "Pronunciation, or Delivery of a Discourse," and deviates from Blair primarily to add more specific instructions about teaching young children (as in his discussion of loud tones, where he describes children who have been "taught to read in large rooms" or taught by instructors "imperfect in their hearing" [vii]). The introduction ends with advice to teachers to "exercise their pupils" before they are called on to read aloud, suggesting that such "preparatory" reading will "improve their judgment and taste" (xvii). Murray again follows Blair's lead in his criteria for selecting texts, valuing those showing "purity, propriety, perspicuity" and "elegance" (iii).

Such rhetorical interests distinguish readers in English from the more philological Latin and Greek readers that precede them. The classical readers typically dispense with prefaces, notes to teachers, or introductions about "the art of reading." Classical readers printed in the United States show their dependence on both a teaching canon (the choice and ordering of selections remains remarkably similar across various titles and publication dates) and set of procedures established by German textbooks of the previous century. The earliest U.S. Latin readers reprint or adapt a widely used German edition, Jacobs and Döring's *Latin Reader* (1825), and the Greek readers reprint another German edition, Jacobs's *Greek Reader* (Boston, 1832). These classical readers, often keyed to or supplemented by grammars,[34] focus attention on expertise in language, and few reflect the English readers' concerns about "improving" or "modernizing" the materials or procedures for learning. The subtitles suggest some of the components and expected instructional uses. Walker's *New Latin Reader* (1829) is billed as "containing the Latin text for the purpose of recitation; accompanied with a key, containing the text, a literal and true translation, arranged in such a manner as to point out the difference between the Latin and the English idioms." McClintock's *Second Book in Latin* (1853) explains in its subtitle that it contains "*syntax and reading lessons in prose, . . . imitative exercises and a vocabulary.*"

Compared to advanced English readers, classical readers are generally shorter (180–220 pages) with brief reading selections.

Their affiliation with the study of grammar often occupies the final half of the volume, with extensive sentence exercises, a dictionary or lexicon, and notes about language, vocabulary, and usage (usually rendered in English). Exercises proceed through levels of syntactic complexity and focus on recognizing and composing particular grammatical structures: for example, Harkness's *Second Latin Book* (1853) directs students to "construct three Latin sentences, one with infinitive as subject, one with infinitive as predicate, and one with infinitives both as subject and predicate" (201).

Reading of Latin and Greek declined across the nineteenth century except as a sign of advanced achievement. In 1745, the entrance requirements to Yale College had proposed that students be able to "Read, Construe and Parce" a set of standard Latin texts (qtd. in Nietz, *Evolution* 155), but, a century later, many students pursued the "English" rather than the "classical" course of study, and their entrance examinations shifted attention to English syntax, modern languages, and more modern texts. Although U.S. colleges continued to encourage students to "read" Latin compositions—Rufus Griswold noted that "the number of Latin orations before our colleges has been very large" (25n)—by the 1830s, the "decline" of classical expertise was cited as advanced warning of a general "crisis" in literacy in the United States. Classical languages figured in concern about abstract or outmoded knowledge; modes of teaching reading through the classics were critiqued as antiquarian, tedious, and divorced from reading's "applied" practices of writing and public speaking. In 1846, Griswold claimed: "Few Americans have written much in the Latin language. The occasions for its use are less frequent than formerly. It is commonly taught however in our schools, and numerous works of unquestionable merit . . . have appeared here to facilitate its study" (25–26). The *North American Review* for July 1836 (28–52) discussed a recent life of George Washington "in Latin, for the use of schools" (Kingsley 28) but complained "the number of writers in America, who have adopted the Latin language, is small. The Latin has been taught in our colleges, and in many of our schools; but, though multitudes have made such progress in the language as to read it with ease and pleasure, few have employed it in writing" (43). By mid-century, Latin readers begin to show the influence of their English analogues and to respond to the challenge to make such study more up-to-date and culturally relevant. Harkness's *Second Latin Book* (1853), for example, offered its American students culturally translated exercise sentences to catch their interest and suggest uses for composition: "Has the number of states been increased? The number of states in the United States has been increased. Will not the number of American citizens be increased?" (92). The traditional Latin sentences about citizens being deprived of their land are displaced by Americanized sentences about students being deprived of their books: "Who deprived you of your books? Will you deprive the Romans of their glory?" (119).[35]

By the 1830s, most advanced English readers printed a fifty- to sixty-page elocutionary introduction that makes such "advanced" readers longer texts than either earlier English or Latin readers. The introductions detail expectations for students and teachers, offer advice on the importance of particular rhetorical practices, and explain why the specific book (or pedagogical system) is appropriate for a designated set of students.[36] They quote experts—reproducing materials from earlier rhetorics, periodical articles, and pedagogical "systems." This apparatus offers advice about what the rhetorics called "pronunciation," which signaled the oral delivery of written text, and so there are often discussions about posture, gesture, and movement, as well as versions of the traditional topics (articulation, inflection, accent and emphasis, rising and falling action, pauses, monotones, parenthesis). Each topic usually offers a series of exercises, short passages of texts (single lines, quatrains, brief excerpts) on which students can practice such principles as "antithesis" or "pitch." Passages that appear in subsequent lessons as authored or contextualized appear in the educational apparatus as discrete practice texts, usually without any attribution.[37] Exercises sometimes call on students to treat text as a printed medium, filling in the omitted words of an "elliptical" exercise or paying attention to italicized words or "emphatics." Punctuation figures as a graphic marker of print, but more importantly as an interpretive mark signaling how to measure pauses, rising or falling action: "when you come to a Period you must stop, as if you had nothing more to read" (Parker, *Progressive Exercises in Rhetorical Reading* 1). Most readers signal verse as a particular kind of reading practice, requiring considerable advice and challenging the most advanced deployment of elocutionary skills. By the end of the century, readers downplay advice to teachers; indeed many late-century readers look more like anthologies of readings, with little pedagogical intervention.[38]

After the educational introduction, most of the pages in a nineteenth-century reader are an anthology of numbered lessons,[39] printing excerpts of select sentences, poetry, fiction, drama, dialogues, historical narrative, descriptive passages, and essays. The lessons may include questions, biographical introductions, or lists of words (vocabulary or likely mispronunciations). Many of the selections show the influence of the elocutionary tradition. An early reader like *The Columbian Orator* (1797) is composed of dialogues (such as the one between the "Master" and "Slave" that Frederick Douglass describes in his 1849 *Narrative*),[40] and elocutionary readers print exemplary speeches from literature or life (Marc Antony's burial speech or Henry V's speech to his troops, or speeches by noted orators like Fox or Webster). Murray's *English Reader* (1799) and Pierpont's *American Class Book* (1823), follow Enfield's *Speaker* (1774) in categorizing pieces as prose or poetry, with subdivisions of narrative, didactic, argumentative, descriptive, pathetic, dialogues, public speeches, and what Murray calls "promiscuous" pieces (i.e., not belonging to a particular category). Poetry and prose are often intermixed but listed separately in tables of contents. Early in the century, the distinction between "prose" and "poetry" (including verse lines from drama) probably signals different expectations for oral performance, rather than a particular affiliation with belletristic interests.

Across the century, readers offer a wide variety of genres and styles, many inherited from older instructional forms. Such genres as fables, model lives, moral reflection, description, poetry, and history appear in the earliest readers. The early moral tales for children are supplanted in the 1830s by more age-appropriate selections: narratives about pets, stories about the care of books and toys, poems about friendship. Mid-century readers include less elevated forms (comic scenes, excerpts from fiction), although none so insistently as *Oldham's Amusing and Instructive Reader* (1854), which proclaims the importance of "wit, humor, and mirth" as the "means of awakening interest, and imparting instruction" (title page). By the 1870s, generic distinctions may also mark literary genres, and older categories ("dramatick," "narrative") reemerge as literary forms (the drama, ballad). Monroe's *Sixth Reader* (1872) adds to prose and poetry a selection of "dialogues and concert-readings," which offer the familiar dialogues of the elocutionary readers and such set pieces as Longfellow's "Paul Revere's Ride" and Dickens's "Two Views of Christmas." John S. Hart, the prolific editor of the Sunday School Union's periodical as well as a rhetoric, philosophy of education, and introductions to English and American Literature, draws from an eclectic set of texts for his *Class Book of Prose* (1845), which shows its interest in "literary" history by arranging selections from "distinguished authors" in chronological order, with biographical and critical commentary. By late century, many readers privilege literary forms, such as stories, poetry, lives of authors, and literary history, while others print a specified content, such as history or science. Marcius Willson's five *School and Family Readers* (1860), for example, focus on natural history as an organizing topic. The *Third Reader* prints 150 pages of readings on "Zoology," with scientific description mixed in with poems, fables, traveler's accounts, and a "Negro" tale about a fiddler staving off hungry wolves (136–39).

Many readers follow the McGuffey series in producing an "eclectic" selection—multiple genres and levels of discourse, texts from England and America, older pieces and "modern" texts—organized into a numbered sequence of lessons. The McGuffey *Readers,* adopting "eclectic" in their titles, were marketed by W. B. Smith as part of a series of "eclectic school books." Suggesting more generally a broad or unfettered taste, the term referred specifically to a volume made up of diverse selections and drawing from multiple systems of instruction.[41] Although eclectic readers print lessons with little overt structure, the numbered sequences often cluster related pieces, on topics like nature, the flag, war, Indians, or memory. There is usually a discernible logic to beginning pieces (often self-referential pieces about reading, elocution, or school) and ending pieces ("sublime" pieces designed to assist the transition to the world or to adulthood and to negotiate "last things"—old age, death, and eternity). McGuffey's 1844 *Rhetorical Guide,* for example, ends with pieces on old age, the closing year, Campbell's poem "The Last Man," industry, and passages from Psalms. Watson's *Independent Sixth Reader* (1871) ends with a section on death, including Wordsworth's "Intimations of Immortality." Several mid-century readers, including McGuffey's *Sixth* (1857), close with Coleridge's "Ode to Mt. Blanc," with its sublime hymn to earth's wonders.

The editors of earlier readers treat selections as material to be adapted "to the uses of the schools." Selections may be retitled—sometimes to suit the theme of the excerpt, sometimes in accordance with contemporary practices of shorthand titles (for example, Coleridge's "Ode to Mt. Blanc"); they are cut, paraphrased, and in some cases radically rewritten for the level and purposes of the particular reader. The preface to McGuffey's *Sixth Reader* (1867) explains the "considerable liberty" taken to "adapt" selections: "Much change and remodeling have been necessary. The lessons are therefore credited as taken *'from'* the author named" (8). By the 1870s, however, textual accuracy became a literary expectation and a selling point, a way of distinguishing a series from its competitors, and readers like McGuffey's *Sixth* (1879) denounced adaptation: the preface announced that "close scrutiny revealed the fact that many popular selections, common to several series of Readers, had been largely *adapted*" (iii).

Many readers include pieces that challenge the efficacy of school instruction and suggest the importance instead of self-culture or immersion in nature. The McGuffey *Sixth* (1879), for example, prints George Arnold's poem about the "jolly old pedagogue" who displaces the educator's subjects ("the Rule of Three, / Reading, and writing, and history too") with a more personal lesson to "learn while you're young" (133–35), and an excerpt from Dickens's *Old Curiosity Shop* contrasts the "noise and drawl of school" with the greater pleasures of being outdoors (136–37). Whittier's "barefoot boy, with cheek of tan" treasures his "knowledge never learned of schools" and enjoys his brief summer's escape before he is "made to tread the mills of toil, / Up and down in ceaseless moil" (317–20). If this reader offers its own self-critique or attempts to associate its lessons with the pleasure of escape and leisure, it also offers a grim picture of students' future expectations. An excerpt by Lyman Beecher warns that American education has failed to fend off the perils of prosperity (228–31), and a piece by Horace Greeley cautions American youth to consider a career in "productive industry . . . in case he shall fail in the more intellectual or artificial calling which he may prefer to it" (398).

One way of representing the change in readers across the century is to say that reading changed from *elocutionary*—from reading aloud, with attention to pronunciation, emphasis, and gesture—to *literary,* reading silently, with attention to meaning and interpretation. Early books more fully emphasize the genres of oral delivery—dialogues, orations, dramatic speeches—and later ones provide selections across literary genres. The earlier readers emphasize the physical aspects of reading—of posture, gesture, and breath—whereas later readers emphasize a text's literary and historical context, authors' biographies, interpretation, and issues of style. *Cyr's Fifth Reader* (1899), for example, includes biographical essays and portraits of major authors (the expected literary figures, but also historians William Prescott and John Lothrop Motley), and smaller signs of its literary affiliations (author and title for each excerpt, brief biographical introductions for each author, copyright information, illustrations of authors and authors' homes). Unlike the cramped design of earlier readers, Cyr's *Reader* has the spacious layout of a nineteenth-century poetry book.

But of course, the change is not as emphatic as those poles might suggest, and it is more accurate to say that nineteenth-century readers show competing uses for shared materials. The elocutionary readers include many selections from authors like Shakespeare, now firmly "literary," but their Shakespeare is a set of orations, descriptive passages, or historical speeches. Shakespeare is also transformed into didactic pieces, as in a scene from *Othello* retitled "The Folly of Intoxication" for McGuffey's *Rhetorical Guide* (1844). A collection like Rufus Griswold's *Prose Writers of America* (1846) suggests the permeable borders of mid-nineteenth-century literary territory, when he announces that he considers "books of every description" as literature and has "confined" his attention to belles lettres, "only passing its boundaries occasionally to notice some of our most eminent divines, jurists, economists, and other students of particular science" (5). Some elocutionary readers include features that move toward literary culture, as is the case with the attention toward authors and authors' lives, but they turn those features to different uses. McGuffey's *Readers* include lengthy sketches of authors, and their indexes of names invite students to read across authors rather than by genre, mode, chronology, or topic. Yet these biographies focus on the authors as educated subjects, detailing their early schooling, their formative experiences, their setbacks and triumphs. They are cautionary tales, or tales of encouragement, that invite students to imagine themselves in the authors' shoes. The more familiar literary sketches included in later readers like *Cyr's Fifth Reader* (1899) invite students to see how different authors are from them in accomplishment and facility with language. They focus on authors' achievements and fame, not the difficulties they overcame.

A more complicated case of overlapping interests is the importance of poetry, a central concern in both elocutionary and literary readers. The elocutionary readers grant a special place to the reading of verse because it is so difficult to read aloud. The very features that make it a valuable cultural text (compressed expression, heightened language, inverted syntax, pauses, line breaks, allusive reference) make it difficult to read, and thereby a useful test case for the educational enterprise. As was the case with religious texts, it is difficult to determine whether poetry gets so much instructional attention because it is difficult, or whether reading develops a sophistication so as to negotiate poetry. Although the readers include poetry as a text for all to attempt, their focused attention suggests it is an "advanced" text only experts can read well. Thus elocutionary attention helps shape the literary place of poetry, and vice versa.

Who "Authors" the Readers?

In the November 26, 1927, issue of the *Saturday Evening Post,* Hugh Fullerton titled an article, "Who Was That Guy, McGuffey?" It is often difficult to determine the authors of textbooks, and even more difficult to learn much about who they were and how they were trained. Perhaps the more important issue, however, is the complications of representing the intellectual work of "authoring" nineteenth-century readers. Readers were sometimes named by association with a distinguished figure like Benjamin Franklin or the British poet Felicia Hemans, who had no explicit connection with the book or its production. Toward the end of the century, readers were named for the publishing firm that sponsored their production. Whatever the formal title, such readers were often referred to in shorthand as the production of a single author, as McGuffey's or Sanders's or Cyr's *Readers.* Yet the "ownership" or "authoring" of the readers remained a complex activity, more collaborative than singular, borrowing on the expertise of editorial committees, educational consultants, and unnamed assistants, and usually extended through multiple revisions well beyond the oversight of the initial "author." New readers often incorporated the structure and content of older readers, reprinting selections, exercises, and choice sentences. Michael Apple has called modern textbooks "managed" texts, "books without formal authors" (95–96). Nineteenth-century readers are also managed texts, but they are books with an overabundance of authors, existing in layers of citation and borrowings.

William Holmes McGuffey is a telling example of such an author. A well-respected teacher, administrator, and lecturer, he had the knowledge and credentials to produce and help sell textbooks. Yet, although hundreds of *Readers, Spellers,* and *Primers,* appearing from 1836 through the present, bear McGuffey's name, he is directly responsible for only the first four of the *Readers,* printed in 1836–37, and had no direct involvement for the editions of 1857 on.[42] Compiling a reader was often a shared and delegated job. One expert would prepare an apparatus, while another, often very differently educated expert would read through current periodicals and textbooks for selections. William's brother Alexander prepared the 1844 *Rhetorical Guide* and the 1838 *Speller,* both of which appear without a named author but are marked ambiguously as *McGuffey's*. In a newspaper interview given in the 1890s, some sixty years later, A. McGuffey described the process of compiling the readers: the publishers "brought over a great load of old school readers from which, as from other and higher sources, I was to make the selections" (qtd. in D. Sullivan 105).[43]

Others took their turn improving or adding to the *Readers* as the demand for new versions increased. Catherine Beecher, who had helped found a female academy and would write her own textbooks, prepared questions for the second editions of the first four *Readers* (Beecher had been the publishers' first choice to edit an eclectic series but had declined). When the series expanded to a *Sixth Reader* in 1857, the task of reorganizing the multiple "advanced" *Readers* fell to A. McGuffey, in collaboration with Dr. Timothy S. Pinneo and Obed J. Wilson, one of the publishers (Sullivan 211). The 1879 revision, which most modern critics cite, was carried out without help from "McGuffey," by the author of a grammar text, a superintendent of schools, a president and professor from a state normal school, and a publisher.[44]

The "advanced" McGuffey readers print a lengthy educational apparatus, compiled by Pinneo, the author of a series of grammars published by McGuffey's Cincinnati firm. Of course, Pinneo is not the sole "author" of the apparatus any more than McGuffey, since the long essay borrows heavily from Blair's *Lectures* without acknowledging its debt and acknowledges its "free use" of other elocutionary treatises and textbooks. Much of the silent citation and borrowing that comprise textbook making in the nineteenth century was accepted in an era when periodicals reprinted British pieces without payment and piracies abounded, and reliance on authoritative past texts was expected to give a book its place in an educational tradition. Changes in copyright laws, and the growing urgency of textbook marketing, made publishers more jealous of their "possessions," more insistent on claims about what made their book new and improved. In 1838, for example, McGuffey's publishers were sued by the publishers of Worcester's readers for plagiarism; they settled the case for a $2000 fee, removal of identical lessons, and other minor changes (Lindberg 72–74; Minnich 39–41; W. Smith 9).

Many of those who worked on nineteenth-century readers were anonymous—some, like those who compiled the many versions of *The New-England Primer,* because, although many of its selections are "authored" ("John Cotton's catechism," "John Rogers' poem," "Isaac Watts' Cradle Songs"), the book appears without any editor or overall author. Others, like Beecher or Pinneo, are anonymous only to modern readers, although they were well-established figures in the educational or publishing worlds of their day. Pinneo's work on the McGuffey *Readers* was no secret—a footnote in the 1844 *Guide* thanks him by name "for much valuable assistance" (5). In addition to the 1844 preface, it is mentioned in advertisements and promotions, especially those directed to educators who would know his other textbooks.

It is difficult to determine influence in nineteenth-century readers. Much of the educational apparatus is taken—whether silently or with credit—from eighteenth-century British rhetoricians like Walker, Mason, Austin, Blair, Enfield, or Sheridan. Murray's *English Reader* cites Blair's *Lectures* and the *Encyclopedia Britannica,* Cobb's *Juvenile Reader* cites Sheridan and Walker's *Critical Pronouncing Dictionary,* and McGuffey's *Rhetorical Guide* quotes two full pages of Walker's *Rhetorical Grammar* ("on this subject we can do nothing better than lay before the student an extract from Mr. Walker's excellent 'Rhetorical Grammar'" [56]). William Russell, whose introductory essay to *The Young Ladies' Elocutionary Reader* (1845) proposes to make the study of elocution "adapted to female readers," cites as experts Mrs. Hemans (the British poet), Lydia Sigourney (a noted American poet and schoolteacher, admired for her 1837 *Girl's Reading Book* and lectures on reading and female learning), and N. P. Willis (editor of the *New York Daily Ledger* whose often anthologized essay, "Unwritten Music," celebrates the female voice). The long quotation from Sigourney is inserted with a subheading "Mrs. Sigourney's Remarks on Reading" and the comment "It may not be inappropriate to introduce here, the just remarks of Mrs. Sigourney"

(16). To lend weight to his project, Russell cites Dr. Rush, the expert on voice management, and his own redaction of Rush (*Orthophony, or Vocal Culture in Elocution*).

Perhaps the most frequently cited American rhetorician is Orville Dewey (1794–1882), unsigned author of a thirty-page article, "Principles of Elocution," published in the influential Boston magazine the *North American Review* in 1829. Regular readers of the *Review,* especially those Harvard faculty and alumni associated with its editorial circle, would have known the review was Dewey's work and would have recognized him as an author worthy of attention.[45] His training, interests, and career suggest the complicated affiliations and expertise that shaped the readers. Graduated in 1814 from Williams College and in 1819 from Andover Theological Seminary, where he studied with elocutionary scholar Ebenezer Porter, Dewey became a Unitarian preacher, first in Boston as assistant to the preacher William Ellery Channing, then in New Bedford, and finally at the Second Unitarian Church of New York City, where, as one biography put it, "he acquired a national reputation as a great preacher" ("Dewey" 5: 47–48).[46] Married to Emerson's cousin, Dewey circulated among the New England religious and intellectual elite and was renowned for his preaching and lectures and as the author of many books of sermons and moral theology. In 1839, he was awarded an honorary doctor of divinity from Harvard, and his three-volume collected works were reprinted multiple times from 1844 to 1883. Emerson described him as one of the "great speakers" and "prophets of the East," and claimed him as one of those "whose manners or unconscious talk set[s] our own minds in action & we take occasions of rich opinions from him as we take apples off a tree without any thanks."[47]

Dewey's thoughts on elocution are such unthanked apples. His article begins with a review of two influential treatises on elocution published in 1827, Dr. James Rush's *Philosophy of the Human Voice* and Ebenezer Porter's *An Analysis of the Principles of Rhetorical Delivery.* The discussion of these treatises is learned, forceful, and engaging, but the part of his review that circulated in nineteenth-century readers was a section that turned "from this general observation" to "descend to particulars" (54–55). The subsequent three paragraphs lay out a program of instruction, from nursery through the schools. "The business of training our youth," Dewey announces, "must be commenced in childhood. . . . There, at least, may be formed a distinct articulation, which is the first requisite for good speaking." Dewey's elocutionary interests focus on schools that "teach the art of reading," which "ought to occupy three-fold more time than it does." Comparing reading with musical performance, Dewey concludes that reading calls for "a constant exercise of mind," "continual and close reflection and thought, and the finest discrimination of thought."

Advanced McGuffey readers from 1837 on reprint these paragraphs, first as a selection in the *Fourth Reader* ("from *The North American Review*") and then as a coda to the apparatus on "Elocution and Reading." The McGuffey version of Dewey's text made "improvements," deleting a too-learned reference and ignoring Dewey's footnote to Gilbert Austin. He is not credited as author, although a different selection from Dewey appears with his name as early as the 1844 *Rhetorical Guide*. Dewey's essay appears as a selection in Sanders's *Fifth Reader* (1867) and the Russells' *Young Ladies' Elocutionary Reader* (1845), where the author is cited as "an eloquent writer in the North American Review" (17). Dewey, like many involved with readers, initially appears anonymous, yet turns out to have been known by everyone and published everywhere.

As this section suggests, the expertise needed to compile a reader is more dispersed than that of a rhetoric or composition book. The analytic rhetorical reader is an extremely sophisticated book— full of condensed knowledge, thoughtful observation of the difficulties of learning to read, and mastery of the valued educational selections of an era or tradition. Elementary readers reflect insight about childhood and the difficulties of learning. But many readers can be seen as borrowing expertise and juxtaposing different kinds of pedagogical concerns into a meaningful order. A reader borrows the insight of the rhetorical theorist who addresses the topics of importance and the order of their instructional value, of the advanced educator who has analyzed how students learn and has a command of educational aims and discipline, and the social purpose of the public intellectual who articulates the culture's changing interests and priorities. It shapes this through the classroom expertise of teachers, who know the habits and failings of particularly situated students.

The act of compiling selections is an extended version of what every educated citizen was advised to do—to produce a "definite aim in reading," a selection of materials on which to practice, a choice about what to read first or with most care. Whether informed or casual, professional or amateur, the act of selecting is shaped by education and taste, by access to materials and speculation about what readers will want or need. Many of the compilers of school readers brought varied expertise to the task: they include dictionary makers, lawyers, publishers, missionaries, clergy, teachers, school principals, natural historians, geographers, and newspaper correspondents.

What Students Use the Readers?

Nineteenth-century readers are, in some sense, designed to allow less privileged students to taste some riches previously restricted to an elite. They compress some of the values of a classical or clerical education into a secularized volume, translated into a modern idiom. A well-to-do gentleman of an earlier decade might have learned to read by studying Cicero and Greek mythology. He might have used a leather-bound edition of Caesar's commentaries, perhaps with learned annotations or syntactical appendices, or a Latin reader that reproduced passages (much like a quotation dictionary) from important texts. As he advanced, he might have read other literary texts in clear-text editions, without educational apparatus or annotations to suggest he lacked knowledge of the text or context. He would have copied passages into a commonplace book or journal, saving important sentences to recycle in his own letters or speeches. A younger son in an earlier decade might have read for the clergy, studying biblical glosses and parallel texts of the Gospels in Greek or even Hebrew. He might have read cramped, double-columned collections of sermons or collections of essays on such topics as "The Immortality of the Soul," and "Divine Retribution." Nineteenth-century reading textbooks do not assume knowledge of Greek or Latin, although they reproduce remnants of that time, offering excerpts on Roman history and heroes or Shakespearian speeches by Julius Caesar and Marc Antony. Most of them do not assume a particular or focused religious purpose, although they offer excerpts on spiritual needs in time of despair or death and encourage a practice of Bible reading or contemplation.

Indeed, the common school readers were so widely recognized as "secular" that religious readers challenged their dominance. The *Metropolitan Readers,* compiled in the 1870s by a "member of the Order of the Holy Cross" (Mother Angela Gillespie, whose work was supervised by an ecclesiastical board and introduced by The Right Reverend Dr. Spalding), contended that the "great fault of our common-school system" is its undervaluing the "religious element in education" (*Fifth Reader* iii). Consequently, these Catholic readers presented a competing selection of texts (substituting Catholic history for the Puritan settlement narratives; replacing protestant divines with Bishop John Henry Newman and J. A. Stapf, a German priest and author of *The Spirit and Scope of Education;* adding excerpts on immigration, Japanese Christian martyrs, and childhood poverty) and proposed to "exclude from the reading-lessons all the poison of noxious principles, and even all worldly and frivolous matter; and we would do this all the more rigidly whenever the poison would become the more dangerous, because latent, or gilded with the fascination of style, or the gorgeous imagery of poetry" (iv). In addition to the vast output of the Protestant tract and Sunday school presses, religious school readers were produced by a diversity of sects.

The status of these textbooks and of the students who use them often remains implicit, suggested by attention to timesaving study or "faults to be remedied." At other times, readers announce the different educational status of their audience, as when the preface to Watson's *Independent Sixth Reader* (1871) offers annotations for the "great mass of students, who do not aspire to *belles lettres*" (v). The McGuffey series proposes reading, and the industry it demands, as fostering aspirations to elite status. In the 1879 revision, the biographies of authors and the excerpts themselves abound with causal links between effective elocution and success; for the democracy, movement across class lines appears readily available to any child willing to invest "indefatigable industry," "perseverance," "practice," or "careful study" in the art of reading aloud. Students might emulate figures like Patrick Henry, who, according to the McGuffey, "began very awkwardly," but "rose to a surprising height" through the power of eloquence (115). British authors are seen as squandering their gifts and privilege through dissipation, petulance, morbidity, or, in the case of Milton, the "evil influence of bitter political controversy" (312). American authors are generally praised, on the other hand, for making the most of themselves, for earning appropriate "marks of distinction" (Bryant, 141) through their "untiring industry" (Timothy Dwight, 419). Literacy becomes, then, the necessary route to and the emblem of worldly success, wealth, and security. Words serve as property to invest or carelessly expend, with successful cultural literacy depending on being able to produce the currency of the culture, to recognize the correct marks by which value is accorded to language, to create language of "due weight."

Books like the McGuffey series, with an estimated 122 million copies printed from 1836 to 1920,[48] addressed a generalized American student, living in a rural landscape, concerned about the fate of the Indians (but not about slavery or the Civil War), about transformations wrought by industrial change and scientific invention, willing to read poems about "last things" but preferring narratives about heroes and rugged individuals. Boys were differentiated from girls by their games, their involvement with the outdoors and animals, and their need to prepare for a public adulthood. Girls, in these readers, were trained to be caretakers—of the poor, the elderly, children, their toys and books. A series of articulation exercises in McGuffey's *Fifth Reader* (1853) suggests a differentiated attention to gender. Out of twenty-six practice sentences, only one refers to a female, and that one, although positive, is remarkably general ("She is universally esteemed."). The fifteen sentences that refer to a male are far more located and material, offering a wider range of behaviors and qualities, suggesting real lives and activities. For example: "He attended divine service regularly." "He graduated at one of the Eastern Universities." "The whole nation lamented him." "He is a man of eminent merit." "He is generous to his friends." "He has contracted a bad habit." "His reputation is ruined." "He is a formidable adversary" (15–16). Advanced readers designated for girls—the Russells' *Young Ladies' Elocutionary Reader* (1845), Pinneo's *Hemans Reader* (1847), Sanders's *Young Ladies' Reader* (1855), and Hows's *Junior Ladies' Reader* (1860) and *Ladies' Reader* (1859)—mark gender differences in more subtle ways. Although often surprisingly similar in difficulty, length, and selections, they articulate the more public purposes of the general readers to the constraints of women's expectations. These readers introduce more reflective pieces (poems about grief or spiritual life), diminish the traditional emphasis on public oratory and politics, and favor the kind of writing about daily life circulating in women's fiction and periodicals.[49]

Other textbooks targeted factory workers, immigrants, or recently freed slaves. Lydia Maria Child, whose antislavery activities damaged her literary career, proposed to James T. Fields, an advanced reader for Freedmen, to extend the instruction offered by the American Tract Society's lower-level readers.[50] She wrote to Gerrit Smith on April 4, 1864, about her "project" of a reader "carefully adapted to their condition, and especially to have a *good moral* effect, and an *encouraging* effect." She planned to have it "sold at the lowest possible price, and the money it brought used to purchase libraries for their schools" (*Selected Letters* 441). The reader was slow to take shape; Child had difficulty persuading publishers that such a venture would sell, and she took great pains adapting texts, searching for suitable materials, and doing original research. She asked her fellow abolitionist, William Lloyd Garrison, for leads to trustworthy information and interviews. In a letter of July 7, 1865, to Garrison, Child outlined the labors of preparing the book:

> I am writing over nearly every prose article I extract, so as
> to give them as *much* as possible in the *smallest space,* and
> to give it in a very clear and simple form. . . .

> I am taking more pains with it than I should if it were
> intended for young princes, or sprigs of what men call no-
> bility. (456)

"Don't let my M.S. get lost or burned," she wrote to Fields on Au-
gust 27, 1865, "for I have been two years preparing it" (460). Child's
Freedmen's Book (1865) was not a commercial or pedagogical success. As she noted in a letter to Lucy Osgood (February 14, 1870),
she spent $1200 of her own money to distribute the book, but the
freedmen's "wages have been so very low, and so badly paid, that
the poor creatures could not buy it, as I hoped they would, to some
extent" (490).[51] Few textbook compilers were as committed and
sophisticated as Child, but the job of "adapting" books to new learners and learning situations was often taken as seriously as that of
original composition. Adaptation was seen, to some extent, as an
extension of teaching, part of "practical" education's need to make
books that students could, and would, find useful.

How Were Readers Produced and Distributed?

These textbooks were commonly called "readers," although early
nineteenth-century books were called "instructors," "preceptors," and
"class books," and advanced books were sometimes designated as
"rhetorical readers" or, following Enfield's 1774 collection, as "speakers." The many titles mark readers' multiple interests and audiences,
as well as their affiliations with diverse rhetorical or educational traditions. Some were named for their compiler—often a teacher like
Ebenezer Porter or McGuffey, or authors like Noah Webster, William
Swinton, and Richard Parker, known for other work on language (compiling spellers, grammars, dictionaries, or composition books). Some
names appealed to a wide audience and use ("model" or "standard"
readers, "popular" lessons); others signaled a focused audience (girls,
ladies, Mohawks, Freedmen, metropolitans) or purpose (evangelical,
historical, Shakespearian, etymological, geographical, nature study).

Readers' names often cited their location and audience: in the
early part of the century, when the publishing of textbooks was a

fairly local or regional matter, readers might be named for a city, state or area (Albany, New York, New England). Many readers suggested a role in the formation of national culture and identity by using terms like *American* or *National* in their titles (Caleb Bingham's *American Preceptor,* 1794). They thus distinguished themselves from Latin readers but also advertised themselves as refiguring the British influence of earlier English readers. In the 1860s, "union" or "national" readers signaled the political commitment to the nation, while others targeted instruction at the south, both from within (*Dixie Readers,* published during the war by a firm in Raleigh, North Carolina) and from without (*Southern Pictorial Reader,* published in 1866 by a southern author, George Holmes, for a northern firm). Once textbook publishing advanced to the national stage, many readers adopted the titles of their publishing houses and were advertised not only as a series, but as an educational system.

In the early decades of the century, readers were published by small printshops across the country and so often showed the signs of local interests or politics. Early primers, for example, could be reworked to address particular needs and populations, as, for example, Daniel Claus's *Indian Primer* (1786), a dual-language text designed for Mohawk children "to acquire the spelling and reading of their own: As well as to get acquainted with the English Tongue, which for that purpose is put on the opposite page" (title page). After the advent of stereotyped editions and with a shift toward mass printings, "model" readers were often adapted to address cross-cultural uses.

Although nineteenth-century readers have been idealized as vehicles that produced a shared national culture and that promoted "correct" English as a national language,[52] they circulated a complex valuation of multiple languages and modes of speaking. Reissued in translated and bilingual versions, the readers carried out ideological concerns about the importance of the English language and "American" culture. McGuffey's and Swinton's *Readers* were translated and reissued for Spanish-language students in Mexico and Latin America, and the McGuffey *Readers* appeared in dual-language versions for missionaries to Japan.[53] These multiple forms also recognized the practical politics of the diverse languages used for instruction within the United States. The number of German-language versions of popular English readers attests to the many students for whom German was the approved language of instruction.[54] Readers also appeared in Swedish, Spanish, French, Italian, Welsh, and Native American languages, as well as in experimental forms such as the Mormon phonetic alphabet (*The Deseret Books*, by the "Regents ov the Deseret Yioonivursity," 1868) and the phonetic alphabet (Longley's *Furst Fonetic Reader*, 1852). The format of the nineteenth-century reader was also adapted to teach foreign languages to the U. S. audience, and *translation* was promoted as a valuable exercise both for learning foreign languages and for improving English.[55]

The 1873 Dakota reader (*Wayawa Tokaheya*, translated as *First Reader*), prepared by Stephen Return Riggs, is a telling example of a "model" reader adapted for other students and literacy situations. Riggs, a missionary teacher to the Dakotas, devoted many years and much expertise to transcribing the Dakota language, creating a grammar and dictionary, and publishing translations of a hymnal and *Pilgrim's Progress*, as well as a 239-page ethnographic study for the Department of the Interior. The 1873 reader uses as a template a reader published by a mainstream Chicago firm, J. Russell Webb's *Model First Reader* (1873). In his "Preface" and "Hints to Teachers" (2, 3–7), Webb advocated the object lesson, a familiar strategy in composition books of the time, in which objects or pictures help produce language. Webb argued, "Words, *as words*, obscure thought; but words as thought media, are transparent. Reading is grasping thought from language. . . . Recognizing and pronouncing words, as words, is *not* reading" (2). Both the English and Dakota versions of this reader are beautifully illustrated, using color to dramatize adjectives (a black-and-white page shows a top hat or a rose, followed by a colored page showing a "black hat" or a "red rose"). Webb claims his use of the "Sentence method" is closest to the "Method of Nature" (the book's motto is: "When Nature teaches, it is sport to learn"). Children are to "look *through* the words recognized by the eye, to the thought only," with the words as "simply servants to unload the mind of its ideas" (4).

Webb's English reader is converted to a dual-language edition by inserting Dakota words into the spaces between English lines. The English version is appropriate for such cultural translation, offering little overt regional identity, no direct references to historical events, public figures or places, or to specific religious or political groups. Nevertheless, its lessons enforce clear distinctions of gender and class, with one sequence of lessons comparing children's horses: Howard and Della have real ponies, Freddy has a fine wooden rocking horse, and Tommy has a stick horse. Tommy's lesson concludes: "His pony is not at all like Howard's and Freddy's. But Tommy has no other pony. Tommy seems to be very happy on account of his pony" (see fig. 4). The illustrations show well-dressed white children, riding in goat-carts, playing with hoops, and flying kites. Their names are Howard and Della and Freddy and Tommy, and they appear thus, untranslated, in the Dakota version. The clash between text and audience is extreme in this case, but it is a useful clash. Riggs would not have thought such absurd scenes portrayed Indian experiences, rather his situation as a missionary and religious worker made the use of a ready-made text an economic necessity. The addition of Dakota text can intervene only in small ways in the model reader's text. Some crowded pages are simplified to create the needed space for Dakota text, poems are turned into prose, and occasionally a phrase is refigured (Della's pony is "clean" in Webb's reader, but "not dirty" in Riggs 87). The Dakota's lesson on birds omits the sentences about it being "wrong to club or stone" birds for sport, and it leaves off Webb's final text sending students on "without delay" to the next level reader (112). Webb's preface and instructional material are untouched, but Riggs adds notes to teachers and students on a blank verso page and on the back cover, replacing a full-page advertisement. On the back cover, Riggs comments (in both languages) on the book's bilingual situation, suggesting that in addition to its use as an English reader, a language "difficult of acquisition," it can also help "any English worker in the Dakota field, to make such progress in the language of the natives as to increase his usefulness" (8).

LESSON 39.

1. Here is Tommy on his horse.

Tommy tašunke akan den un.

2. With the whip in his hand he prances about.

Nape en icapsinte hduha nacapcam ya ece.

3. His pony is not at all like Howard's and Freddy's.

Tašunke kin *Howard* tawa qa *Freddy* tawa kin iyecece śni ḣinca.

4. But Tommy has no other pony.

Tuka *Tommy* śunka wakan tokeca yuhe śni.

5. Tommy seems to be very happy on account of his pony.

Tommy tašunke kin on cante wašte ḣinca seececa.

Fig. 4. Lesson from a Dakota-English reader. Stephen R. Riggs, *Wayawa Tokaheya (First Reader)*; adapted from J. Russell Webb, *Model First Reader.* Chicago, 1873, 88.

Such cross-cultural transformations of readers are only a more extreme version of their usual production and reproduction. Readers were published in large numbers, at multiple locations and in multiple versions, and they were also remarkably resilient, remaining in print for decades. The McGuffey series, like other strong sellers, was periodically issued in "new" and "revised" versions that promoted their modernity, with new editions competing with earlier versions that remained in production or that appeared under other publisher's imprints. Indeed, a note in the 1857 *High School Reader* warned that the "New Eclectic Reader" should not be "confounded with the former editions which are still continued in publication" (6). The entire McGuffey series was revised in 1853 and reissued in uniform binding for the major revision of 1879 (with copyrights renewed in 1901 and 1920); the series remains in print today. *The New-England Primer* was an even more varied example. A steady seller, the *Primer* was issued in multiple versions by many different presses across the century. Parts common to the earliest *Primers* (especially the shorter catechism, the pictured alphabet, and the martyr John Rogers's poem to his children) were incorporated in primers adapted to and printed in different geographical areas (e.g., *The Albany Primer, The Pennsylvania Primer*) and to different ethnic groups (e.g., John Eliot's *Indian Primer,* Boston, 1747). The *Primer's* variations reflect political changes (the American Revolution, the evangelical movement of the 1800s), changes in attitudes (toward punishment and sin, toward childhood), as well as changes in children's literature. In later, secularized versions, naughty children are threatened not with tempests and the consuming fire, but with losing "Oranges, Apples, Cakes, or Nuts," and the grim poem of the martyr is printed in uneasy conjunction with Isaac Watts's soothing "Cradle Song." An 1800 version even replaces the trademark illustrated alphabet with a milder verse, "A was an apple-pye."[56]

Readers also are produced developmentally, printed as a graduated series of primers and readers with attention to age differences in cognitive ability, interest, vocabulary, and genre. Very early language books like *The New-England Primer* offer a single book for learners of all ages, printing the culture's most valued texts, however difficult or threatening they might be. Vocabulary is not organized by developmental principles in such books, but by numbers of syllables, by Latinate or non-Latinate words, or by clusters of meaning (words having to do with agriculture). In graduated readers, small children read fables and animal stories, older children read about natural history, and the most advanced read literature, history, and moral philosophy. The advent of the female academies pressured an interest in reading's less public uses, in texts for the parlor and for personal reflection. A composition book or speller may appear in both an elementary and an advanced form; by century's end, reading instruction is dispersed across six or seven volumes, moving from a primer through numbered volumes to an "advanced" reader. Readers not only proliferate across levels of learning but also are adapted to differently situated learners, with versions for "young ladies," for "home use," and for "normal schools."

According to Nietz (*Old Textbooks* 102–3), the earliest "graded" series were the *New York Readers,* 1–3 (1812–15) and Cobb's *Juvenile Readers,* 1–3 (1830–31). Publishers often initiated a new reader by printing an advanced volume and later adding more "elementary" volumes to create a series. Elocutionary readers were issued as a single advanced volume, although successful readers, like Murray's and Pierpont's, were followed by "prequels" or "sequels." Pierpont produced his five readers backwards, beginning in 1823 with the most advanced, the 480-page *American First Class Book,* and working to the most elementary, with publishers adding a "third reader" in 1854. As Nietz argues, "the idea of a series apparently was an afterthought, for they were prepared in the exact reverse order to the sequence in which other later series were compiled" (*Old Textbooks* 68).

The McGuffey *Readers,* on the other hand, began in 1836–37 as a series of four readers, adding a *Primer* and a *Speller* in 1838, a *Fifth Reader* in 1853 and a *Sixth* in 1857. The materials for "advanced" work were thus redistributed as the series expanded, so that the "advanced" *Fourth Reader* printed in the 1840s corresponded to a *Fifth* and then *Sixth Reader* in later printings. The publishers also issued other forms of readers, such as the *Juvenile Speaker* (1860), the *Eclectic Speaker* (1858), and the *High School Reader* (1857). This advanced reader marks a different tradition from the series readers by leaving out the educational apparatus; its preface announces the excision of all "collateral matter, such as Rhetorical Rules and Notations, Exercises in Articulation, Definition, &c., &c., which have been so extensively treated of in the other volumes of this series as to render further instruction unnecessary" (7).[57]

The most influential advanced reader was the *Rhetorical Guide; or Fifth Reader,* which, confusingly, is a different book from the *Fifth Eclectic Reader* (1853) that was part of the graduated series (to differentiate, I refer to it as the *Rhetorical Guide,* although it was known familiarly throughout the century as "The Fifth Reader"). In 1844, when this reader first appeared, the series included a primer, speller, and four readers. Like other series' "fifth readers," this volume is an elocutionary/literary reader, with extensive instructional materials, more lessons, selections drawn from more advanced discourses (philosophic essay, literary criticism, foreign authors). Used in the academies and high schools, fifth readers also served as anthologies that adults kept long after formal schooling. The *Guide* was so popular that it launched "Fifth Reader Clubs" that sponsored competitions and conferences (W. Smith 24–26). Its "principles of elocution" (composed by Pinneo) and many of its selections found their way into other advanced McGuffeys and *The Hemans Reader for Female Schools* (1847), which Pinneo edited. The *Hemans* preface indicates the borrowing: "These 'Directions for Reading' are taken, with some modification, from McGuffey's Eclectic Reader, for which they were prepared by the compiler of this work" (12).

An advertisement at the beginning of McGuffey's 1853 *Fourth Reader* (2) explains the gradations of the series—both in terms of age level and subject matter. The "pictorial primer" is designated "for little children"; the *First* and *Second Readers* print "lessons in reading and spelling" for "young pupils"; the *Third* prints "chaste and instructive lessons in prose and poetry" for "middle classes"; the *Fourth* prints "elegant extracts in prose and poetry" for "more advanced classes"; the *Rhetorical Guide* is designated a "rhetorical reading book for the highest classes"; and the *Hemans' Reader* offers "elegant extracts" for "Female Seminaries." The decision to print five or six volumes in a series remained, as the McGuffey ad suggests, somewhat arbitrary. Books did not correspond directly to grades— Nietz's theory is that the first four readers would be "studied for eight years" with the fifth available for academies and high schools (*Old Textbooks* 103)—and the organization of the school year and sequence was only standardized around mid-century in urban areas and considerably later in more remote parts of the country. Not until the 1890s (with series like Ellen Cyr's) did readers emerge as eight books corresponding to eight grades, and even then traces of an older system remained (Cyr's *Fifth Reader* remains the most "advanced" reader, although she adds three more graduated readers).

The complication of specified readers is a far cry from the early part of the nineteenth century, when students in a single class might well have studied from multiple texts—using whatever books were handed down from parents or older siblings, or whatever the school system could gather. These graduated systems saturated the educational field, creating a different kind of dominance from the time when students worked from a single book for many years, studying "Pierpont" or "Murray" as their one route to learning to read. By 1857, the McGuffey "system" assumed progression through the series so subsequent volumes could build on (or move beyond) earlier instruction. And yet even within such a system, there were multiple routes to take, as students moved out to specialty interests or ahead to differently constituted "advanced" achievement.

To Those Engaged in the Business of Teaching

It is thought a great feat for a child to learn to read. The process is not a trivial one which is accomplished every day, and is going on in our nurseries and schoolhouses, by which the infant learns to distinguish letters, to spell them into words, to look through written characters, to interpret words into thoughts and feelings, and do all these so readily that the skill seems literally to have "come by nature." It is indeed a great feat, as we see plainly when a full-grown man

or woman attempts it for the first time, and as we mark the
slow and painful steps by which such persons must halt and
stumble for years, in order to master the mechanical part
of the process. (Noah Porter, *Books and Reading* 28)

Lyman Cobb ends the preface to his 1831 *Juvenile Reader, No.
3* with the confident assertion that "those engaged in the business
of teaching" will readily understand his motives and aims in producing an elementary reading book. But by 1870, when Noah Porter
wrote *Books and Reading,* such confidence was considerably qualified.
Porter depicts the learning of reading as fraught with difficulty, oc-
curring across the nation at many levels and through a complicated
and "painful" process. Many comments about reading in the nineteenth century critique "school" reading as dry and disciplinary, out
of touch with more practical or worldly concerns. And Porter was
not alone in suggesting that reading was perceived as a difficult and
"pains-taking" subject, one that required guidance and practice to
"acquire," and one that depended on the circulation of well-designed
and up-to-date textbooks. Like mathematics—or in today's climate,
computer literacy or sciences—reading was depicted as a challenging subject, one that marked both novice and expert, and that ac-
counted for subsequent success or failure in life as well as school.

Porter's comment on the teaching of reading brings together two
powerful understandings of the process, (1) that it somehow "comes
by nature," as part of a chain of natural events leading from the
nursery to adult skill, or (2) that it is a "great feat," a slow and painful struggle of learning and unlearning. Nineteenth-century readers exemplify both of these concerns, often in contradictory or competing ways. They advise students to read as if conversing, to stand
with natural grace, to gesture with feeling, and to speak from the
heart. Yet students do so under extreme monitorial instruction,
using books that point out their every fault in voice, body, articulation, and understanding. These books select appropriate texts,
framed by elaborate "systems" for self-conscious management of the
voice, and marked with minute rhetorical distinctions about tempo,
pitch, modulation, or emphasis.

The outcome of such systems of reading instruction was often justly criticized, even within the school readers, as pompous, artificial, or mechanical. Horace Mann, secretary to the Massachusetts Board of Education, complained in 1840 in a lecture, "On District School Libraries," that schools attended primarily to *"mechanical"* instruction ("the ability to speak the names of words on seeing them"), slighting the more important *"intellectual"* ("comprehension of an author's ideas") and *"rhetorical"* ("the power of giving, by the tones and inflexions of the voice and other natural language, an appropriate expression to feeling") aims (*Lectures* 276).[58] Mann charged that in his common school education he "never heard a question asked, either by teacher or scholar, respecting the meaning of a word or sentence in a reading lesson. . . . The exercises had no more significancy than the chattering of magpies or the cawing of ravens" (277). The outcome of such instruction was the "mechanical reader," the "mere grinder of words. If he reads without any attempt at expression, it is mere see-saw and mill-clackery; if he attempts expression, he is sure to mistake its place, and his flourishes become ridiculous rant and extravagance" (279).

The earliest treatises on reading, however, articulate the same concerns with mechanical and artificial reading, and each succeeding "system" vows to address the problem. In theory, the intricate artifices of *learning to read* were to dissolve away to produce a natural and unaffected *performance of reading*. Repetition, imitation, syntactic analysis—these were all proposed to address students' unfamiliarity with language, embarrassment, and physical awkwardness. It seems evident now that one effect of making students so minutely self-aware was a stratified or prejudicial labeling of those with recognizable "faults." Yet despite the many problems of such an analytic system of instruction, it was at its best democratic, treating privileged forms of literacy (elegance, grace, and self-possession) as something not "natural" but socially constructed, and therefore a lesson ordinary students could both study and practice. Nineteenth-century reading instruction proposed to enable all students, at whatever economic or regional distance from the centers of culture, to "acquire" powerful literacy abilities. As the McGuffey *Sixth* suggested, reading was to teach not simply a technical practice, but the "secret of acquiring a graceful style of gesture," of learning how to simulate what others have by "natural advantages" (56).

The seeming impossibility of "acquiring" what is "natural" emerged as a central issue from the early British treatises and shaped readers like the McGuffeys. "Study Nature," advised John Mason in 1748; "Avoid Affectation; never use Art, if you have not the Art to conceal it: For whatever does not appear natural, can never be agreeable, much less perswasive" (*Essay* 31). Studying nature was largely a process of imitation: students should listen to good readers and read texts written "in familiar stile . . . nearest to that of common Conversation" (19). As John Walker argued in his influential *Rhetorical Grammar* (1785), imitation offered the "plain simple path of nature" leading to "the beauty of a natural and unaffected simplicity" (2). William Enfield (1774) stated the case for both sides, arguing that "Follow Nature" was the "fundamental law," without which rules could "only produce affected declamation, not just elocution," and then arguing that such "general precepts are of little use till they are unfolded, and applied to particular cases." Enfield defined the agenda for a pedagogy of reading, in which rules function as "the observations of others, collected into a narrow compass, and digested in a natural order, for the direction of the unexperienced and unpracticed learner" (17–18). As Enfield suggested, "following nature" was never easy or, for that matter, natural. Most teachers needed considerable advice on how to read well, and no matter where reading instruction began, students were figured as already having "ill habits" needing to be corrected. More importantly, textbook writers began to understand both faults and skills as complex procedures, needing to be named, dissected, and studied.

To construct a theoretical and pedagogical system, reading theorists turned for advice to the classics, in particular to Quintilian's discussion of reading in *Institutio Oratoria* (I.8), where he announces that the "one direction" for learning to read is that the student must *understand what he reads* (I.8). Despite this claim, Quintilian focuses on the specific problems of delivery, listing the skills only "practice" can teach: "when to take breath, where to divide a verse, where the sense is concluded, where it begins, when the voice is to be raised or lowered, what is to be uttered with any particular inflection of sound, or what is to be pronounced with greater slowness or rapidity, with greater animation or gentleness than other passages" (I.8.1). This passage outlines most of the instructional topics proposed throughout the nineteenth century, topics like management of the voice, rhetorical pause, reading verse, rising and falling action, articulation and emphasis, tempo, and modulation, and proposes *understanding* as preparatory study rather than the desired outcome.

The *art of reading,* defined by Walker as a "system of rules, which teaches us to pronounce written composition with justice, energy, variety, and ease" (*Rhetorical* 29), circulated in the United States in reprintings of British treatises, college lectures and elocutionary instruction, and redactions for use in the schools. But it reached its widest audience in the educational introductions to nineteenth-century readers. Advanced readers like McGuffey's *Rhetorical Guide* (1844) quoted Walker on the "cultivation and management of the voice" and Sheridan and Blair on pronunciation, but they also borrowed without attribution the terms and structure (and large portions of word-for-word text) of rhetorical instruction.

The first concern was usually remedial, proposed to correct the effects of prior bad teaching and habit, to address what students brought with them to the initial lesson in reading. Ever more specific depictions of "faults to be remedied"—from speech defects such as stammering or lisping to errors in articulation or emphasis—marked the student population as needing extensive correction before "natural" practices could emerge. In what became a familiar opening gesture, Mason blamed the "Reading-School" where "children generally get a Habit of reading in a high-pitched Key, or a uniform elevated Voice, without any Regard to Emphasis, Cadence, or a graceful Elocution" (*Essay* 6). But he also mentioned regional and class "problems" (Irish brogue, for example), as Walker mentioned the "London" practice of dropping *h*'s or using *w* for *v*, and McGuffey mentioned rural drawl, all of which presumably marked students more deeply than did a year of bad instruction. J. Hamilton Moore's *Monitor* (1760) proposed to "Eradicate Vulgar Prejudices and Rusticity of Manners" (title page). The advice about faults was, as an exercise sentence included in McGuffey's *Rhetorical Guide* (1844) articulated: "Learn to *un*learn what you have learned amiss" (41).

What Walker disseminated as the "surest method" to make students, especially children, "read well," was a tutorial of imitation, an idealized, labor-intensive process requiring expert teachers and persistent students, a practice long applied to the teaching of Latin. "Let them hear good reading," Walker advised, and "make them imitate it as closely as they can" (1). The teacher had, in this method, two roles: (1) to be a "good reader" worthy of emulation, and (2) to mark the faults in the student's reading and explain "how every fault is to be rectified." Reading lessons were necessarily brief since students had to repeat them many times to approximate "good reading." Walker warned that "the mind cannot attend to many things at once, with the same advantage as to few; and perplexity ought to be avoided as the greatest enemy to instruction." Teachers had to be careful not to overload their students with correction, especially "if a pupil's faults are numerous, not to mark too many at first, but to point out those only that are the most prominent, and to proceed to the rest by degrees" (8).

The art of reading served as a valuable substitute for this earlier model, offering a system that would instruct inexpert teachers, produce a predictive portrait of beginning readers' faults and needs, arrange instructional topics, and organize texts in increasing length and difficulty. Two books from the 1830s, Ebenezer Porter's *Rhetorical Reader* (1832) and Richard Green Parker's *Progressive Exercises in Rhetorical Reading* (1836), adapted the elocutionary exercises of Walker and Sheridan for a new U.S. student population. Both of these readers went through multiple printings: an edition of Porter's with additional exercises was copyrighted in 1855, although the earlier edition continued to be printed as well, running to the "300th edition."

Porter's exercises were initially addressed to his divinity students, but he adapted them to a more elementary and general student population, including those who would not advance to positions requiring public speaking—"the whole of one sex, and all but comparatively few of the other" (13). Students are urged to pursue a "constant and *practical application* of theoretic principles" (vii), following elaborate "rhetorical notations" on such features as monotone, high and low pitch, slow and quick movement, plaintive sound, and rhetorical pause. Porter's system expands Walker's oral lessons (in which a student reads to a teacher who corrects the reading so the student can read again) and makes preparatory study a writing exercise. Students are first to study the text (read it silently, copy it out by hand, then mark it in *pencil* with rhetorical notations), then read it aloud to the teacher who corrects their performance; they then erase any inaccurate marks on their copies, memorize the corrected text, and read it again. Porter strenuously challenged the "incessantly repeated direction 'BE NATURAL,'" arguing that the advice is opaque to a beginning student whose "nature" is inadequate: "You tell him perhaps, that he must drop his reading tone, and be natural; but he understands nothing of what you mean" (16). He defended his "system of notation" by comparing it to punctuation marks in printed text and by arguing that it allowed students to work to "form new habits" (iii).

Parker's *Rhetorical Reading,* designed for young students and articulated with his *Progressive Exercises in Composition,* proclaims the virtue of following "Nature" (its cover carries the motto: "Natura Duce" or "Nature leads"). His preface contrasts the "lifeless, monotone manner" students bring to their assigned reading with the "animation and correctness" they bring to "their story books" (iii). Nevertheless, his reader is a far cry from a story book, and its analysis seems anything but "natural." The first nineteen lessons focus on punctuation, elaborating the length of pause that each mark signifies or its indication about rising or falling action, and analyzing graphic marks like the asterisk (*) or obelisk (†) that would allow a student to negotiate complicated printed texts.

But the innovation of the reader is in its exercises, many of which show the influence of Parker's thinking about composition, and which extend well beyond young learners. Parker brings instruction and reading passage together, dispersing the material usually located in an introduction across forty lessons, each containing numerous passages. His exercises unfold the possible activities of "studying" a text, showing the uses and procedures for punctuation and rhetorical notations. They are a fascinating analysis of how English is composed, and how an attentive reader can read its omissions, unspoken oppositions, syntax, and focus. Parker's elliptical sentences do not simply mark an exercise omission; instead they mark in parentheses what poetic expression has elided or left unsaid: "What sought they thus afar? (*Did they seek*) Bright jewels of the mine? (*Did they seek*) The wealth of the seas? (*or*) the spoils of war? (*No they did not seek either of these, but*) They sought a faith's pure shrine" (74). Exercises teach students to decode long, imbedded, and often literary, sentences, by analogy to more colloquial expressions and by analysis of key terms and antithetical structures: "Why did you drive your hoop so fast to-day?" vs. "Why looks your Grace so heavily to-day?" "Go tell your father how naughty you have been, and ask your mother to reprove you." vs. "Go show your slaves how choleric you are, and bid your bond men tremble." Such exercises encourage students to address difficult texts and syntax, and to see a relationship between their interests, postures, and expressions, and those more elevated or more urgent.

Parker's treatment of reading is close to what Emerson in "The American Scholar" (1837) called "creative reading" (*Collected Works* 1: 58). His system figures texts as composed, capable of being revised, and actively supplemented by those who read them. A good reader of Parker's exercises understands how to read (and perhaps revise) sentences to distinguish key phrases that should be brought "into strong light" from those best "thrown in the shade." Instead of proposing one correct performance, he offers differently marked versions of the same sentence, varied by context, meaning, and readers' preference. Parker ends the exercises warning that since "no rule can be given to aid the pupil in the discovery of the prominent ideas in his reading lessons," students should be "left to study and reflection" (120).

The elocutionary tradition was perhaps most widely disseminated by a less pedagogically explicit reader, McGuffey's *Rhetorical Guide* (1844), which offered "elegant extracts in prose and poetry," with "copious rules and rhetorical exercises" (title page). The *Guide* is a much less insistent textbook than Parker's or Porter's readers, which, perhaps, accounts for its more extensive success. As Mark Sullivan's 1927 interviews suggest, many students thought of it primarily as an anthology of readings rather than as an instruction about reading (10–16). It offers less advice about how to read its materials, its notations are less frequent and less noticeable, its instructional material is clustered in the front matter, and its selections are longer. There is a variety of reading practices scattered through the text, usually in brief references or signaled by code. Part 3 of the lessons marks difficult words and invites teachers to add examples so students can "judge of the *meaning* of words by their *connection*" (171). This last part omits rhetorical notation because "it is believed that the pupil may now, with advantage to himself, rely upon his own judgment, with such aid as the teacher may think it judicious to give" (170).

The McGuffey system, from the *Primer* through the most advanced readers, adapts the art of reading for use by a general population, yet its less strenuous approach is also powerful, shaping students' taste and practices in less visible or acknowledged ways. Attitudes about reading permeate every structure and detail, from the choice of illustration to the apparently casual arrangement of reading selections. The lower-level volumes replace earlier readers' frontispieces of classrooms and strict pedagogues with intimate scenes of children reading, in hammocks and trees, sprawled comfortably on the ground, secluded in an arbor or window seat, thus proposing reading as a more pleasurable, "natural" activity aligned with play. The *Sixth Reader* challenges that pictorial argument with a foreboding and emblematic steel engraving that suggests reading is both highly referential and dangerous. The educational apparatus challenges the insularity of school attention to correctness ("Did I say it correctly or incorrectly?") by directing students to study a host of contemporary speech acts: a voice hailing a ship (*ship ahoy!*), a sailor's reply (*aye, aye*), an officer's commands to his troops (*march! halt!*), a hunter (the *crack* of a rifle), the sound of a mother scolding a child (*a' a' a' a'*).

The eclecticism of the McGuffey allows contradictory positions to be represented at the same time its apparatus teaches students how to regulate differences in text, language, position, and value. One lesson praises those who conform to social constraints, another rewards those who flaunt their independence. Success, or getting away with it, seems a more overarching standard than does any specific moral code. Students are trained to make fine distinctions in emphasis and position; they are taught to understand that every term exists in opposition, that every singular text implies its other. Elocutionary drills teach them to give one opposing term a down inflection, the other an up inflection: "If you care not for your property, you surely value your life," or "It is your place to obey, not to command." The *Guide* acknowledges that the ability to reproduce the tones of learned culture is a subtle expertise: "very slight, requiring an acute and educated ear to discern it, and it is difficult to teach pupils to distinguish it, though they constantly use it" (28). From a modern perspective, however, it is apparent that students were learning more than to rise and fall as speakers. Technical exercises also taught structured antitheses: that nature opposes culture, that women write from the heart and men from the head, that poets are "falsifying gentry" and orators are "men of practical action." Although the *Guide* redefines "correct rules" as a "record of good usage . . . authorized by a majority" (36), it is instrumental in producing that record, in shaping what a majority will believe to be natural.

With an emphasis on learned performance as opposed to acquired knowledge or philosophic insight, nineteenth-century readers hold out to middle- and lower-middle-class students the promise of social success, of rising to positions of power and financial benefit through industry, careful study of successful models, and watchful concealment of any gesture or thought that would give away personal position. The power of the upper class is presented as a "manner" or "grace" of speaking, behaving, writing, and living—a grace that can be learned and that will conceal the "natural awkwardness" of the unlearned.[59] Thus the newly literate are not necessarily less powerful speakers because less educated or less intelligent but because they are not used to speaking; they exhibit a "natural" nervousness in their new "positions" and "postures" that exposes them to ridicule and makes their words ineffective. Such reading systems teach students how to appear to be at ease; as the McGuffey *Rhetorical Guide* claims, it teaches a student to become "familiar with his position" (57). Students practice the gestures, inflections, and modulations of those to whom such speech is "natural," and the success of the instruction depends on being able to cover over the tracks of learning, to cultivate "manners, implying freedom from all embarrassments, and entire self-possession" (58).

Postscript: Words as Gold

The persistence and reach of the readers is exemplified by the curious circulation of early treatises and quotations, well beyond their time, place, or literary context. In 1806, British scholar Gilbert Austin wrote *Chironomia,* a six-hundred-page treatise on rhetorical delivery. In 1829, a Unitarian preacher quoted that text in a periodical essay. In 1844, a compiler of an introduction "borrowed" three pages (and the quoted passage) for inclusion in an advanced school reader. Because of this house-that-jack-built chain, a British argument from 1806 functions as reading instruction well beyond its initial coterie, place, and time; it travels out across the century, the nation, and diverse populations of students into our present moment, as it remains in facsimile copies of the McGuffey series used in the twenty-first century for home schooling. The passage is an argument about how words persist, retain value, and come to be "spent":

> Words . . . should be delivered out from the lips, as beautiful coins, newly issued from the mint; deeply and accurately impressed, perfectly finished; neatly struck by the proper organs, distinct, in due succession, and of due weight.[60]

This passage would have resonated with contemporary audiences that often heard language compared to money, and the association was rooted in biblical texts (Proverbs 25:11 advises that "a Word aptly spoken is like apples of gold in settings of silver"). The comparison altered under the shifting economies of the times, replete with financial speculation, gold prospecting, and confidence games. Emerson wrote in *Nature* (1836), that "old words are perverted to stand for things which are not; a paper currency is employed, when there is no bullion in the vaults" (*Collected Works* 1:20). Osgood's *Fourth Reader* (1871) advised students to "Dig for Knowledge as Men Dig for Gold" and to consider leisure moments as "sands of precious gold. Properly expended, they will procure for you a stock of great thoughts" (242). By 1883, the trope had shifted from its earlier appreciation of beautiful coins, as in James Johonnot's *Natural History Reader:* "Words, like bank-notes, are regarded, not for their intrinsic, but for their representative value. In so far as they clearly reveal the gold of thought, they may be taken for genuine coin, but, failing in this, they are worthless counterfeits" (iv). As this example suggests, the history of nineteenth-century readers is marked by borrowing and adaptation, and by the persistence of traditional associations and definitions that nevertheless adapt to changing times and values.

Studying such a vast and changing archive as that of nineteenth-century readers illuminates reading's articulation with other traditions of literacy study—with rhetoric and composition, spelling and grammar, elocution, and literary study. And it illuminates reading's marked interconnection with social and cultural practices outside the academy, its role in the dissemination and diversification of educational interests. It is startling to compare the archives of reading textbooks with those of rhetorics or composition books: readers appear in many more versions, are reprinted in greater numbers and with more frequency, and are adapted to more diversified and specified student populations than either of the other two traditions. Because of the readers' considerable commercial value, publishers issued significant numbers of titles, going through many graduated and adapted versions, and responding to changes in publishing technology and styles. It is difficult to streamline such a scattered field of materials, to mark a single line of influence or change, or to do justice to the many local innovations and interests. Here, however, are some of the broad claims of my archival study:

- In their theory, arrangement, and many of their treasured selections, readers were closely linked with classical and eighteenth-century rhetoric, particularly through the elocutionary texts and through the analytic "art of reading."
- Readers offered study of small linguistic units—letters, syllables, words, and sentences—and the analysis of larger pieces and courses of reading. The shift of emphasis cannot be resolved as the movement of elementary to advanced, or simple to complex; it is more accurate to suggest that nineteenth-century readers proposed rich engagement with language at multiple sites as a shift from more abstract to more contextual study.
- Readers frame an instructional project in terms of the body—and often of particular bodies, by focusing on the organs of pronunciation, gesture and stance, the regulation of the eye, and the modulation of the voice, and by developing distinctions about gender, class, educational level, and authority. Such attention does not necessarily eliminate issues of interpretation or understanding, nor does it simply position students. It acknowledges—and pays attention to—the physical and located performances of reading (to such factors as embarrassment, or disability) often obscured in more neutral or generalized instruction.
- Readers were, at various points, realigned with spelling and grammar, as educators debated the value of first learning abstract procedures before moving to a reading of important texts versus the value of investigating grammatical or syntactic questions in the context of a specific (interesting) reading.
- Readers attended to punctuation not as an issue of grammatical correctness but as a coded system, initially as a significant feature of elocutionary instruction (a system for

marking pauses and emphases) and subsequently as a feature for negotiating the graphic markers of printed text.

- Readers were closely linked with composition through offering model selections, stories about writing, pages of handwriting, and materials about which students could write. In more substantive ways, the readers' turn from recitation to analytic study proposed writing as a significant activity in learning—a way of understanding, recording, and demonstrating knowledge.

- Although instrumental in perpetuating rhetorical and elocutionary instruction across the century, readers also prepared the way for literary instruction, by transmitting valued selections, by developing a language about authors and genres, by prefiguring procedures for stylistic analysis and interpretation.

- Readers served as a forum in which significant cultural difference and change played out across the nation and century, in which different kinds and categories of students were positioned and addressed. Among nineteenth-century literacy textbooks, readers are particularly responsive to the interests and languages of their diverse student populations.

3 / Constructing Composition Books

> [Exercise in composition], instead of being attended to once a
> month, or once a quarter, should be attended to daily. It
> should be put on the same footing as reading and spelling. It
> should begin long before the study of Grammar, and should
> continue year after year as a part of the daily routine in school,
> until the study is finally merged in that of Rhetoric.
>
> —John S. Hart, *First Lessons in Composition*

In the language arts or English classes of today's schools and colleges, *composition* is a commonly used critical term and a regular
critical practice. A second grader composes a description of the family cat; a middle school or secondary school student is introduced
to a composing process and analyzes a character in a short story.
College students develop what they have learned about writing by
exploring the interdependence of composition and rhetoric, by de-
ploying complex writing strategies suited to particular rhetorical
contexts, and by inhabiting a range of personae and lines of reasoning. We also speak of composition courses, composition faculty, a
composition sequence, a composition program, a composition director. And while we may attach different sets of values to the terms
compose or *composition* in each of these settings, composition today
is widely understood to refer to a discursive text, to a school subject that teaches the practice of writing a discursive text, to an academic practice that students are expected to be able to perform with
proficiency(ies), or to a field of study.

It was not always so.

Until well into the nineteenth century, composition was a critical term that, while carrying a wide range of meanings, especially
in the scope of the knowledge and the work that the practice en-
tailed, often signaled a particular feature of a text, or a characteristic attached to composing a text, whether oral or written. John Gage,

for example, traces some of the early understandings of the term, noting that for Dionysus of Halicarnassus (first century BCE), "composition" meant "arrangement or order," and that in Roman rhetoric, "compositio" referred to a stage of the writing process that focused on appropriate and effective syntax (16–17). British scholar Ian Michael, in his volume *The Teaching of English,* notes that sixteenth-century writer Thomas Wilson wrote of "Composicion" as

> an apte joynyng together of wordes in suche order, that neither the eare shal espie any ierre [i.e. jar], nor yet any man shalbe dulled with overlong drawing out of a sentence, nor yet muche confounded with myngelyng of clauses, such as are nedelesse, beyng heaped together without reason, and used without nomber. (272)

And eighteenth-century writer John Lawson, lecturer in oratory at Trinity College, Dublin, thought of composition as a "branch of eloquence" that meant the "due Arrangement of Words with Regard to Signification and Sound" (227).

Understandings of composition as a critical term and as a critical practice also varied in nineteenth-century composition textbooks, especially in the first half of the century. In *Rules for English Composition* (London, 1811; Poughkeepsie, 1816), John Rippingham argued that "The art of English composition consists of two distinct branches: one is grammar which teaches the correct dependency of words: the other is a practical union of logic and rhetoric, which teaches order and elegance in the conception and arrangement of ideas" (v). At mid-century, F. Brookfield dedicates the first catechistic lesson of his *First Book in Composition* (1855) to establishing the meaning of "composition" for students, concluding that it consists "in 'putting together,' in a natural order, thoughts belonging to a subject" (10).

Whether from treatises or rhetorics or composition textbooks, these definitions represent a sample of the historical understandings of composition; they and many others, however, also suggest a gradual move from an understanding of composition as a tightly focused aesthetic practice, often oral, in which care was taken not to dull the ear of the listener with "overlong drawing out of a sentence," to Simon Kerl's definition of composition in his 1869 textbook, *Elements of Composition and Rhetoric,* as "the art of finding appropriate thoughts on a subject, and expressing them in proper language and order" (7), a definition that prefigures the work that contemporary writing teachers associate with composing. An even larger change in the meaning of composition is that while it remained an individual practice, it also became a school subject in the nineteenth century and a school subject around which textbook traditions were created.

As many scholars have documented (see especially Elson's *Guardians of Tradition*), textbooks typically reproduce the values and moral views of the dominant culture; composition textbooks are no exception. Early in the century, students wrote about abstract subjects like idleness, greed, obedience. Like textbooks in other subject areas, composition books reflected the culture's commitment to helping students acquire "mental [or formal] discipline"; students were asked to memorize, to recite, to imitate, all with the goal of exercising their mental faculties.[1] Mid-century, and especially after the Civil War, composition textbooks also offered what their authors understood as "practical" knowledge to teacher and student alike: emphasis on writing original text grew; students used writing to demonstrate their understanding of subject matter in other disciplines; and students were asked to manipulate and to interact with written language and to compose in a range of genres, including, in some cases, forms of business correspondence. While different agencies determined the use(s) of the books in individual contexts, the books are themselves repositories of what their authors (who in most cases were teachers) believed were the practices that would best help students, at whatever level of schooling, to inhabit the intellectual space in which they would learn to compose. The books, in other words, were material artifacts designed to improve the life of the mind as well as to give students the literacy skills they needed for everyday life. In the sections that follow, I look at the emergence and growth of the tradition of composition schoolbooks before and after the Civil War, and I offer a reading of the books, their pedagogies, and the watersheds they marked in the history of writing instruction in nineteenth-century U.S. schools and colleges.

The Intellectual Lineage of Composition Schoolbooks

By century's end, composition books were written specifically for high school and college students; at the beginning of the century, however, very few high schools existed, and college students were reading rhetorics. The need for a composition textbook appeared first in the schools, where young students were beginning the practice of composition.

Writing activities in the lives of nineteenth-century children and adolescents did not begin or end with formal instruction in composition but, rather, premiered and were practiced in many other sites, including infant schools, common schools, and home schools (where students sometimes had a private tutor). Beginning students copied alphabet letters and numbers and short words onto their slates; they responded to assignments in school readers (important to remember that school readers have a longer history than composition textbooks) and practiced what they learned by "filling in the blanks" of a passage, a practice often known as "ellipticals." Older students translated passages from Latin or Greek into English or wrote a version of a published text in their own words; and students of different ages imitated model passages, wrote letters to family members and friends, wrote in their journals or diaries, and as Susan Miller describes, kept commonplace books. When formal instruction in composition became a school practice, specialized textbooks were required, the students' needs shaping the books, and the books shaping not only what and how the students wrote but also the values attached to composing.

Innumerable demographic, educational, and technological forces—some we can name, others we probably cannot begin to recognize—contributed to the creation and growth of the nineteenth-century composition textbook. Among them were the increased numbers of students attending school, a growing awareness that youngsters learned differently from adults, and the proliferation of new publication and transportation technologies.[2] In addition to these factors, two strands of intellectual genealogy contributed to the growth and development of the composition textbook. The first strand embraced not only the writers and rhetoricians whose thought and language influenced the authors of the new genre, but also the intellectual property conventions of compiling or borrowing that marked nineteenth-century authorship; a second strand of intellectual genealogy that contributed to the emergence of the nineteenth-century composition book (but has been little studied) was the nineteenth-century grammar book for beginning students.

For a nineteenth-century writer, the reproduction and representation of the received wisdom of the culture was a sign of accomplishment. A failure to deploy the culture's values or writings in one's own work could well have been viewed as the mark of an author who was not respectful or knowledgeable of the work that had preceded his. Textbook authors, therefore, taught students to assimilate the culture's great works by the readings they incorporated or the writing topics they deployed, but they also incorporated earlier writers' work into their own writing to mark their credibility. When David Irving wrote in the preface to *Elements of English Composition* (London 1801; Philadelphia 1803), "In the following pages the reader needs not expect to discover any originality of observation. I desire to be regarded in no other view than that of a mere compiler" (vii), or when William Cairns began the preface to his 1899 *Introduction to Rhetoric* with the sentence, "This book makes no claims to originality of matter" (iii), they were no doubt assuming a conventional posture of humility. They were also, however, inhabiting the convention that ascribed significance to demonstrating mental indebtedness.

Here I offer examples, some extended and some more limited, of ways that authors of nineteenth-century composition textbooks borrowed from the past as they created work for new settings. Many scholars have documented that the work of George Campbell and Hugh Blair played a major role in rhetoric and writing instruction in the early American college. Not surprisingly, authors of early composition textbooks, some of whom were graduated from Harvard College where these texts were a standard part of the curriculum, frequently invoke or borrow from the British rhetoricians as well. "Purity," "propriety," and "precision," the characteristics Hugh Blair attaches to "perspicuity," show up again and again in the composition books as part of an established value system (see Parker's *Aids* and Quackenbos's *First Lessons*, for example); and in sections of composition books on letter writing, Blair's words appear almost verbatim.[3]

As Robert Connors has documented in *Composition-Rhetoric*, another important and long-recognized authority whose work inflects composition textbooks is John Walker, author of *The Teacher's Assistant in English Composition* (London, 1801; Carlisle, PA, 1804). It was Walker who formalized distinctions among "Themes," "Regular Subjects," "Easy Essays," and "Narratives" and included dozens of models for students to imitate; it was also Walker who embraced the pedagogy of asking students to listen to a text that a teacher read and then write what they could recall of it in their own words. As I will elaborate, Walker's work is especially visible in Richard Green Parker's 1832 *Progressive Exercises in English Composition*, but it is also redacted in work that follows Parker's.

Yet other contributions that inflected the nineteenth-century composition textbook came from Comenius, Locke, Rousseau, and later, from reform educators Friedrich Froebel and Johann Friedrich Herbart. The most powerful influence on the nineteenth-century composition book for young students, however, was Swiss education reformer and humanitarian Johann Heinrich Pestalozzi (1746–1827).[4] Pestalozzi believed that children learn best not from abstract concepts but from concrete and familiar objects; thus textbook writers who endorsed this understanding began, in earnest, to ask students to write about the concrete and the familiar. The first composition book to instantiate this pedagogy was, I believe, John Frost's 1839 *Easy Exercises in Composition*. Frost had edited the work of Elizabeth Mayo (who, with her brother Charles Mayo, is credited with introducing Pestalozzian ideas into England), and borrowing from her work, he created composition exercises based on objects, asking students, for example, to describe an apple, a piece of glass, a sponge.[5] Many later textbook writers included assignments asking students to write about an object.[6]

In thinking further about the ancestry of composition textbooks, I find that issues of intellectual property are pervasive. Sometimes authors named their indebtedness to one or more writers, and sometimes they borrowed silently. For contemporary scholars, tracing a silent borrowing is complicated business at best. In Parker's *Progressive Exercises in English Composition* (1832), he names three texts he is indebted to, Walker's *Teacher's Assistant* (1801), David Booth's *Principles of English Composition* (1831), and George Jardine's *Outlines of a Philosophical Education* (1818). In this list, Parker doesn't name Blair, but, indeed, he borrows heavily from Blair, and he cites those borrowings (99 and following, for example). When he uses a sentence derived from Quintilian's *Institutes of Oratory* ("An aim at too great correctness may possibly cramp the genius too much, by rendering the pupil timid and diffident; or perhaps discourage him altogether, by producing absolute despair of arriving at any degree of perfection"), he doesn't tell us he is borrowing from Quintilian (I:II:IV:107) or, more likely, from Walker who used a very similar sentence in his work (1808, 7). When writers do name their indebtedness, they do not always tell us the particular parts of a text they are borrowing. Walker, for example, acknowledges his debt to William Jones's *Letters from a Tutor to His Pupils* (1780), but he does not offer any specific citations to this indebtedness.

In some cases, the source of a silent borrowing can be difficult to identify because several writers will have used the same or similar language without attribution. In Walker's text, for example, his list of the "Parts of a Theme" is identical with the list that John Holmes used in the *The Art of Rhetoric Made Easy* (1739). And like Holmes—a public grammar school master in England who created a short Latin "verse" to help students remember the parts of a theme ("*Pono* [Proposition], *Probo* [Reason], *Firmo* [Confirmation] , *Simil* [Simile], *Exemp* [Example], *Testeq* [Testimony]; *Claudo* [Conclusion]") (21)—Walker also versifies the parts of a theme as a mnemonic device (15). But nowhere does Walker credit Holmes or any-one else for this part of his work. In *Progressive Exercises,* Parker uses the same list of "Parts of a Theme" that Walker does, and he credits Walker. Thus, when Frederick Knighton includes in his 1853 book a slightly modified version of the "Parts of a Theme" (138) that appears in Holmes's *The Art of Rhetoric* (1739, 21), Walker's *The Teacher's Assistant* (1808, 14), and Parker's *Progressive Exercises* (1833, 73), the reader is hard pressed to know if Knighton is bor-rowing from Parker, Walker, Holmes, or yet another unnamed source. I would speculate that like many other borrowings, his is multilayered, and he is indebted to more than one author.

I don't intend the sources and models I name here to constitute a straightforward intellectual genealogy of the nineteenth-century composition book; rather they serve as examples of the kinds of borrowings that Emerson explains (and praises) in "Quotation and Originality" and that were characteristic of much nineteenth-cen-tury work. I also hope these examples suggest (a) that while con-temporary scholars can recognize some of the dimensions of intertextuality that inflect a nineteenth-century textbook, we may not have access to all of the writers or thinkers who helped text-book authors, in whatever nuanced ways, to shape their texts; (b) that "authority" (more than originality) was a powerful cultural value in the early nineteenth century, and invoking authorities whose reputation was significant was a certain way to establish the credibility of a book and to gain the respect and support of a po-tential readership; and (c) perhaps most importantly, that over time, ideas that were once attributed to a particular person became assimi-lated into the intellectual commons, and authors no longer felt a need to credit the originator of those ideas (English essayist Augus-tine Birrell, 1850–1933, quipped, "Ideas, it has always been admit-ted, are free as air. If you happen to have any, you fling them into the common stock, and ought to be well content to see your poorer brethren thriving upon them" (qtd. in Lindey 1).

A second (but less often studied) strand of the intellectual lin-eage of the composition textbook for young students is the nine-teenth-century grammar for children. Rollo Lyman's *English Gram-*

mar in American Schools Before 1850, a 1922 dissertation written at
the University of Chicago, remains an important source for understanding the evolution of grammar instruction in early U.S. schools.
Lyman's study makes clear that the teaching of the vernacular, including grammar, had "entered seriously into American education"
by 1750 (68), and that like reading instruction and school readers,
both grammar instruction and grammar books for children (often
with a phrase like "grammar for children" in the title), predate composition instruction and composition books. Writers of grammars
for children were not constructing new treatises on the structures
of English grammar; rather, they were adapting an established grammatical system, often Lindley Murray's, to meet the perceived needs
of a young audience.[7]

The earliest and most typical of these grammars for beginning
students were written by church officials or teachers and included
the four traditional sections of study: orthography, etymology, syntax, and prosody. Punctuation was viewed as a system similar to that
of elocutionary marks, a way of showing how to read an author's
"sense," and therefore it was studied more in readers than in grammars.[8] If punctuation appeared in grammars, it most often was included in prosody. Underscoring the value of mental discipline,
these early grammars emphasized pedagogies that imitated or du-
plicated the pedagogies used to teach and learn Latin grammar: they
included some combination of memorizing, reciting, correcting false
syntax, and parsing. Because parsing required the application of
principles (the parser analyzed the components of a sentence in
terms of their grammatical properties), it was more interactive than
memorizing, but none of these early pedagogies taught students to
apply the rules they were learning by constructing sentences. Goold
Brown's *Catechism of English Grammar; with Parsing Exercises. Designed for the Youngest Class of Learners in Common Schools* (1827)
is an example of what I would call a traditional grammar for young
learners: it is catechistic, emphasizing memory, recitation, and parsing; it quotes from texts intended for an adult audience (by authors
such as Addison, Dryden, and Pope); and it offers no graphics or
illustrations or playfulness to help students learn.[9]

While not dismissing the values of mental discipline, some writers, even contemporaries of Brown, began to tailor their grammars to the developmental needs of the child and to interactive pedagogies. This marks the onset of the grammars that prefigure, in a variety of ways, the composition books that would appear a decade later. John Locke, principal of Cincinnati Female Academy, is among the earliest grammar writers who made this move. In the preface to his *English Grammar for Children* (1827), Locke wrote that when he asked a child, "What is the difference between a featherbed and a stone," the child responded, "Nominative case governs a verb" (x). Locke thus argued that children were so indoctrinated in the tradition of memorizing without understanding that they automatically read a question as an exercise in parsing, rather than as an act of communication. His solution was to argue for a pedagogy grounded in what I would call Pestalozzian epistemology, leading the child to understand an abstract concept or term by showing the child an object that manifested that property. Students could best understand "transparent," for example, if the teacher showed them a piece of glass. John Locke (reminder that this is the nineteenth-century textbook writer) also recommended that teachers begin not by giving students definitions to memorize, but by teaching them names of everyday objects—chair, table, house, book—then the qualities of those objects—square, round, high, soft, hard. It was thus a quick leap, he argued, for student to understand that the objects were named "nouns" and that qualities describing these objects were "adjectives" (xiv).

In *A Practical Grammar of the English Language* (1830), Roscoe Greene argues that young learners have trouble remembering the variations of a verb in different moods and tenses, so he offers comparative graphics addressed to the "untutored minds" of children, illustrating the relationship of one verb form to another. To show the present tense of the verb "to write," a boy sits behind a desk holding a pen and writing on a piece of paper, and the accompanying verb form is "write"; to show the imperfect tense "wrote" (what we would call the past tense), the pen and paper remain on the desk, but the boy and his chair are pulled back from it (29). In Greene's

1835 *Grammar for Children,* he uses a page of illustrations of common objects and/or activities to illustrate each part of speech. And in the preface to William Bentley Fowle's *North American Grammar, Part First* (1842), he notes that he wrote his book for "the comprehension of the very young," and in his text, he includes illustrations of common objects, people, and scenes to teach grammatical principles. He uses one illustration, for example, to teach students how to use adjectives to compare nouns. The engraving shows three girls of different heights, each holding a hoop (see fig. 5). And to the young learners, Fowle writes that if it were said that all the girls were short, it would be correct to say, "No. 1 is a *short* girl, No. 2 a *shorter* girl, and No. 3 the *shortest* girl" (23).[10]

While adapting their instruction to what they imagined as the learning style of a child, some writers pushed one step further. In Frost's preface to his *A Practical English Grammar* (1842), he wrote

COMPARISON OF NOUNS BY MEANS OF ADJECTIVES.

[No. XVIII.]

1   2   3

We not only use adjectives to distinguish nouns from each other, but also to compare them together. Referring to cut XVIII., I may call the first the *tall* girl, the second the *middling-sized* girl, and the third the *short* girl. But if it be said they are all *short* girls, I should say, No. 1 is a *short* girl, No. 2 a *shorter* girl, and No. 3 the *shortest* girl.

Fig. 5. Example of an illustration to help students understand a grammatical concept. William Bentley Fowle, *North American Grammar, Part First.* Boston, 1842, 23.

that since his goal was not "to offer any new theories on the subject of grammar" but rather "to suggest improvements in the methods of teaching" (iii), he wants students "to reduce their knowledge to practice, as fast as it is acquired" (iv). Thus, he writes, he introduced pictures to help students to practice what they were learning. The task accompanying an illustration entitled "The Village School," reads, "Write sentences referring to this picture, including *nouns in both numbers, articles, pronouns, verbs, adjectives,* and *adverbs*" (94).

An emphasis on mental or formal discipline never disappeared. To make the chore of memorizing more palatable, an author in at least one case used verse as a mnemonic device. Lambert Wilmer's rationale, he writes in the preface to his 1849 *English Grammar,* was, "If any part of the great highway of education requires smoothing and embellishment, grammar is that part" (2). Here is a selection of a ditty he asked students to sing to learn the parts of speech.

Air—"Auld Lang Syne."

1

Nine sorts of words or parts of speech
  In English are embraced:—
Noun, Article and Adjective
  First on the roll are placed.

2

Next Pronoun, Verb and Adverb take,
  Then Preposition greet;
Conjunction, Interjection come
  To make the list complete.

(8)

Creative approaches to memorizing notwithstanding, an important breakthrough in the early reform grammars for beginning students was the adaptation of instruction, in a range of ways, to what was understood as the developmental learning patterns and the psychological needs of the child. To that end, some writers used object lessons; some used graphics; and some asked students to write sentences that used particular parts of speech. All of these approaches to learning prefigured pedagogies that would be visible in composition books for young learners.

Given that the purpose of studying English grammar, borrowed from studying Latin grammar, was not only learning to speak but also learning to write correctly or, expressed another way, learning to write the English language with propriety, a second way that writers of grammars for young students anticipate or contribute to the development of composition instruction and the composition book is in their discussion of this problematic: how to sequence studying grammar and learning to compose text longer than a sentence. Some writers stated unequivocally in their preface that the two tasks were separate, that grammar came first, and that students weren't capable of writing until they had a mastery of grammar. Others, however, as early as Daniel Jaudon in his 1811 *Union Grammar,* added material on composing (that he borrowed largely from Walker or perhaps Holmes) to his grammar. Richard Green's 1831 *Inductive Exercises in English Grammar; Designed To Give Young Pupils a Knowledge of the First Principles of Language* includes an appendix called "First Lessons in Exercises of Composition"; Charles Morley's 1836 *Common School Grammar* includes an appendix called "Directions for Composing"; in 1845, Bradford Frazee adds lessons in composition to his *Improved Grammar,* so that, he writes, the two branches can mutually "promote the acquisition of each other" (viii); and in 1854, Peter Bullions, in *Practical Lessons in English Grammar and Composition,* moves toward an integration of the study of grammar and composition by asking students, for example, to write sentences using the part of speech just studied. In Bullions's words, "Analysis and Composition are carried on together" (iv).

While this is an unremarkable idea to contemporary teachers, it challenged long-held assumptions of eighteenth- and early-nineteenth-century teachers about the primacy of grammar instruction, and it encouraged the development of freestanding books on the teaching of composing that reverse the pattern of the earlier books; whereas the grammars sometimes had included a section on composing, composition books began to appear that included a section on grammar. In the preface to Frost's 1839 *Easy Exercises in Composition,* for example, he advised, "if [the child] begins the study of grammar at the same time [as he studies the writing of composition], I believe he will make greater progress in both studies . . . than he would in either separately" (6).

Repositioned Readings

Before I work with individual texts, I offer two suggestions, based on my traversals of the archive in its relationship to nineteenth-century culture, for a fresh reading of nineteenth-century composition textbooks. The first is this: to assume that the relationship between students and their composition books in the nineteenth century was the same as it is today would be a mistake. While it is true that schoolbook publishing flourished mid-century, it is highly unlikely, for example, especially in the first part of the century, that each student had a book of her or his own, let alone the same book that other students and the teacher had. An exception would have been the private school or academy that required students to purchase a book; Louise Stevenson's documentary history *Miss Porter's School,* for example, includes an 1855 invoice to the parents of a girl enrolled at the school showing that they were charged $1.00 for "Quackenbos's *[First Lessons in] Composition*" as part of the school's annual fees for their daughter (55).

Several factors affected a student's ownership of a textbook; availability was one. Occasionally, a secondary source will claim that a certain number of copies of a textbook were printed or sold, but there is nothing to indicate how that number was attained and no easy way to check its accuracy. Estimates provided by advertisers or publishers might well be inflated. Gathering reliable numbers of copies printed would require locating and studying publishers' records; some of these records no longer exist, and when they do, they use very different (and irregular) categories for tallying numbers. Gathering reliable data, therefore, about the number of copies of composition books printed or sold in the nineteenth century would require long and tedious work, work that as far as I can discern has not yet been done. What we do know is that the number of textbooks printed did not begin to equal the number of students who were in school.[11]

Expense was a related and overlapping factor that affected student ownership of books. Working from model budgets for the 1850s, Stevenson shows that a "working family's annual income of $600 allowed less than ten dollars a year for reading matters and other amusements" ("Home, Books, and Reading" 4). She thus argues that a book of 75 cents was a luxury. Integrating that data with the textbook costs that are catalogued in Orville Roorbach's *Bibliotheca Americana*—Frost's *Easy Exercises,* for example, rang in at 25 cents (207); Parker's *Progressive Exercises* at 38 cents; and the heftier Parker's *Aids to English Composition* at 80 cents (414)—it is unlikely that a family of modest means and a family with more than one child attending school would have purchased a book for every child, every year. Henry Perkinson writes that into the 1880s, as many as one million students did not attend school because they could not afford the textbooks (xiv–xv). And Alfred Lawrence Hall-Quest reports that while some cities provided free textbooks to students before the Civil War (Philadelphia, for example, in 1818), Massachusetts was the first state to require districts to provide free textbooks for all students—and that didn't occur until 1884 (48–49).[12]

Finally, a third factor suggesting that students did not each own a copy of the same book is that some of the books, at least in part, were addressed as much to teachers as to students. The first books that were written for young writers (and addressed the students as "you") often included a "Note to Teachers" about some aspect of teaching; these notes were occasionally integrated into the body of the text, sometimes were placed at the bottom of a page and appeared in a small font, and sometimes appeared at the beginning or end of a book in a page or two. Even after the Civil War, some books that were billed as textbooks for students were addressed primarily to teachers; this is especially true of the large books intended for students of varying ages. Simon Kerl's 1869 *Elements of Composition and Rhetoric,* weighing in at 408 pages and designed for academies and colleges, for example, contains page-length passages addressed to teachers, explaining the rationale or method for implementing a particular pedagogy. Consider this advice about responding to student writing:

> All commendable efforts should be duly praised by the teacher; and the beauties and imperfections of composition should be brought out by him in the most interesting manner. A little flattery, and frequent help and encouragement, may be highly beneficial. He should particularly beware of criticising [sic] too severely or personally. Children easily despair when they already lack self-confidence; and a very slight touch may break off a tender bud. (137)

In effect, this book and others like it functioned as both teacher's guide and student text, and the heavy emphasis on instructions to teachers, as well as the size of these texts, strongly suggests that in a class where a teacher was drawing on this book for pedagogical advice, not every student owned a copy.

And the significance of this awareness that a student's relationship to a textbook in the nineteenth century was not what it is today? I would argue that the lack of uniform textbooks was a major contributing factor (sometimes as cause, sometimes as effect) to the dominance of many nineteenth-century pedagogies—memorizing and reciting and listening and copying and parsing—all of which were institutionalized, none of which required that a student have the same book in hand that every other student had.

My second preliminary consideration for a fresh reading of nineteenth-century composition texts is a caveat about reading the critical terms of these books (or their absence) as if they were stable. Just as the meanings of *composition* have evolved, so have understandings of many other terms that were common in nineteenth-century books and remain in use today. *Writing,* for example, merits attention because it is a term contemporary teachers use in a number of contexts; we speak of writing centers, of writing classes, of writing instruction, of school writing. In each of these cases, we affiliate the term "writing" with composing text. Sometimes "writing" also referred to composing in the nineteenth century, but in the seventeenth century, the eighteenth, and into the early part of the nineteenth, "writing," borrowing from the English tradition, more often signaled "handwriting." Learning to write in primers and early readers meant learning to form letters and words; the teacher might have been a "writing master," and the pupils might have attended a "writing school" where, as E. Jennifer Monaghan notes, the focus was on form, visual properties, and a range of "hands" (styles).[13]

Another important term that merits a repositioned reading, and unlike *writing* has not been elaborated by scholars, is *exercise*. Perhaps echoing earlier uses of the word "exercises" (Richard Whately and John Walker used the term, for example) or perhaps drawing on even earlier instantiations of the practice (such as the writing exercises of Aphthonius known as *progymnasmata* or Quintilian's suggested exercises for young orators), many nineteenth-century authors used "exercises" in the titles of their books. For these writers the term did not mean low-level activity, signifying repetition. Nor did it refer to easy-answer questions or fill-in-the-blank drills. Rather, in contrast to those instances when learning to write meant memorizing rules, "exercises" suggested a pedagogy based on practice, the use of performance-based (as opposed to recognition-based) activity to improve one's level of fitness in composing, not unlike today's use of exercise to signal a means of enhancing fitness or strength or musical proficiency. William Russell, for example, in his 1823 *A Grammar of Composition* writes:

> Pupils who have entered on the practice of composition, will find the following exercise . . . useful and pleasing. Let them, every six or twelve months, write a piece on the same subject,—compare the one composition with the other, observe what improvement has been made, and in what the improvement consists. The learner is thus enabled to avoid former errors, and is animated by the consciousness of advancing in the refinement of his taste and his style. (150)

For textbook author Richard Green Parker, "exercises" began with the writing of simple sentences and progressed to the writing of a full-length theme; for John Frost, "exercises" referred to the different kinds of essays a student might write with the help of his textbook, a description, for example, or a narrative in response to an illustration. John S. Hart, who wrote college texts as well as a range of school texts, used the concept of exercise as late as 1870 and articulated its value in the preface to his *First Lessons in Composition*, where he wrote that teachers who tell a youngster to write a composition without the preliminary training that exercises provide might as well tell him to make a steam engine (1886, iii). And as college catalogues at the end of the nineteenth century demonstrate (see many examples in John Michael Wozniak's dissertation), "exercises in composition," which meant practice in writing compositions, themes, orations, and declamations, were a frequent requirement for college students.

Books Before the Civil War and Their Composing Strategies

In the July 1832 issue of *American Annals of Education*, an unsigned article titled "Schoolbooks in the United States" lists the textbooks that were used in U.S. schools in 1804 and in 1832; the writer does not claim the lists are complete, but, rather, useful approximations.[14] For 1804, he lists 13 spelling books, 28 readers, 16 grammars, and 1 composition book. For 1832, he lists 45 spellers, 102 readers, 48 grammars, and 5 composition books (377). The five composition books he lists are David Irving's *Elements of Composition* (London, 1801; Philadelphia, 1803); Caleb Bingham's *Juvenile Letters* (1803); John Walker's *The Teacher's Assistant* (London, 1801; Carlisle, PA, 1808); William Russell's *Grammar of Composition* (1823); and Parker's *Progressive Exercises* (1832). Of these, I would argue that Irving's book is a rhetoric with no exercises; Walker's is intended for teachers; and Russell's is intended for older students. These books use heavily embedded syntax, pages of text with little white space and almost no formatting, and vocabulary beyond a child's understanding (Russell, for example, uses this silently borrowed phrase from Blair, "Precision . . . means retrenching all superfluities" [35]). Bingham's book consists of a series of letters that model the letters students might write: a letter to parents or siblings when one was away at school, or a friendship letter. While the seeds of composition instruction as it came to be understood appear in these early works, it is Parker's 1832 *Progressive Exercises* that marks a change in the form and content of composition books for school students, and might be seen as the first of many nineteenth-century texts that were written for and accessible to students who were beginning their study of the school subject called composition.

Early on, the authors of these books were sometimes ministers; more consistently, they were teachers, often noting in a preface that they wrote the book based on their own teaching experience and that the student writing in the text was that of their own students. By mid-century, as men left the classroom for higher-paying jobs, the number of women teaching beyond the infant school grew, but most of the textbook writers remained men. Mary Hyde, who taught composition in the State Normal School in Albany, and Lucy Chittenden, who taught English in an Ann Arbor high school, are among the growing number of women who wrote composition textbooks after the Civil War.

The new composition books bear many physical resemblances to the readers and grammars: they were small, usually fewer than one hundred pages (readers were often much longer), often close to 4" x 7" in size. Front and back covers (most often tan, brown, dark green, dark red, or dark blue) were cardboard; on them were printed the book's full title, author, intended audience, and publication data. Sometimes a cover was illustrated; some early books included a Latin phrase on the cover. Before mid-century, most books were printed on rag paper; as the demand for books increased, they were printed on paper made from wood pulp that was not acid free. Hence the older books often are in better condition today (fewer chipped corners, less foxing) than the later books. The type font was most often small, and section or lesson headings were often in bold.

By the end of the 1830s, illustrations of students' everyday life at home and at school began to appear. The use of paratexts—those liminal devices that Richard Macksey (in his forward to Gerard

Genette's *Paratexts,* xvii) claims form part of the complex mediation among book, author, publisher, and reader—was irregular. So while prefaces appeared fairly often, a table of contents or an index was less common in the early decades. Sections of the book were called "Lessons," not chapters, and, for the most part, each lesson numbered just a few pages. Not every book included the same lessons, and there is no consistent order in which the books treat topics, but a number of topics were common. Word- and sentence-level topics included, for example, the use of words, the construction of sentences, qualities of sentences, tropes, style, and punctuation. When punctuation was included, it received little of an author's attention and appeared most often in the last several pages of the book.

Some books, like Parker's *Progressive Exercises,* followed earlier traditions of asking students to write about abstract topics (such as "Happiness," "Indolence," or "Modesty"), while adding an occasional opportunity to write about a topic such as "Description of a family circle on Thanksgiving, Christmas, New Year's day, Fourth of July, and Election day" (96). For the most part, though, the lessons of the new books for young learners centered on the activities and ideal behaviors of childhood, including, for example, a child's relationship with a sibling, a friend, a toy, or a pet.

Description, narration, and the letter were the genres students were most often asked to write. Occasionally, a book, especially a longer one intended for students of all ages, would include a section on writing poetry, an oration, a sermon, an obituary, a biography, or an argument. Less often, a book would include a section on writing fiction. Length of an assignment was not specified, and students were not given elaborated directions for an assignment. Assignments were called "exercises" or "themes" or "compositions" or "essays"; a label that does not appear for a writing assignment, but one we that commonly use today, is "paper," perhaps signaling that a student's written work was intended to be read aloud in class and thus was more of a "performance" than a "paper." Among the most popular means of assisting students with an assignment was including models; sometimes, these models were written by recognized authors; occasionally, but less often, by students. Among the most popular strategies for offering students topic choices was a "list of subjects." While such a list is often associated with Richard Parker's work in the 1830s (his lists included more than three hundred items), very short lists of topics appear at least a decade earlier in Russell's 1823 *A Grammar of Composition* (141–43) and, before that, in Rippingham's 1816 *Rules for English Composition* (32). Sometimes the list is simply alphabetical; sometimes, as in Russell and in George P. Quackenbos's *First Lessons in Composition* (1851), it is divided into genres. So frequently used were these topic lists that by 1869, Simon Kerl questioned their value, explaining his choice not to include lists in his own book: "Most books on Composition give long lists of subjects or themes. We have never known pupils to make much use of them" (228).

As scholars today read beneath or beyond the surface features of nineteenth-century composition books, the important question, "So how did these books, and the teachers who used them, teach students to compose a text?" is more complex than might appear at first glance. To name just one problematic: contemporary scholars have in many cases focused on what appears to be absent from these books, rather than on what is present.

To construct a reading, then, of how young students might have learned to compose from a textbook before the Civil War, I work closely with two pre–Civil War books: Richard Green Parker's *Progressive Exercises in English Composition,* first published in 1832, and John Frost's *Easy Exercises in Composition,* first published in 1839. While these writers are indebted to earlier traditions, each of them also introduced a maverick approach to composition instruction. Parker wrote the first book to teach young students the importance of practice as they learned to write; instead of asking students, for example, to memorize the definition of a word, or to correct false syntax, Parker asked students to use a word in a sentence. Seven years later, Frost, drawing on Pestalozzian concepts about the way children learned, wrote the first book that relied heavily on illustrations as writing prompts and that begins by asking students not to practice rules but to compose short texts.[15] The two books deploy very different pedagogies, and Parker's approach to composing is certainly more grounded in tradition than Frost's, but over time, their groundbreaking approaches evolved, were hybridized and institutionalized, and even became representative. Beyond that, though, I use these books as examples of how a contemporary reader can resist what has become an established reading of a text (or a group of texts) and thus complicate—and enrich—an understanding of the history of composition instruction.

Parker's *Progressive Exercises in English Composition* (1832)
It is easy, even natural, to rely on associations that we as readers and writers of composition histories have, in the past several decades, attached to the name Richard Green Parker, or just "Parker." And indeed such associations can help us to make new knowledge. But in serious ways, if they are used as disembodied or dismissive short-cuts, they can also impede us from new knowledge. To hear "Parker" and to think "pedagogue" (Crowley, *Methodical* 64) or "professional text book author" (Connors, *Comp-Rhet* 78) or "textbook compiler" and to stop there is to stop short. While Parker was the author or compiler of many books, and while it may be appropriate to apply those labels in particular instances, they represent only part of Parker's story.

Richard Green Parker (1798–1869) was graduated from Boston Latin, and then, in 1817, at the age of eighteen, from Harvard College, where he had studied with Boylston Professor of Rhetoric Joseph McKean.[16] (Parker's father, Samuel Parker, was graduated from Harvard in 1764 and was a distinguished Anglican clergyman and teacher.) R. G. Parker served for many years as a grammar master in Boston schools, including East Roxbury Grammar School (1825–28), Boylston School for Girls and Boys (1828), Mayhew School (1828–29), Franklin School (1830–36), and Johnson School for Girls (1836–53). Parker thus had a lengthy and accomplished career as a teacher of young students, and to overlook that aspect of his history or to erase its importance is to risk overlooking the ground of his work.

The book by Richard Green Parker that is most often cited in contemporary composition history is *Aids to English Composition*

(1844), the book he wrote "for students of all grades; embracing specimens and models of school and college exercises, and most of the higher departments of English composition, both in prose and verse" (cover). A more important work, I would argue, in terms of innovation, is *Progressive Exercises* (1832), written for beginning students while he was principal of the Franklin Grammar School in the mill town of Franklin, Massachusetts, some thirty miles outside of Boston. Parker's *Aids* is simply a more elaborate version of *Progressive Exercises,* repeating most of the contents of the earlier work and adding lessons suited to more advanced students, including an assignment, for example, on obituary writing. It is in the earlier work, the book written for young learners, that he breaks important new ground, and it is this book that I focus on here as I attempt to modify and broaden what we think when we hear the name "Parker."

Two editions of this book appeared in 1832, published both in Boston and in Cincinnati. The first stereotyped edition of the book, known as the third edition, appeared in 1833. The "Advertisement" to this edition followed the convention of noting that because the 1832 edition sold four thousand copies in the first six months, the publishers elected to stereotype it "and thus put it into final form" (iv). The *National Union Catalogue* lists fifty-five different printings from stereotyped plates, and the book was enlarged and revised a number of times and by different writers until the last printing appeared in 1879, published by R. S. Davis in Boston.

I have the 1832 and 1833 editions of *Progressive Exercises* in hand, and I have looked at many of the later printings. I have chosen to work with the 1833 stereotyped edition because this is the edition that would have had widest circulation when the book was still a recent publication. Almost identical to the 1832 edition, the primary changes are additions: new in the 1833 edition are Parker's praise for Samuel Newman's *A Practical System of Rhetoric* and his regret that he hadn't seen Newman's work earlier; a list of what Parker calls "terms connected with the study of composition"; a recommended reading list for students (which includes Blair's *Lectures*); and recommendations for the book itself from a range of sources. In the 1833 edition, Parker has also extended his commentary on letter writing, including, for the first time, sample topics for letters (as well as the audience and purpose for each) that a student might write. The few pages of additions will, Parker writes, "supersede the necessity of using any *abridged* treatise of Rhetorick in connexion with it [his book]" (iv). Parker is also here telling us that in his eyes, the study of rhetoric and the practice of composition, however different, are also interrelated.

Although *Progressive Exercises* has been recognized as one of the first nineteenth-century books to teach students to compose not by asking them to memorize rules, but by asking them to produce text, contemporary scholars have not yet focused on the composing strategies that Parker articulates. In fact, many scholars (and I include myself in this group) have underestimated, even overlooked, his attention to those strategies.

The 1833 *Progressive Exercises* contains 105 pages of text plus a one-page index and two pages of "Recommendations." A note in the front matter reads, "The School Committee of the city of Boston have authorized the introduction of this work into the publick schools of the city." The book has no table of contents, but the index lists the forty lessons as well as a few unnumbered topics. It also includes the two-page preface (the paratext that Borges calls the vestibule of a book, the site from which a reader decides to enter a room or not) that Parker wrote for the June 1832 edition. In that preface, Parker articulates his pedagogy as well as a rationale for his work: "Two great obstacles beset the pupil in his first attempts at composition. The first is the difficulty of obtaining ideas, (or learning to think;) [sic] the second is that of expressing them properly when obtained" (iii).[17] And thus Parker sets out to alleviate both of those problems with a series of progressive exercises.

In brief, Parker's text moves from the part to the whole. In lesson 1, for example, students are asked to write a sentence using the word "surprised"; the model sentence is, "I was surprised by the return of my long lost brother" (5). At the end of the book, students are asked to write original work based on a 302-item list of (primarily) abstract subjects. Between these mileposts, students write sentences in a range of syntactic patterns, practice using figures and tropes, and practice writing in a range of schematic models that Parker borrows from Walker. At the end of Parker's book, after students have written full-length essays from outlines and then full-length original essays, Parker offers a few paragraphs of counsel on style, rhyme, criticism, epistolary writing, and at the very last, six suggestions—on one page—for the mechanical execution of written exercises.

If we read Parker's text as we would read a contemporary composition textbook, looking for the terms that we expect to see in contemporary books, what jumps out is that nowhere in *Progressive Exercises* is there a lesson, a heading, or an index item marking what we might call "the composing process." Parker doesn't use the word "invention" or "arrangement" to signal a strategy for composing, and he makes no reference to "prewriting," "writing," or "revising." Yet to read the absence of these terms as a sign that the work they represent was not part of Parker's instructional plan is, I believe, to overlook his instructional plan. When Parker states in his preface that the two goals of his text are helping students to obtain ideas and to express them properly, I would argue that he is also expressing his book's central concern with helping students learn to compose a text. I begin my reading of Parker by elaborating what Parker called helping students to obtain ideas, a process akin to giving them a series of heuristics.

Embedded in models that Parker borrows from John Walker are not only culturally established truths for the students to live by, but also what Walker considered the required components of a particular genre. Following Walker but elaborating Walker's five-part scheme for writing about a "regular subject" (education, government, war, peace, youth) into a seven-part scheme, Parker called a text on such a subject a "simple theme"; we would label it expository. Parker's seven parts for a simple theme included definition, cause, antiquity or novelty, universality or locality, effects, antithesis, and conclusion and comparison.

Again borrowing from Walker (who in this case is borrowing from Holmes), Parker assigns a seven-part scheme for writing what

Walker calls a "theme," what Parker calls a "complex theme," and what we might now call a persuasive essay or argument. The seven parts of a theme were the proposition, the reason, the confirmation, the simile, the example, the testimony or quotation, and the conclusion. For each of the model themes, each part of the text is labeled so the student writer sees, for example, how the definition of a topic differs from the cause. The student writer also sees the order of the parts, that they are not random but rather follow a prescribed sequence.

My argument is this: for Parker, "simple" and "complex" were technical terms representing different genres, the topics suited to those genres, and Walker's/Parker's strategies for composing a text in one of those genres. So as students practiced writing the required parts of a simple or complex theme in their prescribed order, they were learning to compose in a specialized genre. As students investigated the "cause" or the "definition" of a simple theme, or the "proposition" or "the example" of a complex theme, they were also learning strategies for a kind of invention, and as they followed the order of these points laid out by Walker/Parker, they were learning strategies for what we think of as arrangement. Neither Walker nor Parker affiliates these strategies with our use of the terms "invention" or "arrangement," but the tasks they were asking students to perform in their rules for writing a simple or complex theme were clearly tasks that would assist a writer in generating both content and structure.

Parker's borrowings from Walker and Blair and their prose models dominate his text. But he also includes short sections on description, for example, that are not from Walker. And to guide students in describing an object, a scene in nature, or a person, he poses a series of questions for each category that serve as what he calls "hints" to help the writer begin the description in each category. About these hints, Parker notes, "It is not expected that he [the student] will take them in the order in which they stand; much less that all of them should, in all cases, be embraced in the same exercise" (43). These hints that Parker offered his students are, I would suggest, additional heuristics or inventional strategies, in this case rooted both in classical topoi and in observation. Here, for example, are the hints Parker   .

gave for describing what he called "a sensible object" (a carriage, a schoolroom, a bureau, a writing desk, a paper mill):

1. The time when, and place where it exists, or was seen.

2. The purpose for which it is designed, its name, uses and conveniences.

3. Its novelty or antiquity, general or particular existence.

4. Its figure or form, and position, together with an analysis of its parts.

5. Its resemblance to any other object.

6. Its size, colour, beauty, or want of it.

7. The persons or artists by whom it was made.

8. Materials of which it was made and the manner in which it is constructed.

9. Its effects on mankind by increasing or abridging their comfort, &c.

10. The feelings or reflections which it excited.

11. Its connexion [*sic*] with any other subject. (43)

This list, of course, suggests the Aristotelian topoi, a version of which Parker may have studied with Bolyston Professor Joseph McKean when Parker was at Harvard and which are now part of our intellectual commons.[18] I quote Parker's set of heuristics in its entirety because it strikes me as telling evidence that he was giving his students a procedure, a process, if you will, for generating text and, I would add, a process not all that different from that which contemporary textbooks offer students.[19]

Parker offers yet a third invention strategy; like Walker, he asks students to write from a sketch or an outline that he provides. But following that, he teaches students a skill he calls "Methodising," an exercise in which students write their own outlines or skeletons, with the understanding that for simple subjects, they would need to discuss the nature, the importance, and the effects of their subjects; and that for complex subjects, the explanation, the proof, and the confirmation would become part of their outline. For students to practice writing outlines, Parker offers twenty-six sample subjects ranging from "Benevolence" to "Good society improves the mind"

(87). He follows this with a lesson on "Investigation," teaching students in his words "to investigate a subject, assign causes, trace effects, and draw inferences" (88). As examples, he offers students questions such as, "What art, manufacture, or profession, is most serviceable to mankind?" and "What comforts or conveniences have been added to the sum of human enjoyment, by the discovery of the art of making glass?" (92). Again, with these strategies, Parker is teaching students to generate both text and structure, in the one case by investigating cause/effect relationships and drawing inferences, in the other by drafting an outline.

What might look to a contemporary eye like a haphazard arrangement of lessons, dedicated primarily to sentence-level work, is what Parker's book title and preface promise: a series of progressive exercises that prepare students to write original themes, the final work that they are asked to do in the book. Prior to this final task, students have read models, practiced imitating models, memorized prescribed parts of particular genres, learned observational strategies, practiced writing outlines, and written simple investigations into cause/effect relationships. In short, they have learned a series of strategies for generating and arranging text.

Partly because Parker uses the word "style," his attention to this aspect of a composing process is, at first glance, more visible than his attention to invention and arrangement. Borrowing from Blair's Lecture XIX (212–15), Parker gives clear rules for helping students develop what he calls "a good style." These rules include studying clear ideas of the subject, composing frequently and with care, studying the style of the best authors, avoiding servile imitation of a particular author, adapting one's style to the subject and the audience, and not letting concerns with style override a necessary "higher degree of attention" to the thought of the writing (100).

In stark opposition to contemporary anecdotal understandings of nineteenth-century writing instruction, Parker does not equate style with correctness, as we sometimes do today; neither does he focus on sentence-level correctness. Parker does not teach by negative example (asking students to correct false syntax as some grammars did and some composition books continued to do), and he does not focus on right or wrong. Instead, he asks students to practice a large number of stylistic moves, including, for example, varying sentence structure and using tropes in their writing. Parker's only direct mention of correctness occurs on the last page of his text when, offering suggestions for the "mechanical execution of written exercises," he writes to teachers that "No abbreviations should be allowed; and neglect of punctuation and errors in spelling should be particularly noticed" (103).

In response to what the student wrote, the teacher's job was, in Walker's words, "to inspect what is written, and correct what is improper," taking care not to "affect too elegant a style in his corrections, but, as much as possible, to make them of a piece with the pupil's own production" (6–7). Repeating Walker's suggestion (who, in part, was borrowing from Quintilian I:II:IV), Parker added that

> An aim at too great correctness may possibly cramp the genius too much, by rendering the pupil timid and diffident; or perhaps discourage him altogether, by producing absolute despair of arriving at any degree of perfection. For this reason, the teacher should show the pupil where he has erred, either in the thought, the structure of the sentence, the syntax or the choice of words. Every alteration, as has already been observed, should differ as little as possible from what the pupil has written; as giving an entire new cast to the thought and expression will lead him into an unknown path not easy to follow, and divert his mind from that original line of thinking which is natural to him. (103)

Thus, not only does Parker not emphasize "correctness" to the exclusion of other aspects of composing, he is careful to say that too great an emphasis on correctness may inhibit the pupil and detract from his authority.

Frost's *Easy Exercises in Composition* (1839)
John Frost (1800–1859) studied at Bowdoin College for one year. In 1819, he transferred to Harvard College, entered the sophomore

class, studied with Boylston Professor Edward T. Channing, and was graduated in 1822, one year after Ralph Waldo Emerson, five years after Parker, six years after Samuel Newman.[20] Also in 1822, Frost was named the winner of Harvard's Bowdoin Prize (Emerson had won the prize in 1820 and 1821), an annual award presented for the best original dissertation in English, Latin, or Greek.[21]

In 1845, Frost took up book compiling as a full-time labor and worked in that capacity until his death. The *NUC* cites him as author of more than three hundred books, most of which were compiled with a team of associates for a general audience and some of which sold many copies, including, for example, the *Pictorial History of the United States*. Before turning to full-time writing and compiling, Frost taught school from 1823 to 1845, at both the elementary and secondary levels, and in 1843, he received an honorary LLD from Franklin and Marshall College. He served as principal of the Mayhew School in Boston (recall that Parker also taught at this school) from 1823–27; as director of a school for young ladies in Philadelphia from 1828–37; and from 1838 until 1845, as Professor of Belles-Lettres at Central High School in Philadelphia, the second oldest public school in the United States and a school (like Boston Latin and Miss Porter's School) that remains in existence today. He published two grammar books,[22] but *Easy Exercises* is his only composition book. He wrote it while he was teaching at Central High, and the book was adopted there for student use.[23]

Unlike Parker's *Progressive Exercises,* Frost's 1839 *Easy Exercises in Composition* was not widely used in the nineteenth century (WorldCat shows the last printing occurred in 1843, not 1841 as *NUC* suggests and as I wrote in *The Young Composers*). Although named in several dissertations, *Easy Exercises* has been almost unnoticed by contemporary scholars. I work here with the second edition, published the same year as the first, 1839, but as a stereotyped edition; like Parker, Frost reports in the preface to this new edition that the quick sale of the first edition (three thousand copies in a month) galvanized the need for additional availability of the text. In this preface, Frost also provides interesting data about the changes from the first to the second edition. He writes, "It is printed page for page, from the first, the only variation consisting in the addition of a picture, here and there, at the bottom of a page, where the space allowed it, and the insertion of a Section on Dialogue Writing, on page 78" (vi). A note in the stereotyped edition reports that in March 1839, the Board of Controllers of Public Schools in Philadelphia authorized the use of *Easy Exercises*, at the discretion of teachers, in all the public schools.

Just as it is easy to read "Parker" in predetermined ways and dismiss his work, it is also easy to dismiss or devalue Frost's work, in his case because copies of his books were not as numerous (or as easily located today) as Parker's and because we haven't, for the most part, read him into our histories. I argue, however, that *Easy Exercises* is a critical text in helping us to read the history of the composition schoolbook.

Unlike Parker, who begins his text with many lessons on the sentence and moves slowly but steadily to asking students to write a longer text, Frost begins with what he calls "exercises in composition," what we could call assignments asking students to write a paragraph or short essay; that is, Frost begins not with teaching rules, but with asking students to compose. Also unlike Parker—and this is a major distinction—Frost makes deliberate and extensive use of illustrations as writing prompts. Divided into thirteen small sections, the first seventy-eight pages of Frost's text invite students to write brief narratives or descriptions in response to illustrations of simple objects or scenes. Only in the final third of his text (the last thirty-nine pages) does Frost offer students instruction in sentence writing and in the use of tropes. In the introduction to this section, he writes that having been encouraged to write "freely and boldly" in earlier parts of the book, the pupil has begun to feel "at home" with writing and at this point in his development as a writer, "will be much less embarrassed and disheartened than he otherwise would on entering upon a systematic course of exercises in the analysis and composition of sentences" (79–80).

The most striking significance of the formal arrangement of the text, however, is that it is a trope for Frost's approach to the composing process, an approach that is uncanny in its anticipation of contemporary understandings. Midway through Frost's book, in the headnote to a section called "Subjects for Descriptive and Narrative Writing," he offers what I read as a summary of his book's approach to composing, an approach that begins with teaching students invention strategies, that emphasizes natural expression, and that reserves "correcting" until later in the process:

> Our next series of pictures . . . relate to several of the useful trades and professions. The pupil will obtain information on the subjects which they suggest, by conversing with the persons who exercise these trades and professions; or, if that should not be found convenient, by making inquiries of his parent or teacher. If any pupil should feel disinclined to pursue the subject farther than a simple description of the picture, he may find in that species of writing an ample field for the exercise of his best powers. Let him note each object in the picture carefully, and describe it as fully and at the same time as naturally and unaffectedly as he can. Above all it is necessary in these initiatory exercises that he should write freely and boldly, using such expressions as suit his own feelings, and his own understanding of the subject. Hereafter we shall endeavor to give him some instruction in the art of correcting his own composition. But the first and most important thing is to be able to originate observations on the subjects presented and to express them in such language as his feelings prompt. If he feel a constant solicitude lest he should make a trifling mistake, this will chill his feelings and give his writing an unpleasant air of stiffness and constraint. (58–59)

Like other nineteenth-century composition textbook authors including Parker, Frost does not foreground a composing process in the way that authors today do. And although his pedagogy differs in some ways from Parker's, Frost, like Parker, nonetheless places a powerful emphasis on teaching young writers to generate text. In the preface to *Easy Exercises,* Frost articulates the philosophy from which his use of illustrations as writing prompts springs. He argues that some textbooks for young students "direct the attention of the learner to words and phrases, to the entire neglect of *things*" (5), and thus that these books impede rather than enhance the student's learning. Further arguing that "things . . . form the substratum of thought" (5), Frost explains his rationale for making pictures and real objects the foundation of his book.

In one small section of the book, Frost teaches students to write what we would think of as an expository essay with an argumentative edge. Foregoing the visual prompts he offered for the narrative and descriptive essays, Frost teaches young writers another kind of invention strategy, what he calls "the process of investigation." For an essay about Columbus (a popular essay topic in many nineteenth-century books), Frost instructs students:

> Find out from conversation or books when and where Columbus was born; how he passed his early life; what led him to suppose that there was land in the great western ocean; what courts he applied to for assistance; how he fared at each; how and when he succeeded; how his expedition was fitted out; whence and where it sailed; what happened on the voyage; and how the new world was discovered.
>
> You may then conclude with your own reflections on the important results of this grand discovery, or you may follow Columbus through the remainder of his career; and close with your own view of his character and services to mankind. (73)

Again, rather than offering a set of rules, Frost offers an example, a model for how a student might proceed in writing this genre of essay. In fact, he is offering students what contemporary textbooks often term a process of journalistic inquiry ("the five w's and the h") as an invention strategy.

Because so many of Frost's writing prompts call for narration or description, the organizational strategy he assumes is chronological or spatial. And in some cases, the framing text for the visual prompt suggests a particular chronology. Underneath an illustration of one young boy pulling another young boy out of swampy, reedy water, the text reads, "Suppose a story. Boy insisted on climbing a tree to rob a bird's nest. His companion dissuaded. Boy would not be advised. Limb of the tree broke. The picture tells the rest. Make a different story if you choose" (52).

A second way Frost's text teaches organizational strategies is by a version of modeling. Frost does not, in his text, explain or list abstract, categorical ways for organizing a paper. He uses the framing text that accompanies an illustration as a model for how a writer might structure an essay. The text that frames an illustration of a garden, for example, reads, "Description. Different kinds of gardens. Their uses. Pleasures of gardening. Its utility in promoting health and contentment" (49). Without including the words "classification" or "cause/effect," the prompt invites students to use those topoi as ways of thinking about and organizing their papers.

And finally, while Frost doesn't focus on argumentative writing in his text, he does help students to anticipate constructing an argument by inviting them to observe similarities and differences between objects, arguing that "all reasoning or argument is founded on the discernment of those relations of things which are discovered by comparison" (68). As practice for this work, Frost offers students a list of items for comparison, including, for example, "An acorn and an apple," "A wheelbarrow and a coach," "water and air" (69). He follows this task by asking students to perform a slightly more difficult task, to describe the analogy between paired objects. Examples here include, "A school and a ship's crew," "Painting and engraving," "A lamp and the sun" (70). In Frost's design, therefore, students begin with writing narrative or descriptive responses to an illustration and then move toward analytic pieces.

The last sections of Frost's book, the sections he calls "Structure of Sentences" and "Figurative Language," address sentence-level composition, correctness, and the use of tropes. Following an explanation of a topic (a topic would be, for example, the parts of a sentence, or simple and complex sentences, or subjects, predicates, objects), Frost invites students to recognize the elements in other sentences and to create their own sentences. In some cases, he also uses the pedagogy that asked students to correct errors in a sentence, a strategy that predated asking students to produce their own sentences. Unlike the material in the first part of Frost's book, much of this work is borrowed from other sources. Without naming the particular selections, Frost tells the reader that he "copied freely" from David Irving's *Elements of Composition,* from John Murray M'Culloch's *Manual of English Grammar,* from Shepherd, Joyce, and Carpenter's *Systematic Education.* And Frost makes clear that in his subsection called "Qualities Essential to a Perfect Sentence," he is borrowing directly from Blair, not only the qualities Blair assigned to a sentence (clearness and precision, unity, strength, and harmony) but also the language Blair used for the guidelines that govern the use of these qualities.

In constructing this argument for rereading the strategies that nineteenth-century textbook authors offered for composing, I do not want to equate past practice with present practice, or to suggest that the value of the past lies only in its anticipation of the present. I do want to suggest, however, that the absence of headings like "invention" and "arrangement" does not mean these books and their authors did not attend to these matters. I would argue that they do teach strategies akin to what contemporary teachers offer, and that these strategies deserve notice.

After the Civil War: Language Arts Books

Considerable changes affected the institution of school following the Civil War and the accompanying postwar industrialization: the number of students, teachers, and schools grew; the number of days per year that students attended school increased; teaching was increasingly professionalized; statewide centralization continued to grow; new subjects were studied, including, for example, history and what we would call "civics" or "social studies"; students wrote not just on slate but also on paper; and as the nation's commitment to free secondary education grew, the number of newly established private academies diminished, and the number of public high schools grew.

Ross Finney reports that in 1870, the United States had 160 public high schools; in 1880, nearly 800; in 1890, 2000 (153).

Perhaps the change that stands out as having the single greatest impact on the figure of American education is that after the Civil War, the one-room school house, except in rural or remote areas, began to disappear, and the "grading" of elementary schools was becoming institutionalized. In Europe, Comenius had advocated a graded school system as early as the seventeenth century, and graded schools flourished in Prussia in the late eighteenth and early nineteenth centuries. In the United States, the move toward the class/graded school occurred in urban areas roughly between 1820 and 1860 and was due in large part to the work of Horace Mann, who had traveled abroad visiting schools and, in his 1843 *Seventh Annual Report to the Massachusetts Board of Education,* praised the Prussian system:

> The first element of superiority in a Prussian school, and one whose influence extends throughout the whole subsequent course of instruction, consists in the proper classification of the scholars. In all places where the numbers are sufficiently large to allow it the children are divided according to ages and attainments, and a single teacher has the charge only of a single class or of as small a number of classes as is practicable. . . . Let us suppose a teacher to have charge of but one class, and to have talent and resources sufficient properly to engage and occupy its attention, and we suppose a perfect school. (qtd. in Cubberley, *Readings* 287–88)

Education historians report that Mann's advocacy of a Prussian method of organizing school met with some resistance from U.S. educators. John Philbrick, however, principal of Quincy Grammar School (formerly principal of the Mayhew Grammar School, later Superintendent of Boston Public Schools, and author of several textbooks, including the 1868 *Primary Union Speaker*), was so persuaded of the idea's value that he oversaw the construction of what is considered the first graded school in this country. In 1848, the new

Quincy Grammar School was four stories high, had 660 seats, and offered twelve separate schoolrooms, one for each teacher. The building also contained a freestanding desk and chair for each student, a clothes closet, an auditorium, and a principal's office. Such a physical organization allowed dividing students into grades and required determining what instruction was appropriate for each year.

With these postwar changes in industrialization and in school necessarily came changes in textbooks. Given the spurt of transportation and communication technologies, neither writers nor schools needed to rely on local publishers, and as the number of students increased, and as more educators began to call for students to receive free books, the market for textbooks grew. The kind of literacy books that writers were producing for school students also changed.

In 1896, Michigan's Burke Hinsdale published a book for teachers called *Teaching the Language-Arts*. In the early pages of that work, he explained that one of his goals was "To state fully and illustrate clearly the principles that underlie all practical language culture, whether it assumes the form of speech, reading, or composition—what I have ventured to call the language-arts" (4). This is the first mention I find, perhaps it is even the first naming, of what we today know as "language arts," and these post–Civil War books were the forerunners of the books teachers today use in today's language arts classes. They also signaled a new tradition among composition books.

In the 1830s, and in some cases even earlier, some textbooks for beginning students, arithmetics and readers, for example, began to appear in a systematic or graded series for students at different levels of learning. Before the Civil War, some authors of grammars published books for more than one level of student, just as Richard Parker, George P. Quackenbos, and others published a book for beginning composition students and a book for older students. But composition books, like the rhetorics, do not systematically appear in a series before the war in the same way that readers do. After the war, however, as more schools were organized by grade level, authors such as Mary Hyde, John S. Hart, and William Swinton began to write language books in a series, tailoring individual books to students at different levels of learning.

The language arts books published after the Civil War are easy to recognize. In almost every case, the word *language,* the word *lesson* (or both) appears in some combination in the titles. The words *composition* and *grammar* often drop out of the title (an exception is the 1897 *Rand-McNally Primary Grammar and Composition* by William D. Hall), signaling a new approach to language and literacy instruction. Composition does not appear in a separate section of the text but rather is integrated into the study of topics or lessons. So, students might be asked to write an essay practicing a grammatical construction they had just learned, or to write an essay about a poem in the book.

Because of their limited goal (to provide instruction for one grade or group of students), the books are much less dense than many earlier books that were designed to be comprehensive. Consciously tailored to young learners and taking advantage of improvements in publishing technologies, the books include fewer items on a page and make generous use of white space to enhance their attractiveness and readability. In addition, they use formatting features such as varied-size type fonts and bold print for titles and headings; they routinely use illustrations as an integral part of the text; and because it was increasingly common for the students to have the book in their hands, the language of the books is for the most part selected for young learners and appears in large font, not unlike books for students we use today. A sign that the language textbook for young learners was stabilizing as a material artifact is that these books use paratexts, and the same paratexts, fairly consistently; while the use of an index is not yet routine, more often than not the books include both a preface and a table of contents.

Unlike the writers of the earlier books, whose goal was often to teach students a kind of mental discipline and/or to give them the scientific knowledge, say, of grammar that would enable success in higher education, the writers of these books geared their instruction to students whose education might well not have extended beyond elementary school. The focus of these books, therefore, has moved from a strong dedication to teaching habits of mind to teaching students the practical: what they need to know for daily living; many of the books, for example, teach the days of the week and the months of the year. The composition emphasis is on teaching students to write for practical ends, and the method is grounded in practice.

The preface to William Swinton's *Language Lessons* (1877) reads, "A word as to the exercises. *These are the book.* They are numerous and graduated, and are given from the first with a view to composition—the immediate object of the grammar taught in the common school" (iv).[24] William D. Hall notes that he arranges his 1897 *Rand McNally Primary Grammar and Composition* so that "grammar may be rendered tributary to the art of expression" (4). Throughout these language arts books, therefore, students are asked to write. They begin with writing sentences to show they can use parts of speech or compose particular structures. Very quickly, though, the books ask students to write a longer text, sometimes in units of discourse called a "paragraph," as part of learning a lesson in some aspect of language use.

Sometimes a book will include a section on a particular genre— description, for example—but more often, the genres the students are asked to write—description, narration, and what Metcalf and Bright called "Information Lessons"—are scattered throughout the book simply as lessons in composition intended to reinforce a particular language lesson the student is learning. In one lesson, for example, in Hyde's *Practical Lessons in the Use of English,* students practice the correct uses of "has" and "have" by writing about their pets. The author includes a series of questions about each of several pets (for "My Rabbits," the questions are "How many rabbits have you? Where did you get them? How old are they? What do you call them? Where do you keep them? What do they like to eat? How did you tame them? How do they play with you?" [29]). And a note "To the Teacher" instructs, "Before taking up this lesson, talk with the children about their pets. Find out what pets they have, and lead the pupils to tell about them. Then let each child write about his or her own pets. The pupils should read their exercises to the class" (28). Here we also recognize that while pupils are no longer studying a passage on "benevolence" and then writing about it in their own words, they are still absorbing this cultural value, but in their own context, in this case, in the care of their pets.

In other words, the new emphasis on "the practical" signaled that the institution of school was serving a larger and more diverse student body than it had before the Civil War, including an increasing number of students whose needs for literacy would be located exclusively in the activities of daily life. So while teaching habits of mind such as memorizing remained important, what also mattered was teaching students practical literacy skills. The composition genre that perhaps would have had the most practical value to students not pursuing higher education was the letter, and this genre receives particular attention from authors.

Often in a separate chapter in the book, students learn to write "friendship letters" to parents, grandparents, and friends and even short business letters, ordering an item from a shop, for example. At first, they read hints of what to include, and then they are simply given a context in which they are asked to generate a letter. Predictably, the lessons include attention to letter-writing form: addressing the envelope; using abbreviations; and placing the date, inside address, salutation, and closing. Arrangement, capital letters, and punctuation are also part of the instruction, and some authors more than others stress that the appearance of the letter is a sign of the writer's character. No doubt due in part to the increased mobility of the U.S. population after the Civil War, letter writing assumes a newly important function of long-distance communication, so important that Hyde advises teachers to ask students to write a letter "as often as once a week" (43) and that Alfred Welsh, in the preface to *English Composition,* his 1889 book for high schools, writes, "As, in the cases of a very large number of pupils, no higher skill in Composition will ever be required than ability to write a letter properly, it has not been forgotten that one of the great objects of instruction is to make good letter-writers" (vi).

The use of models, a pedagogy that was extremely popular in earlier books, does not disappear, but it is both attenuated and revised. When samples from published authors are included, they are most often by American writers like Longfellow, Lowell, Whittier, and Hawthorne. Mary Hyde includes writing by Lucy Larcom; and Robert Metcalf and Orville Bright use work by Louisa May Alcott, Alice and Phoebe Cary, and Lydia Maria Child. While in earlier books, models were samples to be imitated and memorized, in these later books, more often they provide information upon which students can draw and about which they can write. In a number of cases, the selections teach students about an object or creature in the natural world. Metcalf and Bright, for example, include selections from a natural history book about honeybees. After reading two short informational passages, the students are asked to participate in a "conversation exercise" about the bee, and then to write a composition about what they have learned. The students are also invited to add information they have gained from personal observation or from other books.

The composition pedagogy that prevails in these post–Civil War books moves away from a heavy emphasis on external authority and external knowledge and asks students to compose text generated by their observation of real-life objects or their observation of the details in an illustration. Teaching students "to observe" occurs again and again as a goal: Mary Hyde writes, "the aim is to lead the pupil to see for himself—to cultivate his powers of observation at every step" (iii); Benjamin Conklin advises, "the child should be directed to observe carefully the things with which he comes in contact in his daily life; such as *flowers, fruits, trees, architecture, scenery, pictures,* etc., so that he may be able to describe them at least with tolerable accuracy" (21). Harvey even asks students to observe a teacher performing a particular action, opening a window or clapping her hands, for instance, and then to write a description of what they saw (70).

When Frost used illustrations as writing prompts in the late 1830s, he was a pioneer, forging his way into new pedagogical territory. In the last decades of the century, however, this method for teaching students to compose, what came to be called a "picture lesson," became a dominant pedagogy. Students were asked to observe (we might say "read") a picture in their textbooks and to respond to a series of questions or "hints" that accompanied the picture. In many cases, students responded orally before they responded in writing. And in some cases, the textbook includes a sample dialogue that a teacher and student might have about a picture. Here is one sample dialogue from Thomas Harvey's *First Lessons in the English Language* (1875); it appears directly beneath an illustration of a boy sitting on a log, fishing (see fig. 6).

> **Teacher.** If you wished to tell me that you once took a walk by the bank of a river, and saw a boy fishing like the one in the picture, how would you begin your story?
>
> **A pupil.** I should say, "When I was walking by the river, the other day, I saw a barefooted boy sitting on a log fishing."
>
> T. Very well. What else would you say?
>
> P. "He had just caught a fish, and was taking it off the hook when I passed by him."
>
> T. Could you tell me any thing more?
>
> P. Oh, yes! "There were two fishes on a string which was fastened to the log. A box for bait was on the log near the boy. I talked with him for some time. He told me that he was catching fish to sell, for his parents were poor."
>
> T. Did he tell you any thing more about himself?
>
> P. Yes, "He went to school in the winter; but had to work the rest of the year. When he could not find any work to do, he went fishing. A hotel keeper bought his fish, and he gave all the money to his mother."
>
> T. Now read all that you have written. (61–62)

Even though the author does not articulate writing strategies in this dialogue, several are in play. The student writer is asked to construct a version of a life: "If you wished to tell me that you once took a walk." And in the example the teacher offers, the "pupil" takes on the subjectivities of a boy from a poor family, suggesting that student writers might do the same, constructing not only their own life, as the child walking, but also constructing the life and the values of the poor boy who is fishing and of the culture in which he lives: he gives the money from the sale of the fish to his mother. Secondly,

35. Picture Lessons.

IV.

Teacher. If you wished to tell me that you once took a walk by the bank of a river, and saw a boy fishing like the one in the picture, how would you begin your story?

A pupil. I should say, "When I was walking by the river, the other day, I saw a barefooted boy sitting on a log fishing."

T. Very well. What else would you say?

P. "He had just caught a fish, and was taking it off the hook when I passed by him."

T. Could you tell me any thing more?

P. Oh yes! "There were two fishes on a string which was fastened to the log. A box for bait was on the log near the boy. I talked with him some time. He told me that he was catching fish to sell, for his parents were poor."

Fig. 6. Illustration that serves as a prompt for a teacher-student dialogue. Thomas Harvey, *First Lessons in the English Language*. Cincinnati, 1875, 61.

conversation is modeled as a generative strategy. And third, the teacher models the role of audience.

In some cases, students were invited to write their own version of a story, different as it might be from a model. Teachers were encouraged, "Let them do so, and assist them, by suggestions, in arranging the details" (Harvey 63). Thus picture lessons not only taught students to observe but also invited them to use their imagination to create stories suggested by a picture. Metcalf and Bright, for example, underneath a picture of an old man rescuing kittens from a pond, instruct students, in 1889, "Write a story from the picture, making it as interesting as you can" (62). Early signs of attending to the culture of the child that poked through the ground in Frost's *Easy Exercises* are now in full bloom as authors ask students not to recreate a story as accurately as they can, but, rather, to create a new story.

With the help of a group of starter questions and the discussion those questions sparked, students were thus practicing invention strategies for a short personal narrative or description or expository text, but they were doing so inductively and experientially; that is, students were, in the words of Edward Gideon in the front matter of his 1888 *Lessons in Language,* learning "to do by doing."

Finally, unlike earlier books for young learners written primarily by teachers, these later books were often written by teachers who went on to become school supervisors or superintendents; in some cases they were written by college professors or by normal school teachers. The number of normal schools and teacher institutes increased dramatically in the second half of the nineteenth century, but the number of teachers who had professional training nonetheless remained low.[25] Those who did not have that training relied on their own education as their model, and that education had often been grounded in systems of rules and memorization, what Mariolina Salvatori would call *didactics,* not pedagogy. Thus the language arts books often include a short section called "Suggestions to Teachers" as part of the front matter of the book and often include suggestions for implementing a particular lesson throughout the book. The end of William Hall's 1897 book includes several pages of suggestions, consisting primarily of lists of books: literary texts useful for composition work, nonfiction suited to "literary composition and study," and pedagogical texts that a teacher might find useful in teaching language lessons and composition. Hall recommends, for example, Fred Newton Scott and Joseph Villier Denney's *Paragraph-Writing* (1891) and Arlo Bates's *Talks on Writing English* (1896).[26]

Correlated with this growing emphasis on pedagogy—and in contrast to the freedom students enjoyed in imagining the activities in a picture lesson—comes an expanded emphasis on correctness at the sentence level. Unlike the early writers whose books gave minimal attention to correctness—Parker, for example, includes one page about "correctness" at the end of his book—the writers of these books integrate correctness issues into the lessons throughout the book, and the value-laden words *correct* and *accurate* replace some of the earlier value words like *reputable* or *present*. The importance of correctness often appears in a directive to teachers: "require pupils to be particular in the use of capital letters, and to give the reason for the correct use of each" (Conklin 50); "See that all the words are spelled correctly, that each sentence and every proper noun begins with a capital letter, and that a period is placed at the end of each sentence" (Harvey 12–13); "let [the answers] be given in complete and accurate sentences" (Hadley 9); and "Insist, from the beginning, on correct *form* in composition" (DeGarmo 9). John S. Hart's *A Manual of Composition and Rhetoric,* a book for older students first published in 1870, includes a four-page section entitled "Correcting Compositions," and, anticipating the handbooks that would emerge in the early twentieth century (see Connors, *Comp-Rhet*), he includes a list of abbreviations a teacher might use to mark what he calls "mistakes" (1891, 347–50).

The directives to teachers about correctness of pronunciation and articulation that appeared in early readers are now also appearing in composition books. John Benjamin Wisely's 1896 *Language for the Grades,* for example, includes a fairly specific and severely stated task for teachers. I quote it at some length because it suggests that writers were alerting teachers to the diverse needs of an immigrant student population:

Let every teacher keep beside her on the table, a pencil and notebook, in which she can write down all the mistakes in English which her children make during a month. . . . These mistakes will differ, to some extent, with different sets of children. German children will not make all the mistakes made by English children and they will make some mistakes which English children do not make. The mistakes of Swedes will differ to some extent, from both the others. . . . There will be defects in pronunciation, double negatives, wrong forms of pronouns, pronouns used for adjectives, verbs that do not agree with subjects, mistakes in the use of the principal parts of irregular verbs, auxiliary verbs used incorrectly, etc.

Now after the teacher has discovered what mistakes the children make, let her set to work consciously and systematically to drill them out of the language of the children. Take up one at a time and let the oral work and written work be directed against it. (18)

And still other forms of prescriptiveness emerge. Thomas Harvey's book includes sections called "Incorrect Language" in which he lists "Cautions" for students and gives examples of incorrect usage. In one of these sections, he writes "Do not use *aint* for *is not* or *am not; haint* for *has not* or *have not;* or *'t aint* for *it is not*" (38). Some writers, now that students are studying paragraphs, extend their prescriptions to the students' writing, asking them to determine the number of paragraphs in their composition before they begin, or to write one paragraph for each point in an outline. So while these later books contained fewer topics and less subject matter than earlier books, advising teachers and students of particular forms of correctness became increasingly common.

Finally, the post–Civil War books for school students demonstrate the effects—both light and dark—of a national market and of centralizing education in the lower grades. Once the profession settled on "the language arts" as the business of elementary school, the books also stabilized. And the pedagogy was valuable not just because it was child-centered and grounded in observation, but also because the increased uniformity of the books probably helped curtail the use of less effective pedagogies and allowed students to transfer easily from one school to another. The shadow side, though, to this uniformity is at least two-fold: the earlier composition texts by Parker and Frost stood out from other books of their day when they were first published; they also stood apart from each other; and there is no confusing them in a casual reading. At the end of the nineteenth century, when an accepted rubric is in place, a new composition book appears, what we would call a "language arts" book. Not only is there a look-alike quality to the books, but I don't see any mavericks, books that approached the teaching of writing in breakthrough ways. And therein lies a trade-off.

One way to understand composition instruction in the schools at century's end is to read the educational reports that were emerging. In mid-century, an increasing professionalization of teaching took hold in earnest: a growing number of states developed a teachers associations, and the National Teachers' Association was constituted in 1857 and, in 1870, renamed the National Education Association, an organization that continues to work on behalf of teachers and students today. Supporting a growing interest in the uniformity of school organization, the NEA, in 1893, commissioned the Committee of Fifteen to study three areas of elementary education: the organization of school systems, the coordination of studies in primary and grammar schools, and teacher training. In the portion of the committee's 1895 report that addresses the teaching of language arts, the text emphasizes that language studies is at the core of learning. Students should practice much "in writing exercises and original compositions" because the act of composing is an important means of reinforcing what students are learning in other subjects; the report also reflects a move away from mental or formal discipline as a primary or singular educational goal and toward the inclusion of learning subject matter for its own sake:

> It is thought by your Committee that the old style of composition writing was too formal. It was kept too far away

from the other work of the pupil. Instead of giving a written account of what he had learned in arithmetic, geography, grammar, history, and natural science, the pupil attempted artificial descriptions and reflections on such subjects as "Spring," "Happiness," "Perseverance," "Friendship," or something else outside of the line of his school studies. (90)

Another way to understand composition instruction at the end of the century is to recognize how writers of language arts books build on the pedagogies instantiated in books by writers like Parker and Frost and teach what Swinton called a "living language." Students learn the concept of a paragraph, they write from outlines, they begin to write "impromptu" essays, and, with great frequency and predictability, they use their imagination to write from picture lessons. At the beginning of the century, Parker included a lesson in his book called "Allegory." As part of that lesson, he included a sample theme a student had written to explain the power of imagination:

As I was reclining one morning at the bottom of a beautiful garden, in an arbour overhung with honey suckle and jessamine [sic] of the most exquisite fragrance, I saw a most hideous monster standing before me. I tremblingly enquired his name and wish. He replied, in a voice of thunder, I am the Genius of composition, and am come to require the tribute that is due to me. For a few moments I stood amazed, not knowing how to reply. At length I was relieved by the approach of a beautiful nymph, who called herself Imagination; at whose appearance the hideous monster disappeared. (51–52)

At the end of the century, the Genius of Composition, his voice thundering in the writer's ear about issues of correctness, is nearby, but in many ways, it is the Nymph of Imagination who becomes a central feature of composition instruction as young writers are asked, simply and routinely, "to tell what you see in this picture," "to write a story."

High School and College Composition Books at Century's End

A singularly important educational development after the Civil War was the growth spurt of urban public high schools. Since the early decades of the nineteenth century, privileged youth had been able to attend Latin grammar schools, academies or other private college preparatory schools, or schools that featured an "English curriculum."[27] By mid-century, and especially after the war, as the number of students completing the lower grades increased, and as the desire of and for students to have further education became a national concern, urban public high schools grew in number, not replacing but complementing the classical schools. While the urban public high school sometimes offered a classical course of study, the innovation of this school was that it also offered "the general course," a curriculum that focused on useful learning and drew a population of students who were not preparing for college. It was well into the early decades of the twentieth century before adolescents of the lower middle and working classes were attending what we think of as high school and before curricula were developed with any level of standardization, a reform due in large part to the Committee of Ten Proposal in the 1890s to help set an English curriculum for secondary schools.

With the increasing numbers of high schools serving the needs of a new population came a corresponding need for books for literacy instruction. Among these books were the readers that morphed into the study of "Literature"; others focused on language, selectively including, or not, attention to grammar, to style, to genres of composition, to poetics, to rhetoric. Perhaps what is most visible among the books used for high school language classes at the end of the century is their variety in audience and content. More cogently than the Committee of Ten Proposal, the books themselves elaborate the wide-ranging diversity in high school language study at the end of the century as well as the lack of agreement about the instructional goal(s) of that study.

Some of the textbooks for secondary school language classes (variously titled, for example, "English Grammar and Analysis,"

"English Composition," "Composition and Declamation," and "Rhetoric") were not unlike those that had been marketed for multiple audiences since the 1840s and were dense, thick tomes rich with materials on language and rhetoric. They used small print and little white space, and if illustrations appeared, they were the exception and not the rule. Many of these books were intended for a double audience; Hart's 1870 *Manual of Composition and Rhetoric,* "A Text-book for Schools and Colleges," is an example. Hart's book is almost four hundred pages and covers a tremendous range of subjects: punctuation and capitals, diction, sentences, figures, versification, poetry, and prose composition, including such forms of out-of-school writing as editorials, reviews, essays, treatises, travels, history, fiction, and discourses. He ends with a long section on school-based writing, with smaller sections, for example, on writing about objects, transactions, abstract subjects, and instructions for writing personal narratives and descriptions. In many ways, this book and others like it functioned for high school students as a manual or guide (as opposed to a book students would use on a daily basis); it is also an example of the hybrid formation of composition-rhetoric text that developed toward the end of the century.

A second category of books self-designated themselves, either on their title page or in their preface, "For High Schools" or "For Use in Secondary Schools" or "Adapted to the Wants of High Schools, Preparatory Schools, and Academies." Even within this newly coined category, tremendous variety and overlappings are visible. Some books looked both back to the grammar lessons of the common schools and also ahead to rhetorical principles and strategies, suggesting some students needed more work in grammar, and some students might be bound for college and thus would benefit from an introduction to rhetoric. Lucy Chittenden's 1884 *The Elements of English Composition* is subtitled "A Preparation for Rhetoric" and is, she writes in her preface, intended "for the lower grades of the high school" (iii). She begins with a lengthy section on punctuation and capitals, moving to some grammatical rules and some stylistic suggestions, and ends with composition, letter writing, and paraphrasing based on poems by writers such as Elizabeth Barrett

Browning, William Cullen Bryant, and John Greenleaf Whittier, as well as by lesser-known writers such as Mary Brine and Grace Knapp. Alfred Welsh's *English Composition* (1896), for high schools, calls itself "a sequel to the ordinary text-books on grammar, and an introduction to the study of rhetoric proper" (v) and features sentence-level exercises as well as letter writing and essay writing.

Other books focused exclusively on composing, omitting any attention to grammar or mechanics. A key example here is Scott and Denney's 1897 *Composition-Rhetoric*, "Designed for Use in Secondary Schools." While the authors accord some attention to sentence syntax, the primary emphasis of their 350-page text is on directives for composing; they include a large section on "paragraphs" and other lengthy sections entitled "How To Say It," "What Order To Say It," "How Much To Say," and "What Not To Say."

Unlike the language arts book that in some ways was codified by the end of the century, books for high school students were much more diverse, but diverse without major innovations, either in pedagogy or content. In other words, the category of a high school composition book was new, but the material of the books was eclectic. As the high school English or language arts teachers struggled to identify and serve the needs of several audiences, so, too, did the textbooks.

Scholars who have interrogated the history of writing instruction in the nineteenth-century college (James Berlin, John Brereton, Robert Connors, Sharon Crowley, and Nan Johnson, for example) document that composition instruction per se did not exist in a college curriculum until the third quarter of the century.[28] Prior to that, students read a British rhetoric by Hugh Blair or George Campbell or an increasingly available American rhetoric by Newman, Day, or others. Students who were preparing for college through the mid-nineteenth century would have studied at a Latin grammar school (such as Boston Latin) or with a private tutor, and they would have had extensive experience with writing orations and themes. College matriculants were expected to be proficient in composing oral and written text in a range of genres and in both English and Latin. John Silas White, for example, the Harvard senior who gave a congratulatory address on behalf of the student body at the installation of Harvard president Charles W. Eliot in 1869, delivered his oration in Latin.[29]

But while composition was not listed as a formal subject of college study, the curriculum emphasized the practice of writing themes and declamations and would often list a weekly time slot for what were called "exercises in composition," a practice that might have included forensics and translations, as well as composition. The 1820 Harvard College curriculum, for example, required sophomores to study Blair's *Lectures on Rhetoric* as well as to practice "Exercises in Declamation and Composition once a fortnight" (17). The 1840–41 *Catalogue of the Officers and Students of Williams College* documents that the curriculum required seniors to participate in "A critical exercise in composition every Friday afternoon" (17). And in 1850–51, Mount Holyoke Female Seminary prescribed Newman's *Rhetoric* for sophomores but showed that "all the members of the school attended regularly to composition" (Wozniak 39).

After the Civil War, however, as college enrollments increased, and more students were matriculating who had limited experience (and in some cases limited proficiency) with written composition, a composition course requirement was instituted in some colleges. Just as new categories of the composition textbook were created earlier in the century for students in lower schools, after the Civil War for the subject area named language arts, and toward the end of the century for the increased number of high school students whose literacy goals were, for the most part, practical, a new genre of textbook was also created for the college students who were required for the first time to take a course in composition; this was the last of the composition textbook genres to emerge and is the forerunner of the books used today in first-year college writing classes.

A difficulty in studying late nineteenth-century college composition books is the blurring of boundaries: first, some of the books, especially those that emphasized practice, were used in upper grades of high schools, in academies, in colleges, and in normal schools (Hart, *Manual;* Newcomer, *Practical Course*), suggesting that institutional curricula differed widely and were not stable; second, the migrations and the overlappings between "rhetorics" and "composition books" sometimes resulted in hybrid texts that defy easy categorization. The move in most college classrooms was clearly toward increased instruction and practice in writing, but rhetoric was long seen as the province of college instruction, and textbook authors were slow to abandon that title even when they incorporated composing strategies into their books. Many books, for example, include both composition and rhetoric in their titles even though one of those areas might be dominant in the book itself (Hart *Manual*, Kavana and Beatty, Kerl, Mead). It is also tricky to rely on the title of a book to accurately represent its contents. Especially at the beginning of the nineteenth century, some books that called themselves compositions were really rhetorics, focusing on teaching the matter of rhetoric rather than the practice of composing (Irving); and others that called themselves rhetorics devoted instructional space to both composition and rhetoric (Kellogg). Perhaps the point to be made is that while some books focused primarily on composition (Chittenden; Newcomer, *Practical Course*), and others focused primarily on rhetoric (Genung, *Practical*), composition and rhetoric were increasingly tangled in the college classroom.

A distinguishing characteristic of books used for college composition courses, whether they featured composition or rhetoric or some distillation of both, incorporated the often-studied practice of asking students to compose texts in the modes of discourse. While composition books for school students routinely asked for description and narration and sometimes what we would call exposition (the schoolbooks would have said "information lessons"), the college composition books—with, of course, exceptions—added argument to those genres; they also understood the study of writing as modal but without consensus about the designation of the modes (Cairns, for example, names 4; Bain, 5).

John Franklin Genung's 1887 *The Study of Rhetoric in the College Course* offers what the author considers an ideal composition class, one that is not "a mere demand for so many written productions," but "a systematically ordered, progressive series" (25). He continues:

the beginning is made by assigning subjects requiring simple observation or imagination; and afterwards the student is introduced to subjects requiring exercise of thought. He is not required 'to read up' at all; nay, the subject often precludes reading. But he must use eyes and ears . . . and he must lean wholly on his individual powers. . . . Descriptions, to begin with, of such objects as might be studied from reality, or imagined from pictures and models. Then come narratives, constructed from outline data, or related from personal experience. These are followed by subjects requiring study and interpretation of general ideas, as embodied in terms, propositions, and extended passages. Finally comes work in argumentative composition, preparation and debating of such questions, and the like. (27–28)

While Alexander Bain is the first to systematize what were hints of modes of discourse in Newman and Day, Genung here argues that the task of a college composition course was to teach students to compose in the modes he names. Important to notice, though, is that the strategies he recommends are eclectic: they resemble the pedagogies that first emerged in the textbooks for school students, especially description based on observation of material objects or pictures and narration based on personal experience; and they include borrowings from classical rhetoric, especially the study of argument.

In sum, composition books for college students were the last of the composition textbook traditions to appear. With some exceptions, most of these books retained a clearly marked identification with rhetoric and included the study of argument, but also, and unlike the earlier rhetoric textbooks (such as Newman's), they taught students to compose text. Although most of today's composition courses for first-year students offer very little formal training in rhetoric, rhetorical principles continue to ground the curriculum of many of these courses, and it is common to call one category of book used there (the *St. Martin's Guide,* for example) a rhetoric; it is also significant that many of the books used in today's first-year college courses are inflected by the pedagogies that emerged first in the nineteenth-century composition textbooks for beginning students.

The Watersheds

To a contemporary eye, nineteenth-century composition books can appear ineffable, otherworldly, opaque, and, yes, wonderfully charming. The exercises they suggest, the illustrations they offer, the sample writing they model, the habits of mind they emphasize are all deeply rooted in nineteenth-century cultures and value systems. And absent are some of the qualities that contemporary teachers value, the self-reflexivity, for example, that characterizes so much work in classrooms today.

My work on the archive of nineteenth-century composition books has sought to respect the particular project of individual books and to read the emergence of the different categories of composition books in their historical and educational settings, and in concert with the needs of students and institutions. Broadly conceived and broadly stated, these are the watersheds I locate in nineteenth-century composition books:

- "Writing" was transformed from "acts of writing" to "acts of composing."
- With the culture's growing understanding of the culture of the child, composition instruction was increasingly tailored to what was understood as the developmental level of the student.
- "Memorizing" and "Recitation" and "Imitation" never disappeared as pedagogies for acquiring certain language skills or habits of mind, but "Practice" became the way students learned to compose, and as the neoclassical mindset gave way to romanticism(s), students were more frequently invited to write original text.
- The practical values of literacy—its potential for contributing to success in the world of business—were articulated, even for young students.

- "Experience" joined "Authority" as a source of knowledge.
- Emphasis on the skill of observation grew.
- Imagination came to be prized.
- Graphics became a valued and regular part of textbook instruction.
- Books—and sheets of paper—became more widely available.
- Textbook publishing became a business, new technologies allowing not only for increased numbers of textbooks but also for their wider distribution.
- A grouping of literacy studies—reading, speaking, composition, literature—known as the "Language Arts" emerged.
- "Composition" in the schools became part of the "Language Arts," an enterprise larger than itself, and the "composition book" for younger students came to be called the "language arts book."
- Meeting the needs of the growing population of high school students, several categories of high school composition books were created, their diversity suggesting the different courses of study that high schools began to offer as well as the lack of consensus about the task of high school language classes at the end of the century.
- When composition became a discipline in the college curriculum in the fourth quarter of the nineteenth century, the last category of composition book emerged: the textbook for the college composition course that linked practice in composing to a foundation in rhetoric.

Of the three textbook traditions we investigate in this book—rhetorics, readers, and composition books—the composition books are the youngest. In the epigraph with which I open this chapter, John Hart argues, in 1870, that exercise in composition should have the same importance as exercise in reading and spelling, and that practice in composing should be a routine part of school until it merges with the study of rhetoric. Reading the archive of composition books makes visible that the earliest books, those written for beginning students, were at once indebted to the even earlier readers and rhetorics, and, further, that the books written for the college composition course, the most recent category of composition book to be developed, are indebted not only to rhetoric and to rhetorics, but also to the practices that emerged first in the books for beginning students. Finally, what I suggest here is that the story of the emergence and growth of the composition book, in its different forms and for different settings, is an ongoing story of affiliations and recomposition.

Coda

Here are ten lessons from *Archives of Instruction:*

1. Textbooks are complex material and discursive artifacts. Addressed to different audiences, they are collages of arguments, procedures, and routines whose principles of arrangement are never simply transparent.

2. Although topics, passages, and exercises persist for decades in textbooks, surprising innovations in arrangements, arguments, and pedagogical strategies respond to changes in the culture and audience.

3. What is important is often apparent in small, routine gestures of a textbook in ways not necessarily visible in a preface, table of contents, or index. Local details or variations—in, for example, a biographical headnote, the exercises a student is assigned to do, or a listing of the common tropes—can signal the changing interests of the larger project.

4. Rhetorics, readers, and composition books form distinct textbook traditions, but there are important migrations of materials across traditions and levels of instruction. Instruction is often a sequenced or accumulated process, and it is important to read advanced work in relationship to the often less visible work that came before.

5. The characteristic features of textbook traditions often derive from little-recognized or -valued contributions—the work of abridgement, translation, or compilation; the writing of questions or exercises; the selection of reading passages; or the responses of teachers.

6. Textbooks are compiled rather than composed. Accepted and regular practices include copying, adaptation, and reordering of earlier texts in ways that challenge received assumptions about authorship, intellectual property, and originality.

7. Textbooks are unusually complicated bibliographic items. Many were reprinted frequently, and others were adapted for different audiences or purposes. Attending to details about printing meth-

ods, publishing venues, and forms of circulation helps to determine questions of influence and the changing preoccupations in the culture of literacy.

8. The writers and compilers of textbooks had diverse intellectual formations, expertise, and careers. Some were surprisingly eminent. Many were teachers at different types and levels of institutions; others were preachers, lawyers, and literary figures. Some produced a single book out of a personal or professional interest. Others were professional textbook writers who worked across disciplines and grade levels: John Frost, for example, compiled more than three hundred books in response to pedagogical and commercial opportunities.

9. Several influential and still-familiar writers work in each tradition—the triumvirate of Blair, Campbell, and Whately, for example, or McGuffey—but many now nearly anonymous figures also make decisive contributions. As a result, textbook traditions are diversified and complex in ways not readily available from reading only major figures.

10. Close readings across these textbook traditions challenge several familiar ways of characterizing nineteenth-century textbooks. It is more appropriate and useful to understand rhetorics as practical than as belletristic or current-traditional; to see that readers inculcate practices of analysis and notions of propriety while providing training in oral performance; and to understand composition books as prompting invention and composing processes and not simply imposing correctness.

* * *

> How are we to understand the ways in which the form that transmits a text to its readers or hearers constrains the production of meaning? The appropriation of discourse is not something that happens without rules or limits. Writing deploys strategies that are meant to produce effects, dictate a posture, and oblige the reader.
>
> —Roger Chartier, *Forms and Meanings* (1995)

Textual "obligation" is always a double action, a way both of placing restraints upon users and of pleasing them. Textbooks oblige their users in distinctive formal and institutional ways. The "postures" dictated by nineteenth-century schoolbooks are often quite literally physical—they ask students to stand, gesture, and hold their pen in certain ways. Yet such postures also support more general positions within various social, cultural, and ideological systems. Textbooks require students to reproduce certain texts and definitions; they instruct them to write or to speak proper sentences in a pure language; they drill them in the discursive norms of the time. The instructional work of producing and sustaining such postures is considerable, and never entirely successful. Students refuse positions assigned by instructional materials or assiduously misapply their lessons: they slouch. Their textbooks, moreover, are never simply orthopedic exercises. They also produce pleasure, at times making available local occasions of word play and more generally providing access to expansive cultures of literacy.

Our work throughout *Archives of Instruction* describes the complexities of textbook traditions. Because of the continual recycling of materials from earlier treatises and textbooks, almost any detail in a textbook carries with it a history and presents it anew. Textbooks never simply reproduce the past, nor do they start from nothing. They borrow, redact, redistribute, quote, adapt, revise. As passages, or sometimes whole books, circulate to different cultural locations, they show traces of both old and new interests, beliefs, and attitudes. Textbooks, that is, have sedimented layers of meaning. Over time, it becomes harder to appreciate the often-complex appropriations of earlier arguments and conventions that underlie most textbooks. And as nineteenth-century texts have in turn been selectively appropriated and recalled, it can also be difficult to appreciate that what actively survives into the present is only a small part of the total archive, and that there were many options not subsequently developed, many routes that instructional traditions might have taken.

We have challenged received histories and shorthand uses of this past, but we are most interested in seeing how archival inquiry can help us rethink pedagogical and critical practices. By acknowledging the stratifications of past practices, we are better able to see layered investments in present materials. Rereading the past helps to connect what we do in our own isolated classrooms with those classrooms down the hall, operating under a different rubric of English studies or language instruction. It comes as a pleasant surprise, for example, to discover that elliptical exercises, emerging from nineteenth-century rhetorical readers and composition books, are being put to use today in a colleague's creative writing class. It is useful to recall that a simple term for evaluating writing—"Be precise"— has a long history, making it both more difficult and interesting than initially recognized. It is somewhat startling to encounter prosody or versification not as a specialized literary topic but as a general concern of grammars, rhetorics, and elocutionary readers.

We have been drawn both to texts that circulate so widely as to become a kind of brand name and to texts that appear only a few times, or even once, and that were not often imitated or remembered. We recall both dominant tendencies that structure the archive and latent or residual features that were never quite realized. And we want to suggest that understanding textbooks, both past and present, calls for similar attention. Our work, that is, suggests a changed disposition to present textbooks, one alert to sedimented histories of dominant current practices as well as to their occasional playful, experimental, or marginal features that offer a reservoir of possible new initiatives to investigate.

We don't want by any means to idealize nineteenth-century instructional values or practices. Instead, we would like our work to counter an often dismissive attitude to old textbooks, whether that is an interested simplification of varied instructional traditions as "current-traditional" or a profound lack of interest in readers or early composition books. We understand historical research in the nineteenth century less as a foil to our own sophistication than as a prompt to ongoing reflection about the teaching and study of literacy. Wide-ranging historical research can at times challenge fundamental dispositions toward the field, but more focused or local research, or even chance encounters with an old textbook, can allow a teacher to rethink a moment of instruction, to consider anew a familiar term or assignment. Like other forms of theoretical and critical reflection, that is, historical research is an ongoing and open-ended practice. It can be conducted as one's conditions of work permit, and it can have significant consequences at every stage of an investigation.

Every textbook is an archive of instruction—it holds traces of past books and traditions, sometimes literally in silent borrowings or explicit citations, and sometimes in more deeply embedded ways. It carries out inherited attitudes, visible, for example, in a proposed sequence of learning, in notions about student work or progress, in evaluative terms or standards, in its pedagogical routines. We would like this project to recall the value of attending to the material archive, both past and current, in which we are always immersed.

Notes

Works Consulted

Index

Notes

An Introduction to Textbooks and the Cultures of Literacy

1. We generally use the term *textbook* to refer to our objects of study, although at times we borrow the older term *schoolbooks,* widely used by collectors and earlier historians of print culture to signify especially the books used in the public schools. Since many of our materials cross from elementary through college level, we usually prefer the term used for such books that are produced and marketed today, *textbooks.*

2. No comprehensive bibliography exists of nineteenth-century rhetorics, readers, or composition books. A useful bibliographic source is the catalog of the textbooks that were once held by the U.S. Department of Education (see Svobodny), most of which are now held by Harvard's Gutman Library. A number of dissertations offer circumscribed bibliographies: Emma Besig, "The History of Composition Teaching in Secondary Schools Before 1900" (Cornell 1935); Porter Perrin, "The Teaching of Rhetoric in the American Colleges Before 1750" (Chicago 1936); Glenn Hess, "An Analysis of Early American Rhetoric and Composition Textbooks from 1784 to 1870" (Pittsburgh 1949); Edward Burrell, "Authors of English Textbooks Published in the United States, 1844–1855" (Harvard 1964); Nancy McCoy, "A Relationship Between Rhetoric and Poetics: English Studies in Secondary Schools" (Purdue 1994); and Kathleen Welsch, "Nineteenth-Century Composition: The Relationship Between Pedagogical Concerns and Cultural Values in American Colleges, 1850–1890" (Pittsburgh 1994).

3. There is as yet no comprehensive book on the readers, although considerable work has been done on *The New-England Primer,* Webster's speller, and, in particular, the McGuffey *Readers.* On the composition books, see Lucille Schultz, *The Young Composers.* See also E. Jennifer Monaghan, *Learning to Read and Write in Colonial America.*

4. Our understanding of the varied cultures of literacy in the nineteenth-century United States has benefited greatly from studies, for example, of commonplace books (Susan Miller); curriculum and examination standards (Arthur Applebee, Gerald Graff, Miles Myers, David R. Russell, Mary Trachsel); literary clubs (Anne Ruggles Gere, Theodora Penny Martin, Elizabeth McHenry); pedagogy (Kathryn Fitzgerald, Mariolina Salvatori); student papers (Erika Lindemann); and literacy practices (Dorothy Broaddus, Melanie Dawson,

Bianca Falbo, Margaret Ferguson, Harvey Graff, Kenneth Lockridge, Shirley Logan, Jacqueline Jones Royster, Ronald J. Zboray).

5. We found particularly helpful the following: On the history of education, Burton Bledstein on professionalism; Lawrence Cremin; Larry Cuban on teaching; Carl Kaestle; Michael B. Katz; Lee Soltow and Edward Stevens on literacy and the common school; David B. Tyack on urban public schools. On particular levels of education, Norman Brosterman on kindergarten; Edward A. Krug, David F. Labaree, and William J. Reese on high school; Frederick Rudolph, Barbara Miller Solomon, and Laurence Veysey on higher education; Richard J. Storr on graduate education. On the education of African Americans, James D. Anderson, John Hope Franklin, Robert C. Morris, Carter Woodson; on the education of Native Americans, Michael Coleman, Devon A. Mihesuah; and on the education of women, JoAnn Campbell, Janet Eldred and Peter Mortensen, Catherine Hobbs, Linda Kerber, Kim Tolley, and Thomas Woody.

6. On immigrants, see Cremin (*The National Experience* 397). On the literacy experiences of girls, see J. Carr, "Nineteenth-Century Girls and Literacy," Schultz, "Editing *The Jabberwock*," Tolley, and Greer. On early nineteenth-century schooling for African-American and Native American students, see Schultz, *The Young Composers* 16–20.

7. On high schools for African Americans, see J. Anderson 186–237.

8. Tolley discusses the complications of determining levels of difficulty in science textbooks used in the nineteenth century (62–73), suggesting that "the determination of whether or not a text is difficult" depends on several categories, such as "vocabulary level, sentence length, number of pages or topics, format, or mathematical complexity" (62).

9. In 1850, more than three million students, ages 5–19, were in 87,000 primary, secondary and higher schools; in 1870, more than seven million students were in 141,000 schools. Separating out higher education, the U.S. Bureau of Education lists 356 U.S. colleges and universities in 1876 (Cremin, *National Experience* 179–85; 401–9). By 1890, 13 million students in elementary schools and 220,000 in high schools attended 224,526 schools (Cuban 24). College enrollments grew slowly during the century, with only 1.7 percent of people aged 18–21 enrolled in colleges and universities in 1870 compared to 50 percent in 1970 (Rudolph, *American* 486). Harvard catalogues show that in 1821, almost two hundred years after the college's 1636 establishment, undergraduates numbered 277; by 1876, the number had grown to 821. By 1890, Yale College enrolled 1477 students, Harvard 2079 (Veysey 234n).

10. For studies of "mental discipline" and its history as an educational theory, see Payne; Heck; and Kolesnik. Russell distinguishes several usages of "discipline" in the nineteenth-century: moral discipline, mental discipline, and the discipline of corporal punishment (36–37). See also Nye 331–33 and Storr 2–3.

11. The report was published by Yale College and also appeared in the *American Journal of Science and Arts* 15 (Jan. 1829): 297–351. See Rudolph, *American College* 130–35. As Gerald Graff has argued, the very argument about the disciplinary value of classics allowed educators to propose other, more modern, texts as equally challenging to the faculties (72–74).

12. On Froebel, see Brosterman 6–39.

13. The Sheffield Scientific School, formed in 1854 by consolidating departments of science, applied chemistry, and engineering, was the first institution to use funds under the Morrill Act (Hofstadter and Smith 2: 583). The report they cite is the *Third Annual Report of the Sheffield Scientific School of Yale College, 1867–68*. New Haven: Yale, 1868.

14. Eliot's advocacy of such reform persisted throughout his career. In a published lecture, *The Tendency to the Concrete and Practical in Education* (1913), he argued for "inductive" learning based on processes of "observation, record, and inference" (8) and for a wide range of "applied" subjects: chemistry and engineering, writing and speaking, laboratory sciences, case-study, field work, and activities that attended to physical skill (such as those learned in sports and games, drawing, and music).

15. As Rose explains, the practice of abridgment was a significant challenge in eighteenth-century copyright law. A 1740 British case (Gyles v. Wilcox) posed the legal and existential question: "Was an abridgment of an existing book a new work, and was an abridger an author?" The Lord Chancellor found for the abridger, arguing that his "efforts required invention, learning, and judgment," and that he thus was indeed "an author" (51).

16. Copyright in the nineteenth-century United States was a complicated negotiation of older British law, case precedent, and publishers' conventions, inflected by ongoing concerns about democratic access and resistance to publishing monopolies and state censorship. Questions of intellectual property and copyright appear as urgent concerns in the earliest national documents: they are addressed locally in state charters in the 1780s, as a federal issue in the Constitution of 1787, and proposed as federal law in the Copyright Act of 1790. Based on the British Statute of Anne (1710), the 1790 copyright law offered fourteen years of protection with a fourteen-year renewal by a living author. Subsequent laws passed in 1831, 1870, and 1909 extended the initial term to twenty-eight years (1831), and the renewal term to twenty-eight years (1909). All these laws called for books to be deposited in local or regional libraries, or in the U.S. District Court of the region where the author resided. In 1870, copyright management was centralized in the Library of Congress. U.S. law offered no protection for foreign publications until the 1891 international copyright. For discussion of British law and case precedents, see Rose 36–66 and Patterson 151–79. For early U.S. history, see Patterson 180–211 and McGill 45–75.

17. For a related argument about literary publications and giftbooks, see Meredith McGill's discussion of the 1830s–50s as the "culture of reprinting."

18. On the first copyright, see U.S. Copyright Office Circular 1a, 18. On Webster, see Lehmann-Haupt 106, and Nietz, *Old Textbooks* 15–16.

19. One of the most significant precedents was the case of Wheaton v. Peters (1834), involving the rights of a court reporter who claimed ownership of accounts of Supreme Court decisions, a case that raised questions of multiple authors, material in the public domain, and reporting as a form of authoring. Other significant cases involved "new" forms like the poster, the piano roll, and photolithography, translations, books first published in serial form in periodicals, adaptations, and the printing of what was regarded as "factual" knowledge. See Patterson 203–21 and Rose 134–38.

20. The Library of Congress holds the largest number of nineteenth-century textbooks in the United States. The two most significant special collections of these textbooks are the Historical Textbook Collection held at Harvard University's Gutman Library (35,000 volumes) and the Nietz Collection at the University of Pittsburgh (18,000 volumes). Other institutions with significant textbook holdings include the American Antiquarian Society, Antioch College, Columbia's Milbank Library at Teachers College, Illinois State University, Northern Illinois University, Stanford University, Trinity College, University of Kansas, University of Michigan, University of South Florida, University of Southern Mississippi, and the public libraries of Boston, New York, and Philadelphia.

Textbooks are also available on microforms, especially through the American Primer Collection (see Richard L. Venezky's introduction and the *Guide to the Microfiche Collection,* Bethesda, MD: University Publications of America, 1989) and the Early American Imprints collection. The "Nineteenth-Century American Schoolbooks" Digital Collection at the University of Pittsburgh currently offers online 130 full-text versions of schoolbooks. Other digital collections include the African Colonial Schoolbooks collection (available through Aequatoria Archives Research Project). Textbooks are reproduced in facsimile versions by Southern Illinois University Press (Landmarks in Rhetoric and Public Address), Teachers College Press (Classics in Education), and Scholars' Facsimiles and Reprints. There are facsimiles of popular readers, issued by commercial presses (Dover, Applewood), and in growing numbers, of grammars and spellers (addressed to the home schooling audience). The McGuffey series remains in print.

1. Reproducing Rhetorics

1. I take the term from Newman (1835, iv).

2. Broadus's *Treatise* appears nearly yearly to the century's end and claims a 42nd edition by 1926. A revised edition of 1898 does include a bibliography

of selected modern rhetorics as well as scattered footnotes to these texts. See Hoshor 143–49 on homiletic rhetorics.

3. In the classical rhetorical tradition, "elocution" designates the study of style, and its eighteenth-century redefinition as oral performance creates an enduring ambiguity of reference. A few rhetorics use "elocution" in its earlier sense: George Campbell titles his section on usage, "The Foundations and Essential Properties of Elocution," and Getty returns to the classical meaning to head his discussion of style and figurative language.

4. Nineteenth-century publishers' counts, especially of stereotyped editions, are often misleading. Some books are silently reprinted many times; others suddenly claim a high-numbered edition, though no intermediate printings survive. *Orthophony* is a steady seller for over fifty years, but irregularities in its bibliographic record make an exact count of printings problematic: a 12th edition, for example, is issued in 1857, 1858, 1859 and 1861, while there are no records of many later intermediate printings. There are three substantively different editions of this text, the 1845 first printing, an 1846 "improved edition," and an 1882 revised version.

5. See Whately, *Elements of Rhetoric,* part 4. A few rhetorics support elocution: Channing offers a general defense of the elocutionary project in "Elocution, A Study" (*Lectures* 46–59), and Hope specifically argues against Whately's critique.

6. On the restriction of writing solely to efficient communication, see especially my discussion, below, of Henry Day and Alexander Bain. I find J. L. Austin's account of the "performative" aspects of discourse in *How to Do Things with Words* useful in attending to the extracommunicative purposes of discourse.

7. See Howell 529–35 on the emergence of *belles lettres* into English. For later uses, see the entries for "belles lettres" and "belletristic" in the *Oxford English Dictionary.*

8. Apart from Blair, I know of only two rhetorics printed in the States that use "belles lettres" in their title: John Andrews's *Elements of Rhetorick and Belles Lettres* (1813) and Eustace A. Ansley's *Elements of Literature; or An Introduction to the Study of Rhetoric and Belles Lettres* (1849). Both appear in only a single edition. Andrews claims to have substantively completed his text some twenty years earlier, and it may therefore reflect an earlier formation. Ansley identifies his book as a near translation of two French treatises, and it probably represents a late grafting of the French term back into English.

9. See, for example, Crowley (*Composition* 36–42), who argues that a "pedagogy of taste" is central to nineteenth-century rhetoric but addresses neither the derivative treatment of taste nor its function or position in a rhetoric's larger argument. She discusses taste in Newman, Boyd, Quackenbos, and Coppée. Taste is an important analytic category in Newman. Yet in the other three rhetorics, taste is described in a single chapter—Boyd devotes less than

three full pages to the topic—and it does not provide a conceptual basis for other aspects of the books. Boyd's account is drawn almost word for word from James Beattie and Hugh Blair. Quackenbos and Coppée freely adopt several sources and add nothing substantive to these redactions.

10. Nan Johnson (81–83) lists the literary figures Adams Sherman Hill (*Principles*) cites and reprints passages Hill uses to exemplify descriptive writing. Yet she does not mention that Hill also cites many nonliterary passages (from travel writing, biography, or natural history) to illustrate the skillful adaptation of rhetorical principles, especially in expository and argumentative writing, and that most literary passages in Hill's textbook exemplify incorrect usage.

11. Among recent critics of nineteenth-century rhetoric, only Nan Johnson regularly notes the publication totals of rhetorics, using the *National Union Catalogue* for her information. My estimates are generally significantly higher than the numbers she reports and derive from several online bibliographies and research in Nietz Collection of Old Textbooks at the University of Pittsburgh and other archives as well as from the *NUC*.

12. See S. Carr for a full account of the circumstances of Blair's publication history, with some estimates of comparative circulation in relation to other rhetorics.

13. Lois Agnew's account of the "civic function" of taste in Blair is one of the few recent studies willing to grant Blair's views some complexity.

14. The critical response to these lectures has been mixed. Corbett praises them highly and recalls a chance encounter with them as decisive to his rhetorical career. T. Miller (*Formation* 238–39) complains that Blair focuses on local qualities of form and style, to the exclusion of Addison's ideas or relationship to any social or cultural context. This criticism, I think, could be leveled at virtually any stylistic exercise and is not, as Miller claims, specific to "belletristic" rhetoric. Moreover, Blair does allude to context when he mentions, for example, Swift's relation to his patron (XXIV, 253), and his later discussion of Atterbury's sermon (XXX) attends to discursive qualities beyond the perspicuous use of language.

15. Berlin misrecognizes Blair's unusual treatment of eloquence, calling it "the obligatory attention to traditional rhetorical concerns" (26). Nan Johnson (38–40) offers the best recent appreciation of this section. Campbell's comment was added to his 1781–82 lectures on pulpit eloquence sometime after the 1783 publication of Blair's *Lectures:* see Campbell, *Lectures* 167.

16. See J. Tarver on Pearson's abridgment.

17. Bitzer's bibliography lists printings of Campbell's *Philosophy,* though it describes imprint variants as distinct "editions." I identify three American editions to 1830: one circa 1813 (Bitzer's H, I, J, K), another from 1818 (E, F), and a third from 1823 (L).

18. The best account of Campbell on "Reputable," "National," and "Present" usage remains Leonard, esp. chap. 9. Kitzhaber (52–53 and 182–83) notes its popularity throughout the nineteenth century; Nan Johnson (28 and 262 n.7) usefully recalls a related argument in classical rhetoric; Thomas Miller (*Formation* 222–23) observes that these formulations have been little studied. On the scholarly preference for book 1, see, for example, Howell's judgment that "'Of the nature and use of the scholastic art of syllogizing' [book 1, chap. 6] is perhaps the most famous chapter on logic in any rhetorical treatise ever written" (401). The selection of Campbell in Golden and Corbett's widely used textbook reprints most of book 1, but only the first chapter of book 2.

19. See especially Anderson's chapters 2 and 3.

20. See Jamieson's sections 45–53 for some of Barron's contributions, 74–117 for Campbell's, and 54–58 and 118–21 for Blair's.

21. See T. Miller's 1990 introduction to Witherspoon's treatise for full biographical and bibliographic information, and an argument that, I think, overstates Witherspoon's differences from Blair.

22. Among recent critics, only Beth L. Hewett notes some of the substantive changes across various editions and begins to elaborate their significance.

23. See the tables in Wozniak that list "Texts and Reference Books Used in Composition Courses in Eastern Colleges" for each decade from the 1850s through the 1910s. Trench is studied at several colleges in every decade until 1910. His peak years were the 1880s and 1890s.

24. There is little general recognition that these texts are compilations, though Kitzhaber (58) notes that Boyd identifies himself as a compiler, and Johnson several times mentions that Quackenbos shows some form of Blair's influence.

25. Wozniak's tables for 1850–80 show a regular steady use at various eastern colleges, but nowhere near commensurate with Quackenbos's near yearly publication.

26. See Kitzhaber 104–5 and Connors, *Comp-Rhet* 305–8 on lists of theme topics.

27. Historians of rhetoric often follow the title page of later printings in claiming sixty editions, yet such publishers' notices are usually unreliable. I have traced twenty U.S. versions: 1827 (1st), 1829 (2nd), 1832 (3rd), 1834 (4th), 1835 (5th), 1836 (6th), 1838 (7th), 1839 (7th), 1842 (10th), 1843 (12th), 1844 (13th), 1846 (20th), 1849 (30th), undated 50th, 1852 (and thereafter, 60th), 1854, 1855, 1856, 1862, 1894. London editions appear in 1837 and 1846. Newman is, I think, the first and one of the very few U.S. rhetorics to be reprinted in England until late in the century.

28. Compare, for instance, Newman's advice on refutation (37) with Whately's (1, iii, no. 7). Even when Newman largely adopts Whately's views, there can be interesting differences in emphasis; both recommend that writers

narrow broad topics, but Whately values the fullness of treatment this allows (I, ii, no. 2), and Newman, the stimulus to thought it provides (32).

29. Crowley (*Methodical* 58–63) offers the most thoughtful account of Newman on invention. See Connors, *Comp-Rhet* 219–21, and Crowley, *Methodical* 96–100, on Newman's classification of modes.

30. In his influential 1984 study, Berlin dismisses Newman and Day as repetitions of Blair and Campbell, and as exemplars of nineteenth-century "belletristic" or "scientistic" rhetorics.

31. Kitzhaber (201–20) notes the increased importance of "the practical" at this time, though he understands it primarily as leading to a simplification of rhetorical theory and a narrow focus on mechanical correctness.

32. Connors (*Comp-Rhet* 6–16) offers a broad definition of "composition-rhetoric" as that "form of rhetorical theory and practice devoted to written discourse" and identifies four stages: "Early American" (1800–1865), "Postwar" (1865–85), "Consolidation" (1885–1910), and "Modern" (1910–60). He is more interested in the term as a corrective to the dismissive and reductive notion of "current-traditional" than as a fine-grained category of historical analysis.

33. My findings challenge Connors's assertion that "between 1865 and 1890, the exercises of the earlier part of the century were relegated to secondary school texts, while college texts again became treatises" (*Comp-Rhet* 82). Yet texts intended in part for college use foreground exercises (Hart, *Manual;* Kellogg; Coppens), and several others (Hepburn, Day, D. Hill) print a good selection.

34. Women authored several readers, letter-writing guides, and other schoolbooks early in the century, but Lockwood and Waddy are the first women to author school rhetorics. Their work, along with near contemporaneous composition books by writers such as Mary Harper, Lucy Chittenden, and Harriet Keeler and Emma Davis, mark the emergence of women as producers of textbooks for formal writing instruction.

35. See Brereton on the Harvard writing program and its long-term influence.

36. Kitzhaber (141–48) surveys the sketchy treatments of adaptation up to Genung. Nan Johnson (96–101) discerns more interest in adaptation in nineteenth-century rhetoric.

2. Reading School Readers

1. This is the title of an excerpt from Porter's *Books and Reading* included as the penultimate lesson in McGuffey's *Sixth Eclectic Reader* (1879), 457.

2. The fourteen-page advertisement appears at the end of an abridgement of Blair (Concord, NH, 1821). The books include thirty-four Latin and thirteen Greek readers, as well as eight readers in French. Mason's treatise offers

insight on the "nature and benefit" of "self-knowledge" and advice on "the way to attain it" (title page); one way was through reading such books as those on this list.

3. Reading figured in debates about the "new education" of the 1860s. Charles W. Eliot argued in an 1869 essay in *The Atlantic Monthly* for language instruction

> not through formal grammar, but by reading aloud, by committing to memory choice bits, and by listening to a good teacher's commentary. . . . A child can drink in and instinctively appreciate the beauties of a refined or noble style years before he can understand grammar and rhetoric. (Krug, *Charles W. Eliot* 30)

4. Dillaway's 1881 essay praises the common school system for teaching "equality and republican principles; it creates the reading public; it has produced a throng of readers such as was never known before, —countless and never satisfied" (260).

5. Jane Addams argued the importance of merging "school life into the working life" and reported as one of Hull House's first activities, a weekly "reading party in George Eliot's *Romola*" for "young women who followed the wonderful tale with unflagging interest" (106, 101).

6. William Gilmore quotes this address as source for his title, *Reading Becomes a Necessity of Life* (19–20). Harriet Beecher Stowe used the phrase in 1879 to describe freed slaves' cry "for the spelling-book as bread" and "teachers as a necessity of life" (qtd. in James Anderson 5).

7. The inadequacy of libraries in the United States, especially in light of national ambitions for education, was a regular topic of concern, both in and out of academia. On May 20, 1816, George Ticknor wrote from Germany to Stephen Higginson, steward of Harvard: "in America we look on the Library at Cambridge [i.e., Harvard College] as a wonder . . . [but] it is nearly or quite half a century behind the libraries of Europe" (Hofstadter 1: 256). An 1842 review of Francis Wayland's *Thoughts on the Present Collegiate System* claimed that the total number of books in U.S. colleges (520,000 volumes) did not equal the holdings in either Paris or Munich (Bowen 307). This negative comparison became a frequent way of describing the problem. As late as 1881, Justin Winsor, librarian of Harvard University, repeated the claim, although he offset it with a list of impressive private holdings—including Charles Francis Adams, 18,000, and Edward Everett, 7,500 (293). Horace Mann noted that as of 1839, few libraries were public, and most were in cities (*Lectures* 272). The opening in 1852 of Boston Public launched a rise in public libraries; by 1860 there were over 10,000 in the United States with about 8 million volumes.

8. See McHenry on early literary societies 48–83 and newspapers and periodicals 84–102, 130–40 for African American women in the north.

9. The American Sunday School Union, formed in 1826, was committed to universal basic literacy (four grades of instruction in reading, writing, spelling, and religion) (Zboray 90). Rice estimates that by 1830, the union had produced over six million copies of Sunday school titles, launched a teacher's magazine and two other periodicals, prepared two hundred volumes for libraries, and spent $76,000 annually on literacy activities (146). In 1860, there were an estimated forty-eight thousand Sunday school libraries (Nye 364). The American Tract Society, founded in 1825, distributed huge quantities of reading materials free, both at home and abroad. As Zboray has argued, the distribution of cheap or free reading materials drove out other forms of publication, and the form of literacy instruction—largely untrained teachers, infrequent and large classes, lack of instructional sequence—encouraged basic rather than advanced literacy (90–92).

10. The term "extracurricular," as commonly used in college catalogues, signals additional instruction alongside or in relationship to the regular curriculum but has also been used to signal those activities conducted "extramurally," that is, outside the school venue. Rudolph uses the term "extracurriculum" for a wide variety of activities supplementing the formal curriculum of U.S. colleges: clubs, debating and literary societies, literary magazines, fraternities, and athletics. Gere challenges the focus on traditionally male colleges and activities, extending the term to refer to "agencies of intellect" outside academe—to women's clubs, temperance societies, periodicals where people were instructed and practiced their literacies ("Kitchen Tables"). John Brereton argues that such agencies should not be termed an "extracurriculum" but rather "alternative" forms of learning, since they were, in a sense, the primary instructional route for learners not able to attend college (private correspondence). In *Intimate Practices,* Gere refers to "extra-academic" writings (243), thus specifying their relationship to the location of college rather than to a set curriculum. The school readers suggest considerable exchange between school and such "extra" venues, both those closely linked to school and those at a further remove. See Rudolph, *American College* 136–55, and J. Carr, "Rereading."

11. Many scholarly books detail nineteenth-century reading practices. Some draw on individual readers' diaries, commonplace books, or letters for evidence of what and how they read (Kaser 1984; Miller, *Assuming* 1998; Nunis 1964; Sealts 1966). Some analyze the sale and distribution of books (Charvat, *Literary Publishing* 1959 and *Profession* 1968; Hart, 1950; Mott, *Golden Multitudes* 1947). Since the 1980s, scholars in education, history of the book, and literary and cultural studies have investigated reading practices and the accessibility of print matter, asking questions about what reading matter was produced, sold, and distributed, what social organizations and institutions framed the activity of reading, and how different populations were positioned as readers by social factors, schooling, and economic conditions. See Buell; Cornelius;

Davidson, *Revolution and Reading*; Denning; M. Gilmore; W. Gilmore ; Glazener; D. Hall; Johns; Kaestle, *Literacy*; Lehuu; Manguel; Moylan and Stiles; Nord; Saenger; Shannon; Soltow and Stevens; and Zboray, *Fictive*. Textbooks are often omitted from such discussions or positioned as exceptional cases: see Mott, *Golden*, for "a postscript on bibles, schoolbooks, etc." 297–301.

12. On May 11, 1822, Emerson wrote to his Harvard classmate, John Boynton Hill, "we rather improve in the book line. . . . Books are growing *cheaper* because they are imported from France. I bought a Quintilian in 3 Vols, quite a handsome book for 2.50" (*Letters* 1: 113). See Manguel 142 and Williams on the Tauschnitz series, begun in 1841.

13. See Verduin's discussion of differently bound and priced copies of Dante. An advertisement for Houghton Mifflin's "Beautiful Household Edition," printed at the end of Richardson's *Primer of American Literature* (1891), proposed a sliding scale for different bindings of collections like Emerson's *Parnassus* and James Parton's *Humorous Poetry:* calf for $1, cloth for $1.50, half calf or full gilt for $2, tree calf or levant for $3.

14. See Mott, *Golden Multitudes* 68–70, 150–53; Farkas on urban story papers; and Charvat, *Literary Publishing* 64, on "cheap literature." The prevalence of such categories meant that people often represented their acts of reading in more favorable or censored ways, concealing "cheaper" texts and promoting those most approved.

15. James D. Anderson reports that Samuel Armstrong "excluded classical studies" from the Hampton school for African American students because "such training stimulated 'vanity'" and "high-flown notions" (49). Magazines like *The Anglo-African* (1859–65) valued the classics for their very association with "high-flown notions." The title page includes an untranslated line from Virgil, and articles both advocate classical study and assume it as a form of literacy, with quotations from Horace, Cicero, Virgil, and Seneca. In "Education," Beman cites young Haitians who have won "honor" in Paris "for excellence in knowledge of Greek, Latin and Rhetoric" (338) and asks, "Will the dominant race hasten to teach us all that they themselves know—all that which gives them their power and superiority over us?" (338–39).

16. Soltow and Stevens chronicle the economic distinctions in reading materials for the Ohio valley region, 1800–1870 (58–88); see their discussion of "social and economic variables" in determining literacy and illiteracy rates (22–27). See Falbo on differentiated literary editions.

17. Books as varied as Sedgwick's *A New-England Tale* (1822), Marvel's *Reveries of a Bachelor* (1851), Phelps's *Gypsy's Year at the Golden Crescent* (1867), and Alcott's *Jo's Boys* (1886) foreground school activities. Marvel's chapter "School Days" (167–78) discusses reading, punishments, and a school pageant (playing one of Pizarro's chieftains); Sedgwick's Jane Elton performs in one of Hannah More's *Sacred Dramas* (51) and is scandalized when a rich girl plagia-

rizes the winning school composition (54); and Alcott's Jo describes college exhibitions (chap. 18). Such fictions operate in double ways, instructing young readers about the expectations and value of school, but also warning them about social unease, bullying, and punishment. Some "school" fictions, like Alcott's *Little Men* (1871), counter mainstream practices with alternative schools that offer kinder and more practical education.

18. The phrase is from Ik Marvel's *Dream Life* (1851), describing two incidents of "stolen" novel reading, by a boy who is whipped for reading under his desk (34) and by a college student who deviates from the prescribed course by reading historical fiction (104).

19. Child's "instructive games" suggest the learning children needed to perform: arithmetic and geography games, and many language games, such as a French verse to recite from memory, tongue twisters that challenge articulation, rebuses, logogriphs (puzzles in which letters in one word can be used to make other words), conundrums, puns, and anagrams. Some reading selections refer to games, as does a poem addressed to the "fate lady," a fortune-telling toy whose construction is also detailed (81–83). Child includes an excerpt from Maria Edgeworth that depicts children struggling to repeat a nonsense narrative as a memory trial. "I would rather learn a Greek verb," complains little Harry, but his father advises him "it is sweet to talk nonsense in season" (97–98). See Dawson on the literacy of parlor games.

20. Part 3 of Cole's book, addressed to "advanced classes" and for "self-training," offers both elocutionary study and literary/rhetorical study of "expression" and "style" (vi), including a mixture of "genres" (narrative, descriptive, didactic, senatorial, dramatic, and scriptural).

21. For a discussion of the interest in natural history and of gender distinctions in its pursuit, see Tolley, especially 95–125. See Rudolph, *Mark Hopkins,* for discussion of a "Lyceum of Natural History" founded in 1835 by students at Williams College 144–55.

22. In addition to *The Token,* an annual anthology or giftbook for adult readers (1828–43), Goodrich edited the children's magazines *Parley's* (1833–34) and *Merry's Museum* (1841–54). See Mussey for an account of the Peter Parley series.

23. The error list focuses on dropped vowels, difficulties with *u,* dropped *h*'s, mispronunciation of *r* and *w,* and omission of end consonants (*d, k, ng, t, ts*).

24. *Methode* printed an alphabet of script letters organized phonetically and associating pictures and words exemplifying the sound ("th A Thimble") (Hunt 6). *Visible World* printed small woodblocks with a Latin and English text, organized by sound (C. Johnson 17). See also Avery on children's books.

25. See Michael's discussion of the complications about number, constituent letters, and order of the alphabet (*Teaching* 25–32). Well into the eighteenth century, there was considerable variation, particularly around the question of

whether i and j or u and v needed to be listed as distinct letters or treated as vowel and consonant versions. In 1721, for example, Isaac Watts followed the "old and usual Custom" of printing a 24-letter alphabet but complained that "it had been much more proper and natural, if our Fathers had made the v and j Consonants, two distinct Letters, and called them ja and vee, and thus made six-and-twenty" (qtd. on 27).

26. Bailey discusses *spelling pronunciations,* in which pronunciations shift to reflect established spelling (*cowcumber* becomes *cucumber);* he cites Burgess's *Five Hundred Mistakes* (1856), a book that advised speakers to "follow the spelling in pronouncing such words as *celery* (rather than as *salary), clothes' pins* (rather than as *cloze pins)"* (64). By the 1870s, some word books were designed as preparation for spelling bees and tests (Henderson's *Test Words,* 1869).

27. Francis A. March, of Lafayette College, one of the founding members of the Spelling Reform Association (1876), argued for the value of simplified spelling for the many immigrants learning English (Baron 89). See Brander Matthews's discussions of Americanisms and American spelling (1–31, 32–59); M. Sullivan (2: 123–33); Simpson's discussion of dialect traditions (101–18); and West's discussion of dictionaries and the century's predilection for wordplay.

28. For discussion of reading instruction under slavery, using the New Testament, newspapers, and books like Webster's *Speller,* see Cornelius 59–71.

29. For discussions of Webster's innovations, see Baron 41–67; E. Jennifer Monaghan, *Common Heritage;* and Simpson 52–90.

30. Nineteenth-century readers usually credit Blair as the source of the example; his version ("Do you ride to town to-day?") appears in Lecture XXXIII (1833, 369) followed by an example of different import ("Judas, betrayest thou the Son of Man with a kiss?"). "Shall you ride to town to-day?" appears in Mason's *Essay on Elocution* (1748, 25) to illustrate four ways the sentence could be read depending on emphasis (*you, ride, town, today);* "Shall you ride to town to-morrow?" is given as a "trite instance" in Sheridan's *Course of Lectures on Elocution* (1762, 58); and the sentence reappears ("Do you intend to go to London, this summer?") illustrating three senses in Enfield's *Speaker* (1774, 21).

31. See Hirsch's discussion of the "decline of literate knowledge" (1–10), particularly his anecdote about his father's Shakespearian allusions in business letters (9).

32. In July 1833, Dr. Edward Reynolds published an essay about the need to manage the "inordinate use" of the eyes in this "reading age" (qtd. in "Reynolds on the Use of the Eyes" 36). Nietz cites two early readers, Webster's *American Selections* and the *Columbian Orator,* as printed in smaller type (9- and 8-point respectively), whereas McGuffey's *Primer* (1838) appeared in 12-point type (modern primers often use 18- or 24-pt. type) (*Old Textbooks* 3). By comparison, Webster's 1806 *Dictionary* and early versions of *The New-*

England Primer used 3-pt. type. See Casper 195 on font size as a feature of cost, and Manguel 135–47 on the "shape" of books.

33. In 1880, William Swinton published two collections of *Seven Classics* to "supplement" his *Fifth Reader,* one including British authors (Addison, Scott, Lamb, Thomas Campbell, Macaulay, Tennyson, and Thackeray), and the other American (Irving, Cooper, Bryant, Hawthorne, Longfellow, Whittier, Holmes).

34. Andrews and Stoddard's influential *Latin Grammar,* which remained in print from 1836 throughout the century, was marketed as a companion textbook or included in the readers.

35. Harkness's reader is, in educational strategy, length (over three hundred pages), and design, much more like the English readers produced by his publisher D. Appleton, and his analogic sentences are like those in Parker's 1836 English reader, *Rhetorical Reading.*

36. *Appleton's Fifth Reader* (1878) varies this format, by dispersing the elocutionary instruction as selections throughout the volume. The selections are drawn from a treatise on elocution by Mark Bailey, an instructor of elocution at Yale (1878).

37. Indeed, "authored" pieces reappear in other readers (or in other places in the same reader) as if they were anonymous educational bits. McGuffey's 1853 *Rhetorical Guide* prints an antithetical sentence about Homer and Virgil that redacts the volume's selection from Blair (146–47). A lesson, "Tact and Talent," published initially in the British *Imperial Magazine,* appears in McGuffey's *Sixth Reader* (1857), as well as in Sanders's *High School Reader* (1856) and Oldham's *Amusing and Instructive Reader* (1854). Only Oldham cites the source.

38. Barnes's *New National Fifth Reader* (1884), for example, prints one hundred lessons introduced by a two-page preface, complaining that because economically pressed students are leaving school at such an early age, they are too "immature" for the "masterpieces" of literature or, presumably, for systematic instruction in reading (6). Ellen Cyr's *Fifth Reader* (1899) similarly offers no elocutionary apparatus, questions or exercises.

39. There is considerable variation in the number of lessons in readers. In general, however, the most advanced readers, designed for the academies and high schools, follow Enfield's *Speaker* (1774, 268 lessons), printing close to two hundred lessons: McGuffey's *Rhetorical Guide* (1844, 235), the Russells' *Young Ladies' Elocutionary* (1845, 201), McGuffey's *High School* (1857, 194), McGuffey's *New High School . . . for Advanced Classes* (1857, 200), Sanders's *High School* (1856, 163). Single-volume readers from 1800–1820 usually print sixty to eighty lessons: *Columbian Orator* (1797, 84 unnumbered), Murray's *Sequel* (1800, 76), Lyman's *American Reader* (1811, 60); and so do elementary readers in graduated series: McGuffey's *Third* (1837, 66), Osgood's *Third* (1871, 70), McGuffey's *Second* (1879, 71). Advanced readers in graduated series and elo-

cutionary readers print 120–160 lessons: Porter's *Rhetorical* (1832, 126), McGuffey's *Sixth* (1857, 138), Town's *Fourth* (1858, 145), Sanders's *Union Fifth* (1868, 154), *Harper's U.S. Sixth* (1872, 156), *American Educational Fifth* (1873, 133), *Appleton's Fifth* (1881, 146). Parker's *Rhetorical Reading* (1835) offers forty lessons (perhaps to correspond to the forty lessons in his composition book) and 797 numbered passages, from single sentences to longer passages marked with elocutionary symbols.

40. Douglass claims the reader's selections "gave tongue to interesting thoughts of my own soul, which had . . . died away for want of utterance," in particular Sheridan's "mighty speeches" on Catholic emancipation and a dialogue in which a slave persuades his master to free him (51).

41. See the advertisement for "900,000 Eclectic School Books" in McGuffey's *Third Reader* (1842, 4), which also lists "eclectic" arithmetics. Nietz equates "eclectic" with "choice" or "select" (*Old Textbooks* 76), which by the 1830s signified not just a selection but a *first-rate* selection. Minnich links the term with Pestalozzi (37–38), while Lindberg traces it back to the writings of French philosopher Victor Cousin but notes, "the term was quickly absorbed into educational jargon" (xx). In the 1837 *Third Reader,* the publisher bragged,

> The *Eclectic* System of Instruction now predominates in Prussia, Germany, and Switzerland. It is in these countries that the subject of education has been deemed of paramount importance. The art of teaching, particularly, has there been most ably and minutely investigated. (qtd. in Lindberg xx–xxi)

42. The series of books known as McGuffey's *Eclectic Readers* appears in six graduated volumes, issued from 1836 to the present, with many substantive revisions, translations, and redactions. William Holmes McGuffey prepared the first editions of 1–4, although the series continued to be issued under his name, or in subsequent years, simply (and perhaps more accurately) as "McGuffey's." The other volumes and revisions are the product of many hands: Alexander McGuffey compiled 5 and 6, and Timothy S. Pinneo contributed a revised version of the introduction he had composed for the 1844 *Rhetorical Guide.* Pinneo also helped revise 3 and 4 in 1843–44, and 1–6 in 1853. Publisher Obed J. Wilson oversaw revisions of 1–6 in 1853 and 1879. Daniel G. Mason helped revise 1 and 2 in 1844. Amanda Funnelle and Robert W. Stevenson revised 1–3 in 1879, Thomas W. Harvey and Edwin C. Hewett revised 4–6 in 1879. E. J. Whitney selected illustrations for the 1879, with new photo-engravings prepared in 1901. As the number of readers increases from the initial four to six, the materials of the "advanced" volume are redistributed across newly added volumes (the 4th is the most advanced in 1837–44, the 5th in 1844–57, the 6th in 1857-present). Initially printed in Cincinnati, Ohio, by Truman and Smith (1834–41), they are also issued by W. B. Smith (1841–63);

Sargent, Wilson and Hinkle (1863–68); Wilson, Hinkle (1868–77); Van Antwerp, Bragg (1877–90); American Book (1890–1990); and John Wilson (1990–present). The copyright for the series was renewed in 1901 and 1920.

McGuffey left Cincinnati for the University of Virginia in 1845 (see Westerhoff 17–18). According to Lindberg, his contract granted him royalties of 10 percent on all copies of the first four readers sold up to a total of $1,000, *"after which all profits reverted to the publishers"* (xix). His "grateful publishers" gave him a barrel of "choice smoked hams" every Christmas (xix).

43. For Alexander McGuffey's contributions, see Minnich 41–44 (which prints a facsimile of the handwritten contract between Alexander and W. B. Smith for the *Rhetorical Guide*); Ruggles 13; D. Sullivan 105–14; and Westerhoff 17–19. Claims about collaboration and original authorship are difficult to assess, especially when one of the collaborators is a national hero.

44. The compilers were Thomas W. Harvey, R. W. Stevenson, Edwin C. Hewett, Amanda Funnelle, and Henry Vail, who wrote a history of the McGuffey empire (D. Sullivan 204–14). Westerhoff claims, somewhat hyperbolically, that "there are three distinct editions of McGuffey *Readers*—1836–37, 1857, and 1879—each compiled by a new editor, for a new publisher, to meet new needs. Only the name of the Readers is historically continuous" (20).

45. The review appears in vol. 29 (July 1829), 38–67. The authorship of unsigned reviews in *NAR* was an open secret well before Cushing published his index in 1878. In letters of February 28, 1823, to John Boynton Hill, and of January 25, 1830, to his brother Charles, Emerson listed who had written each article for that month's issue of the *Review* (*Letters* 1: 131, 292).

46. In addition to this biography, which appeared in the *National Cyclopaedia of American Biography* in 1891, other biographies appear in *Dictionary of American Biography* (1930) 5: 272, and *American National Biography* (1999) 6: 519–21. See also Griswold, *Prose Writers* 202–6, and Fowler 267–88.

47. Emerson's comments appear in a letter to Henry James Sr. February 28, 1852 (*Letters* 4: 280), and in his journal for October 3, 1847 (*JMN* 5: 385).

48. The numbers of textbook copies sold in the nineteenth century is always an elusive bit of "knowledge." Scholars propose a figure, based on extrapolations from known editions and school populations, publishers' blurbs, or early bibliographic records. Claims for *The New-England Primer,* for example, vary from three to ten million, with most splitting the difference at seven. Ford showed his wariness by offering "an over-conservative claim" based on an "estimate" of three million copies (19). Claims for Webster's *Speller* lie between twenty and one hundred million copies. Minnich estimated forty million (39), whereas Nietz justified his high estimate by quoting an advertising blurb that appeared through the 1866 version (*Old Textbooks* 16). Minnich is the source for this widely reprinted number of McGuffey copies, based on the estimate of

the publisher Louis Dillman, of figures for the "entire sales of Readers, Spellers, and Primers, from 1836 to 1920" (92).

49. Hows's *Ladies' Reader,* for example, offers the "essential rules of elocution, simplified and arranged for strictly practical use" (title page). For further discussions of readers for girls, see E. Monaghan, "Uses of Literacy" and J. Carr, "Nineteenth-Century Girls and Literacy."

50. The society published three *Freedman's Readers* and a *Speller* (1865–66), subsequently reissuing them as a *Lincoln's* series. The periodical *American Freedman* questioned whether there was a reason for such a reader "any more than a Dutchman's or an Irishman's Primer? Are not the so-called Freedmen to learn the same language, spell the same words, and read the same literature as the rest of us?" (qtd. in Morris, *Freedmen's Schools* 2: i–iii). The *Third Reader's* prefatory note suggests the difference was lowered expectations: instructions were "made as brief as possible, for the reason that a few rules, understood and used, are better than many neglected" (ii).

51. In contrast to *The Third Reader,* prepared by Israel Warren, editor of the Tract Society's publications (1859–70), Child's volume opens with a brief letter "to the Freedmen," from "your old friend." Her book, printed by the distinguished firm Ticknor and Fields, looks like an essay collection instead of a school reader, with no numbered lessons, questions, or apparatus, but Child adds informational notes and stars the eighteen pieces whose authors are African American.

52. Writing in 1911, Vail praised McGuffey's *Readers* for teaching "a sound morality to millions of children without giving offense to the most violent sectarian" (64). In 1962, Commager argued they provided "a common body of allusions, a sense of common experience, and of common possession" (70), and in 1987, Ravitch wrote longingly of the "golden age of the school reader" compared to the modern "hodgepodge" (46). M. Sullivan hailed the series for "carrying a democratic point of view" to the world. Despite his dated approach, Sullivan offers a fascinating account of "memories of reading" sent in by adults recalling their school experiences (2: 7–48).

53. McGuffey's *First Reader* was translated into German (1853), Japanese (1871), and Spanish (1879) for use by American educators in the Philippines and Puerto Rico; in 1882, a bilingual version was printed for the Laguna Indians. In 1868, Edwin Leigh published a version of the primer in pronouncing orthography, called *Leigh's McGuffey's Reader.*

54. German came in a close second in the United States as a language of instruction in the nineteenth century, and as many as a third of midwestern students spoke German at home. Non-English instruction was often the case in parochial schools run by Lutherans, Mennonites, and Catholics, for example (see Cremins, *Metropolitan Experience* 126–36), but in some communities, the public schools as well conducted instruction in two languages, sometimes

switching halfway through the day, sometimes for part of the year. According to Kaestle, in Wisconsin "some predominantly German towns had instruction entirely in German, despite a revised education law in 1854 requiring that basic subjects be taught in English" (*Pillars* 165). English-German versions of the major school readers (by Sanders, McGuffey, and Monroe) appeared throughout the century. Publishers in German strongholds like Cincinnati, Chicago, and St. Louis also issued "Lesebüchen" (reading books) explicitly marketed for the "öffentlichen Schulen" (public schools) of those cities. Some of these translated existing English readers, but others featured "choice selections from the best German writers," as did Woodbury's five-volume *Eclectic German Readers* (1852); in other cases, the influence was reversed (Wilmsen's influential German reader, for example, was translated into English in 1845 for U.S. students).

55. See Roemer's *Polyglot Reader* (1855–56), which reproduces its English reader in four translated volumes (in French, German, Spanish, and Italian).

56. *The New-England Primer* also emerged in facsimile form as early as 1843, designated as "the richest treasure that ever human industry and wisdom accumulated" (ii).

57. Although the reader omits elocutionary instructions, it adds historical annotations and notes to its often obscure vocabulary—e.g., "*clepsydra*: a contrivance used by the ancients for measuring time by the running of water" (15).

58. Mann proposed the establishment of common school libraries to help combat the mechanism of reading instruction: "no one thing will contribute more to intelligent reading in our schools, than a well selected library; and, through intelligence, the library will also contribute to rhetorical ease, grace, and expressiveness" (*Lectures* 279). New York state in 1835 authorized district schools to raise funds for libraries, as did Massachusetts in 1837 (269–70). According to Mann, by 1839 there were fifty libraries in the 3,014 common schools in Massachusetts.

59. School readers perpetuate traditions of rhetorical delivery, management of voice, and gesture long after rhetorics have marked such concerns as specialized fields. They prepare generations of students to participate in late-century activities, such as the Delsarte "science of attitude and gesture" (Gere, *Intimate Practices* 35), debating, theatricals, and recitation.

60. Orville Dewey's 1829 essay ("Principles") footnotes Austin's passage (38) as from "Chironomia," but the author remains unnamed ("says one, referring to articulation"); Dewey changed the earlier version's "sharp" to "distinct" (54). McGuffey's *Fourth Reader* (1837) includes the passage as part of a longer selection "On Elocution and Reading" from "N. A. Review" (69). Austin's source for the passage as a whole (Quintilian, *Institutes* XI.3.33) does not mention the metaphor.

3. Constructing Composition Books

1. Walter Kolesnik, following B. B. Hoffman, suggests that a European corollary to mental discipline was the "sloyd" system, a system of manual training in Sweden that emphasized mental gymnastics. Hoffman understood "sloyd" as a means of formal (as opposed to material) education, seeking "to develop the innate mental powers" and "to strengthen character, will-power, memory, perception" (qtd. in Kolesnik 17).

2. See Schultz, *The Young Composers* (1999), for an elaboration of these factors and a study of the beginnings of composition instruction in nineteenth-century U.S. schools. See also the the list of works cited in that volume for an extensive bibliography of composition books, related secondary works, and student writing.

3. See Schultz, "Letter-Writing Instruction in Nineteenth-Century Schools in the United States," 117–18, for a selection of books that borrow directly from Blair.

4. For a discussion of Comenius, Locke, Rousseau, and Pestalozzi, see chapter 3 of Schultz, *The Young Composers*. Friedrich Froebel (1782–1852) is best known for his model of the kindergarten, an important progenitor of the American kindergarten, a place where children, like young plants in a garden, could be nurtured, and where, from their play with the simple toys Froebel designed ("gifts"), they could experience, for example, order and discovery. Johann Friedrich Herbart (1776–1841) is often considered an early advocate of "educational psychology," credited with the concept of the lesson plan, and known for his resistance to the theories of faculty psychology and mental discipline. As scholars of Herbart note, he placed, with William James and John Dewey who followed, great emphasis on "motivation" as an aid to learning. Composition textbook author Charles DeGarmo, along with A. F. Lang, translated Herbart's work into English.

5. Nineteenth-century composition books asked young students to describe objects that would also be familiar to students today, an apple or rice, for instance. Other objects were more particularly centered in nineteenth-century life and might be unfamiliar to today's students; "Indian rubber" is an example. And still other objects might have had a different function or a different importance from what they have today. The sponge, for example, is an object for description in a number of nineteenth-century texts, as early as 1839 in Frost's *Easy Exercises* (1839 stereotyped edition, 67) and as late as 1896 in Metcalf and Bright's *Language Lessons, Part Two* (36). I wondered at the frequency with which the sponge appeared until I learned that in the nineteenth century, it was an important bathing accouterment. In Susan Coolidge's 1873 *What Katy Did at School,* the teacher Miss Jane instructs Katy and the other boarding school students to carry "a bath towel, a sponge, and soap" as they walk from their school to the local bathhouse on Saturday mornings (62–64).

Consider also this humorous passage from a January 15, 1874, letter from Ellen Tucker Emerson (R. W. E.'s firstborn daughter) to her sister Edith. She is writing about their father, Ralph Waldo Emerson:

> The other morning (she [mother] is always arranging plots to make him take a bath you know) I had orders for her to draw a bath for him and then call him. I obeyed, and he took it, as she knew he would, rather than waste the warm water. At breakfast-time he said 'I got into that awkward bath, but I didn't see how I was going to use it. At last I saw a sponge hanging there, my own sponge. That solved the problem at once. Indeed one hardly sees how a bath could be taken without a sponge. The Divine Providence seems to have anticipated our needs—' I caught his idea and exclaimed 'Why Yes! He made sponges so we could enjoy our baths!' 'Yes, it looks like that,' he said. 'Here is the poor man quite helpless in the water, wondering how he shall make it available and suddenly he sees the sponge before him, created on purpose! I had forgotten there ever had been such a thing in the world. I should never have thought of it if it hadn't presented itself.' (2: 119–20)

An example of a student theme written about a sponge appears in Alcott's *Little Men.* Jo (March) Bhaer and her husband, Fritz, direct a boarding school called Plumfield. In their school, Composition Day is a regular event, and on one particular day, the program begins with a ten-year-old student, Nan, reading her composition called "The Sponge" (282). (For the Emerson example, I thank J. Carr; and for the Alcott example, I thank Susan Carpenter, who is studying scenes about writing instruction that appear in nineteenth-century novels for adolescents.)

6. Examples include James Boyd, who, in his *Elements of English Composition* asked students "to enumerate all the parts of your own dwelling-house and out-houses, also of your school-edifice and surroundings" (290); Hiram Hadley, who, in his *Lessons in Language,* asked students to write about objects such as apple, water, bread, and writing paper (34–41); and Alonzo Reed and Brainerd Kellogg, who, in their advice to teachers in *One-Book Course in English,* noted an advantage of asking students to write about objects is that that material is always available, and "the best is always available in every school-room" (4).

7. Lyman notes that 301 grammars were written by Americans and printed in America before 1850; most widely used was the work of Lindley Murray (1745–1826). Born, raised, and educated in the United States, Murray retired in England (after a successful career as a lawyer and businessman); it was there that he wrote his grammar, following the prescriptive systems of predecessors Robert Lowth (1710–87) and Thomas Sheridan (1719–88). The ab-

sence of international copyright law allowed Murray's grammar to be reproduced in the millions in the United States, a tremendous boon to publishers.
Lyman notes that before 1850, nearly two million copies of Murray's grammars,
by both Murray and his adapters, were printed. See Charles Monaghan's *The
Murrays of Murray Hill* (about Lindley Murray's family).

For bibliographies of early grammars and their history, see also Leitner,
Barbour, Huston, Michael, Pooley, Henry Lester Smith, and Tyler.

8. It is likely that modern punctuation evolves from "pointing," the early
practice of marking a text (a psalm, for example) to indicate where the reader/
singer/chanter would pause for breath, or to insure that the proper notes could
be sung over the proper syllable. The first edition of the *Oxford English Dictionary* shows that the usage of "pointing" as punctuation dates to 1400.

See also chapter 2 on the teaching of reading, including the practice of
rhetorical notation.

9. Occasionally, struggling to find a way of delivering grammatical rules
that would be effective for young learners, a writer who emphasized memorization would experiment with a new pedagogy, embedding the grammar rules
in a conversational exchange between a student and a teacher or in a series of
letters; see Ingersoll.

10. As late as 1873, Fowle laments the way grammar was being taught,
arguing that teachers focused too heavily on the rules of grammar, too little
on its use. See the section from his *The Teacher's Institute, or Familiar Hints to
Young Teachers* called "English Grammar," which is included in Salvatori.

11. Helmut Lehmann-Haupt and Charles Madison both include a few
pages about textbook publication in the United States. Each author offers a
useful if quick overview of textbook publication (and how it was part of an ever-
growing publication industry); neither author includes specific citations (that
would be easy to verify) for the numbers or data he offers. For broader views
of book history in the United States, see Casper, Chaison, and Groves; and
Zboray and Zboray.

12. Hall-Quest, in his 1918 study called *The Textbook*, lists what were
considered the arguments for and against schools providing free textbooks for
school students; he notes that the strongest argument against free textbooks
is that they "are likely to be carriers of disease" (53).

13. Monaghan elaborates that William Bradford, second governor of Ply-
mouth colony, wrote *Of Plimouth Plantation* in the italic script, his version of
that script influenced by the rounded quality from the Dutch writing masters.
Monaghan further notes that since Bradford was writing for a public audience,
he used "a version of italic that had most of its letters standing separately from
one another, rather than joined in a true cursive," thus making for a document
"of singular visual clarity." (*Learning*, introduction to part 1).

Composition textbook author Simon Kerl illustrates the difference between "writing" and "composing" in a section of *Elements of Composition and Rhetoric* when he writes to teachers,

> Writing.— Rufus Choate [American jurist] wrote so bad a scrawl that the puzzled printers called his penmanship chain-lightning; and Daniel Webster once jocosely asked him what he meant by those antediluvian bird-tracks. Since the natural tendency of children is to carelessness, and since the haste and bustle of subsequent life are very apt to cause a degeneracy from the mechanical excellence acquired at school, the teacher should, in the writing of compositions, insist on as much neatness and precision as possible. (50)

For a sample of books on handwriting, see the twenty-seven books on penmanship in the University of Pittsburgh's Nietz Collection, especially John Jenkins's *The Art of Writing* (1813). See also Tamara Plakins Thornton's *Handwriting in America: A Cultural History* (1996).

14. As is the case for many nineteenth-century journals, determining the author of an article in early education journals (I think, for example, of the *American Journal of Education, American Annals of Education,* the *Common School Journal,* and the *Connecticut Common School Journal*) can be difficult for contemporary readers (see note 45 for chapter 2 explaining that Emerson knew who had written the unsigned articles in the *NAR*). In some cases, the writer's initials or a pen name appears at the end of an essay, but it is not uncommon for essays in these journals to be unsigned; occasionally, as is the case with some of the journal holdings in Harvard's Gutman Library, a librarian or reader will have determined the author's name and penciled it in. In the case of the article I cite here, there is no attribution. While individual issues of this journal for this year do not have a masthead, the entire year's collection of numbers is bound together with a single collective title page that names William C. Woodbridge (author of many school geographies) as the editor and as the person under whose name the volumes were "Entered according to Act of Congress in the year 1832." It is likely that Woodbridge wrote the article.

15. See Schultz, *The Young Composers* 25–26, for an account of how these books differed from John Rippingham's (1811?) *Rules for English Composition, and Particularly for Themes,* intended "for the use of schools, and in aid of self-instruction."

16. For a history of the Boylston Professorship in the nineteenth century, see Ronald Reid's essay in the *Quarterly Journal of Speech*.

17. In an 1837 lecture delivered before the American Institute of Instruction, Parker uses, verbatim, lengthy passages from *Progressive Exercises,* including large chunks from the preface. The lecture appears in the *Proceedings and Lectures of the American Institute of Instruction: American Annals of Education and Instruction*.

18. Parker was graduated from Harvard College in 1817. A lecture that he would have heard by Professor Joseph McKean (according to McKean's notes, he delivered Lecture XI on October 9, 1812; February 17, 1815; and November 1, 1816) contains this passage:

XI. Constituent parts of Oratory and Invention its importance, sources, & materials.

The attention of every speaker or writer should be first directed to the enquiry what may be advanced on the subject he undertakes to discuss. According to the occasion or kind of composition, he is to explain some truth, describe some thing, to present them clearly & forcibly to the views of others, to prove & illustrate their importance, to confirm & enforce their merits & claims, to dissipate obscurities & answer objections. He is also, with a view to persuade as well as convince, to seek in a due degree to gratify the taste, & interest the affections, & move the passions, of those whom he would not only inform but influence. For these & corresponding purposes is oratorical invention exercised. It brings into requisition all the powers of conception, reasoning, imagination, memory & feeling, to furnish thoughts, arguments, ornament, facts, & pathos: that by these displayed & in due measure & proportion, the great aim & end of eloquence which is persuasion, may be effectually secured.

According to the *Catalogue of the Select Library of the Late Rev. Joseph McKean* (HUG 1546.5.2), published in 1818, several works by Aristotle (including *Ars Rhetorica* and *Opera Omnia*) were part of his collection.

19. The heuristics that Rise Axelrod and Charles Cooper offer students for "describing a scene" in their 1993 *The Concise Guide to Writing* are remarkably similar to those Parker offered in 1833: they ask first-year college students, as preparation for describing a scene, to focus on the sights, the sounds, the smells, tastes, and textures of objects that are part of that scene (31). In a more broadly based list of inventional strategies, they ask students to name the parts of a subject; to determine what the subject is similar to, different from; to think about the origin of the subject, its causes and effects (202–3).

20. An interesting project would be to study the intellectual exchanges among these four writers. We know that Frost left a teaching position at the Mayhew School in 1827 (some sources list 1828) and that Parker joined the faculty of that school in 1828; that Parker praised Newman's work in the 1833 edition of *Progressive Exercises;* and that Ralph Waldo Emerson, in a letter to his brother Edward Bliss Emerson, spoke of conversation with Frost. Apologizing to his brother for not reading his journal, R. W. Emerson wrote,

> And my excuse is that on the first Saturday that I saw it in town Mr.
> Moody and Mr. Frost (Wms Collego-Kennebunko friends) so fasci-
> nated and overwhelmed me with the charms of their conversation,
> that—if ever you have seen either or both of them—you can easily
> conceive that I was unable to read . . . (*Letters* 1: 94)

The footnote reads, "Like George Barrell Moody, John Frost, of the class of 1822, was from Kennebunk."

Each of these writers also studied with a Boylston Professor of Rhetoric: Newman and Parker with Joseph McKean, Emerson and Frost with Edward T. Channing.

21. Bowdoin Prizes, which continue today, were established in 1791 from the income of the bequest of Governor James Bowdoin, AB, who was graduated from Harvard College in 1745.

22. Both Frost and Parker wrote grammars. Frost's are *Elements of English Grammar* (1828) and *Practical English Grammar* (1842). Parker's (with Charles Fox) is *Progressive Exercises in English Grammar* (1834).

23. At least some of the illustrations in Frost's book (showing young children at play, for example) suggest an audience of young students—not the high school students who used the book at Central High. Common practice among those nineteenth-century authors whose pedagogy depended on illustrations was to use the engravings that a publisher/printer might have had on hand; in other words, at least until the Civil War, it would have been unusual for an author to commission art for a book; rather, for the available engravings, he would have created captions that suited his own purpose (witness that occasionally the same illustration will appear in different books, by different authors, used for different purposes). It is likely, therefore, that if Frost did not find illustrations of high school age students, he used what was available, a nineteenth-century form of clip art, if you will. This discrepancy (between the age of the children in the illustrations and the age of the students at Central High) also suggests that, like many early books, *Easy Exercises* could have been used with students of differing ages. See chapter 4, "The Agency of Textbook Iconography" in Schultz, *The Young Composers*.

24. Here is a fascinating snippet of a biography of William Swinton:

> [He] worked for the New York Times [his brother John was manag
> ing editor at the time] in the field as a war correspondent, until ex
> pelled from the army's lines in 1864. A Scottish-born former student
> for the ministry and a teacher, he joined the Times in 1858, four years
> later covering the Army of the Potomac. Knowledgeable on military
> matters, he was often critical of military leaders an [sic] often gained
> his information why what military authorities considered by questional
> [sic] means. On the first night of the battle of the Wilderness, he was

caught overhearing a conversation between Grant and Meade. A few weeks afterward, he angered Burnside with an unfavorable report. As a result, on 1 July 1864, the War Department stripped him of his credentials and ordered him expelled from the lines of the Army of the Potomac. . . . He subsequently was a professor and textbook writer. (http://www.scots-in-the-civil-war.net/newsmen.htm)

25. See Borrowman, Fitzgerald, Herbst, and Salvatori for discussions of normal schools and the professionalization of teaching.

26. The ideas of earlier writers might remain in play, but Blair's *Lectures,* for example, are no longer in print in 1897, and so we no longer see his work routinely recommended as a resource for teachers, as it had been earlier in the century.

27. Because these were often boarding schools, students had occasion for regular letter writing. Their letters to friends or family describe daily life, often in delightful ways: "Boarding school laundry is a great destroyer of underwear"; "Last week, there was a great excitement in the school on account of two girls being expelled for flirting [with two of Mr. Hart's boys]" (Stevenson 174). But they also refer to reading ("I am reading the life of Margaret Fuller") and, in a number of cases, to composition. On October 29, 1859, Julia Ann Clarke of Dubuque, Iowa, wrote to her sister that she had been "writing my composition all the morning" (Stevenson 166); in January 1860, she wrote to her mother, "I spent three hours on a composition this morning" (171).

28. See, especially, Brereton's very important collection of primary documents that both elaborate and contextualize the beginnings of composition studies in U.S. colleges.

29. John Silas White's oration begins, "Convenimus hodie, alumni fautoresque hujus literarum universitatis, ut illum, cujus adventus per hos dies non mediocriter captatus est, praesidem in munere constituamus" (11). Even one sentence demonstrates that this student was not only equipped to compose in Latin, but also that he had mastered the conventions of a celebratory genre, opening as he does with "We gather today . . ." Translated, the opening sentence reads, "We gather today, alumni and patrons of the university of letters, in order that we might place him, whose arrival has for some time been eagerly awaited, into the office of president." (I am indebted to Marie Cleary for this translation, and for reminding me that the root of "alumnus" is "nursling" or "foster-child," and thus by extension, the word can refer to the pupils or students at a school or university.) Charles W. Eliot, the Harvard president in whose honor White gave his oration, was the president who brought electives to Harvard College, who gave new emphasis to English as a language of study, and during whose tenure, his colleague A. S. Hill created the first-year English requirement.

Works Consulted

One of the bibliographic problems of nineteenth-century textbooks is determining which version is under discussion, especially since many of these books were often revised. We think it important to avoid naming often quite complicated print histories as if they were a single book (Blair, McGuffey). We, therefore, offer as full a bibliographic account as we can, especially for selected key texts. In each case we list the date of first printing (when known) and specify the version from which we cite. For certain titles, we provide a fuller entry, indicating major revisions, for example, and dates when the book flourished. This is not a comprehensive bibliography: to do such entries systematically for some of our categories (readers in particular) would be a massive project. We list the books for each of our sections (rhetorics, readers, and composition books), followed by other significant categories of textbooks (elocutionary treatises, grammars, primers, spellers, and others). Many nineteenth-century textbooks indicate in their title or prefatory material their primary category of affiliation, although such self-designations can be misleading. Some textbooks with "composition" in the title may be primarily expositions of rhetorical principles or grammatical exercises. We organize the books to suggest their primary affiliation as reflected by their structure and content. Many book titles are extensive, some running to eight lines of text. We generally print a short title but sometimes retain terms that specify a particular version of the book (e.g., educational level, specified student population, adaptation).

Primary Materials: Textbooks

Rhetorics

Abbott, Edwin. *How to Write Clearly.* London: 1874. Boston: Roberts Bros., 1875. 24 issues to 1914.

Abbott, Edwin, and John Robert Seeley. *English Lessons for English People.* 1871. Boston: Roberts Bros., 1872. 14 issues to 1901.

Adams, John Quincy. *Lectures on Rhetoric and Oratory.* Cambridge: Hilliard and Metcalf, 1810.

Andrews, John. *Elements of Rhetorick and Belles Lettres.* Philadelphia: Moses Thomas, 1813.

Ansley, E. A. *Elements of Literature; or, An Introduction to the Study of Rhetoric and Belles Lettres.* Philadelphia: J. B. Lippincott, 1849.

Bain, Alexander. *English Composition and Rhetoric: A Manual.* London, 1866. New York: D. Appleton, 1867. 10 American issues to 1887. Enl. ed. 2 vols. 1887–88.

Baker, George Pierce. *The Principles of Argumentation.* 1893. Boston: Ginn, 1895. 9 issues to 1905; rev. ed. 1925.

Bancroft, Timothy Whitney. *A Method of English Composition.* 1884. Boston: Ginn, 1885. 3 issues to 1898.

Bardeen, Charles W. *A Shorter System of Rhetoric.* New York: American Book, n.d., copyright 1885.

———. *A System of Rhetoric.* 1884. Rev. ed. New York: A. S. Barnes, 1885.

Barron, William. *Lectures on Rhetoric and Belles Lettres.* 2 vols. London, 1806.

Bascom, John. *Philosophy of Rhetoric.* 1866. New York and Chicago: Woolworth, Ainsworth, n.d., copyright 1872. 6 versions to 1892.

Bates, Arlo. *Talks on Writing English.* Boston: Houghton Mifflin, 1896. 6 issues.

Beattie, James. *Elements of Moral Science.* 2 vols. Edinburgh: Cadell and Creech, 1790.

Blair, Hugh. *An Abridgement of Lectures on Rhetoric.* Cambridge, MA: Hilliard, 1802. Over 85 versions through 1870s.

———. *An Abridgement of Lectures on Rhetoric.* Concord, NH: Hill and Moore, 1821.

———. *A Compend of Rhetoric in Question and Answer Compiled for the Use of the Young Ladies of the Schenectady Female Academy.* Schenectady: Van Veghton, 1808.

———. *Lectures on Rhetoric and Belles Lettres.* London, 1783. Philadelphia and Pittsburgh: James Kay, n.d., copyright 1833. 1st American, 1784. 56 American versions to 1870s.

Boyd, James R. *Elements of Rhetoric and Literary Criticism, with Copious Practical Exercises and Examples, for the Use of Common Schools and Academies.* 1844. New York: Harper, n.d., copyright 1844. Rev. ed. 1846. 21 issues to 1876.

Buck, Gertrude. *A Course in Argumentative Writing.* New York: H. Holt, 1899. 2nd issue, 1911.

Buck, Gertrude, and Elisabeth Woodbridge. *A Course in Expository Writing.* New York: H. Holt, 1899, 1901, 1905.

Buehler, Huber Gray. *Practical Exercises in English: Arranged for Use with Adams Sherman Hill's "Foundations of Rhetoric."* New York: Harper, 1895. 5 issues.

Cairns, William B. *The Forms of Discourse, with an Introductory Chapter on Style.* Boston: Ginn, 1896. 4 issues to 1909.

———. *An Introduction to Rhetoric.* Boston: Ginn, 1899.

Campbell, George. *The Philosophy of Rhetoric.* London, 1776. New York: Harper, 1844. 1st American, c. 1813. 31 American versions to 1880s.

Channing, Edward T. *Lectures Read to the Seniors in Harvard College.* Boston: Ticknor and Fields, 1856.

Clark, J. Scott. *A Practical Rhetoric for Instruction in English Composition and Revision in Colleges and Intermediate Schools.* 1886. New York: H. Holt, 1893. 8 issues to 1898, as well as 2 issues of *A Briefer Practical Rhetoric* in 1891 and 1893.

Coppée, Henry. *Elements of Rhetoric.* 1859. Philadelphia: E. H. Butler, 1860. Rev. ed., 1866. 12 issues to 1887.

Coppens, Rev. Charles, S. J. *A Practical Introduction to English Rhetoric: Precepts and Exercises.* New York: Schwartz, Kirwin, and Fauss, n.d., copyright 1880. 4th edition in 1886.

Day, Henry Noble. *The Art of Discourse.* New York: Scribner's, 1867. 11 issues into 1880s.

———. *Elements of the Art of Rhetoric.* 1850. 4th ed. New York: A. S. Barnes, 1854. 12 issues to 1876.

De Mille, James. *The Elements of Rhetoric.* New York: Harper, 1878.

Genung, John. *Handbook of Rhetorical Analysis.* Boston: Ginn, 1888. 11 issues to 1902.

———. *Outlines of Rhetoric: Embodied in Rules, Illustrative Examples, and a Progressive Course of Prose Composition.* Boston: Ginn, 1893. 9 issues to 1903.

———. *The Practical Elements of Rhetoric.* Boston: Ginn, 1886. Preliminary versions of part 1, "Style," appear in 1884, 1885, and 1886. 16 issues of 1886 stereotype ed. to 1914.

———. *The Working Principles of Rhetoric.* Boston, Ginn, 1900.

Getty, John A. *Elements of Rhetoric.* Philadelphia: E. Little, 1831. 2nd ed. *The Art of Rhetoric.* Philadelphia: Carey and Hart, 1849.

Gilmore, J. H. *The Outlines of Rhetoric for Schools and Colleges.* 1877. Boston and New York: Leach, Shewell, and Sanborn, 1891. 4 rev. eds. in 1877, 1879, 1884, and 1891.

Hale, Edward Everett, Jr. *Constructive Rhetoric.* New York: H. Holt, 1896.

Hart, John S. *A Manual of Composition and Rhetoric: A Text-Book for Schools and Colleges.* Philadelphia: Eldredge, n.d., copyright 1870. 26 versions. Issued yearly, 1870–77. Slightly rev. and newly stereotyped ed., issued some 13 times from 1878 through mid-1890s. Rev. ed. 1897, by James Morgan Hart, issued at least 5 times in the next decade.

Haven, Erastus Otis. *Rhetoric: A Text-Book, Designed for Use in Schools and Colleges and for Private Study.* New York: Harper, 1869. 8 issues, yearly through 1876.

Hepburn, A. D. *Manual of English Rhetoric.* 1875. Cincinnati and New York: Van Antwerp, Bragg, n.d., copyright 1875. Some printings of the Van Antwerp version include 30 pages of exercises (281–310).

Hill, Adams Sherman. *Beginnings of Rhetoric and Composition.* New York: American Book, 1902.

———. *The Foundations of Rhetoric.* New York: Harper, 1892. 8 issues into early twentieth century.

———. *The Principles of Rhetoric and Their Application.* New York: Harper, 1878. 15 issues to 1893. Rev. ed., 1895. *The Principles of Rhetoric.* 7 issues to 1923.

Hill, David Jayne. *Elements of Rhetoric and Composition: A Text-Book for Schools and Colleges.* 1878. New York: Sheldon, n.d., copyright 1884. Rev. and newly electrotyped ed. 1884. Additional printings in 1893 and 1906.

———. *The Science of Rhetoric: An Introduction to the Laws of Effective Discourse.* 1877. New York: Sheldon, 1883. 7 issues to 1905.

Holmes, John. *Art of Rhetoric Made Easy.* London: A. Parker, 1739.

Hope, Matthew Boyd. *The Princeton Text Book in Rhetoric.* Princeton: John T. Robinson, 1859.

Irving, David. *The Elements of English Composition.* London, 1801. Philadelphia: Johnson and Plowman, 1803. 2nd American, 1825.

Jameson, Henry W. *Rhetorical Method.* 1879. 4th ed. St. Louis and New York: G. I. Jones and A. S. Barnes, 1880. 3 surviving issues.

Jamieson, Alexander. *A Grammar of Rhetoric and Polite Literature.* London, 1818. 1st American, 1820. 4th ed. New Haven: A. H. Maltby, 1826. At least 24 issues to 1880s.

Kellogg, Brainerd. *A Text-Book on Rhetoric.* 1880. Rev. ed. 1892. New York: Maynard and Merrill, 1897. 18 issues to 1904.

Knox, Samuel. *A Compendious System of Rhetoric.* Baltimore: Swain and Matchett, 1809.

Lacey, William B. *Illustration of the Principles of Rhetorick: Designed for High Schools, Female Seminaries, and Private Students.* Pittsburgh: Hogan, 1834.

Litch, Samuel. *A Concise Treatise of Retoric: Extracted from the Writings of Dr. Blair, Usher, &c. for the Use of Common Schools and Private Persons.* Jaffrey, NH: Salmon Wilder, 1813.

Lockwood, Sara. *Lessons in English.* 1887. Boston: Ginn, 1892. 12 issues to 1900.

McElroy, John G. R. *The Structure of English Prose.* 1885. New York: A. C. Armstrong, 1895. Issued in 1885, 1886, 1889, 1890, and 1895.

Newcomer, Alphonso. *Elements of Rhetoric: A Course in Plain Prose Composition.* New York: H. Holt, 1898. 5 issues to 1907.

Newman, Samuel P. *A Practical System of Rhetoric.* Portland, ME: William Hyde, 1827. Rev. stereotype ed., 1835. At least 20 U.S. printings.

Nichol, John. *English Composition.* New York: D. Appleton, 1879.

Pearson, Henry G. *The Principles of Composition.* Boston: D. C. Heath, 1898.

Porter, Ebenezer. *Lectures on Eloquence and Style.* Andover, MA: Gould and Newman, 1836.

Quackenbos, George Payn. *Advanced Course of Composition and Rhetoric: A Series of Practical Lessons on the Origin, History, and Peculiarities of the English Language.* New York: D. Appleton, 1855. Copyright 1854. 32 issues to 1889; nearly yearly (1855, 1857–84) with rev. ed., by John D. Quackenbos in 1885, 1888–89.

Quackenbos, John D. *Practical Rhetoric.* New York: American Book, n.d., copyright 1896.

Raub, Albert N. *Practical Rhetoric and Composition.* 1887. Philadelphia: Raub, 1899. Issued in 1887, 1888, 1890, 1891, and 1899.

Scott, Fred Newton, and Joseph V. Denny. *Composition-Rhetoric, for Use in Secondary Schools.* Boston: Allyn and Bacon, 1897. Rev. ed. 1898 and 1911.

———. *Paragraph-Writing.* Ann Arbor, 1891. 3rd ed. Boston: Allyn and Bacon, 1893. At least 8 versions, with several revisions, to 1909.

Spencer, Herbert. *The Philosophy of Style.* New York: D. Appleton, 1871. At least 24 issues.

———. *The Philosophy of Style, Together with an Essay on Style by T. H. Wright.* Ed. Fred Newton Scott. Boston and Chicago: Allyn and Bacon, 1892. 2 issues.

Stirling, John. *A System of Rhetoric.* London: Printed for Thomas Astley, 1733.

Theremin, Francis Franz. *Eloquence a Virtue; or, Outlines of a Systematic Rhetoric.* Trans. William G. T. Shedd. 1850. Andover, MA: W. F. Draper, 1859. The edition was also issued in Boston, New York, and Philadelphia. 1st German ed. 1849.

Waddy, Virginia. *Elements of Composition and Rhetoric.* Richmond, VA, 1888. Cincinnati and New York: American Book, n.d., copyright 1889. Issued in 1889, 1890, and undated (copyright 1889).

Wendell, Barrett. *English Composition: Eight Lectures Given at the Lowell Institute.* New York: Scribner's, 1891. 17 issues to 1918.

Whately, Richard. *Elements of Rhetoric.* London, 1828. Cambridge, MA: James Munroe, 1832. 1st American from 3rd London ed. 15 versions to 1855.

———. *Elements of Rhetoric.* Boston: J. Munroe, 1853. 8 issues to 1861. New York: Sheldon, 1863. 10 issues to copyright 1880. Both versions come from 7th London ed.

———. *Elements of Rhetoric.* New York: Harper, 1852. From 7th London ed. 17 issues to 1893.

Willard, Samuel. *Rhetoric, or, the Principles of Elocution and Rhetorical Composition.* Boston: Leonard C. Bowles, 1830.

Williams, William. *Composition and Rhetoric by Practice, with Exercises, Adapted for Use in High Schools and Colleges.* 1888. Rev. and enl. ed. Boston: D. C. Heath, 1891. 11 issues to 1923.

Witherspoon, John. *Lectures on Moral Philosophy and Eloquence.* 1801–2. Philadelphia: William W. Woodward, 1810.

Readers

The American Educational Fifth Reader. New York and Chicago: Ivison, Blakeman, Taylor, 1873. Reissued by American Book in 1901.

Barnes, Charles J. *Barnes' New National Fifth Reader.* New York: A. S. Barnes and American Book, 1884. Reissued through 1912. Printed in English in Osaka, Japan (1888) and Tokyo (1901).

Bingham, Caleb. *The American Preceptor: Being a Selection of Lessons for Reading and Speaking.* 1794. Boston: Manning and Loring, 1801. This reader went through numerous printings, in Boston; New York; Philadelphia; Troy, New York; Vermont; and New Hampshire, through 1875. *The American Preceptor Improved* appeared in 1819.

———. *The Columbian Orator: Containing a Variety of Original and Selected Pieces; Together with Rules; Calculated to Improve Youth and Others in the Ornamental and Useful Art of Eloquence.* 1797. Boston: Manning and Loring, 1800. Numerous versions through 1865.

Child, Lydia Maria. *The Freedmen's Book.* Boston: Ticknor and Fields, 1865. Rpt. in Morris, *Freedmen's Schools,* vol. 6.

Cobb, Lyman. *Juvenile Reader, No. 3.* Pittsburgh: Luke Loomis, 1831. Cobb's three-volume series was printed 1830–31 in Baltimore and New York as well and was reprinted through the 1840s.

Cole, W. H. *The Institute Reader and Normal Class-Book.* Cincinnati and New York: Van Antwerp, Bragg; Wilson, Hinkle; American Book, 1870.

Cyr, Ellen. *Cyr's Fifth Reader.* Boston: Ginn, 1899. Reprinted in 1901.

The Deseret Sekund Book. Salt Lake City: Regents of Deseret University, 1868. Reader transcribed into the Mormon phonetic alphabet, listed as authorized by the "Regents ov the Deseret Yioonivursity," with illustrations "selected from Willson's Readers" (72). *American Primers* fiche 629.

Enfield, William. *The Speaker; or Miscellaneous Pieces.* London, 1774. 1st American, 1795. Philadelphia: William Wallis Woodward, 1799. At least 8 American printings to 1823.

Gillespie, Mother Angela. *The Metropolitan Fifth Reader.* Intro. by Right Rev. Dr. Spalding. New York and Montreal: D. and J. Sadlier, 1871. A Catholic reader, reprinted in U.S. and Canada through 1891.

Harris, William T., Andrew J. Rickoff, and Mark Bailey. *Appleton's Fifth School Reader.* 1879. New York: D. Appleton, 1881. The *Fifth* was reissued as *The Advanced Reader* in 1887 and remained in print through the decade.

Hart, John S. *Class Book of Prose.* 1845. Philadelphia: E. H. Butler, 1858.

Hillard, G. S. *Sixth Reader.* Elocutionary essays by Mark Bailey. Philadelphia: Eldredge, 1863. Many issues through 1876.

Holmes, George. *Southern Pictorial Third Reader.* New York: Richardson, 1866.

Hows, John W. S. *The Junior Ladies' Reader.* Philadelphia: E. H. Butler, 1860.

———. *The Ladies' Reader.* Philadelphia: E. H. Butler, 1859. At least 7 issues to 1878.

———. *The Practical Elocutionist, and Academical Reader and Speaker.* Philadelphia: Childs and Peterson, 1849.

———. *The Shakespearian Reader.* New York: D. Appleton, 1849. 7 issues to 1875.

Johonnot, James. *Natural History Reader for School and Home.* New York: D. Appleton, 1883.

Leavitt, Joshua. *Easy Lessons in Reading.* 1823. Keene, NH: J. and J. W. Prentiss, 1834. Many issues through 1847. Stereotyped in 1832.

Leigh, Edwin. *Leigh's McGuffey's New Primary Reader, in Pronouncing Orthography.* Cincinnati: Wilson, Hinkle; Van Antwerp Bragg, 1868.

Longley, Elias. *Furst Fonetic Redur.* Boston: Otis Clapp, 1851. A phonetic reader, published in the "Ecselsiur Seriez".

Lyman, Asa. *The American Reader: Containing Elegant Selections in Prose and Poetry.* Portland, ME: A. Lyman, 1810. 2nd edition 1811.

McGuffey, William Holmes, Alexander McGuffey, T. S. Pinneo, et al. *Eclectic Readers.* 6 vols., 1836–present.

    First Eclectic Reader. Cincinnati: Truman and Smith, 1836. Rev. eds. 1841, 1844, 1848, 1853, 1879.

    Second Eclectic Reader. Cincinnati: Truman and Smith, 1836. Rev. eds. 1838, 1841, 1844, 1853, 1879.

    Third Eclectic Reader. Cincinnati: Truman and Smith, 1837. Rev. eds. 1838, 1843, 1848, 1853, 1879.

    Fourth Eclectic Reader. Cincinnati: Truman and Smith, 1837. Rev. eds. 1844, 1848, 1853, 1879.

    Fifth Eclectic Reader. Cincinnati: W. B. Smith, 1844. Rev. eds. 1853, 1879.

    Sixth Eclectic Reader. Cincinnati: W. B. Smith, 1857. Rev. ed. 1879.

———. *McGuffey's High School Reader.* Cincinnati: Wilson, Hinkle, 1857. Rev. ed. *McGuffey's High School and Literary Reader*, 1889.

———. *McGuffey's New Eclectic Speaker.* Cincinnati: W. B. Smith, American Book, 1858.

———. *McGuffey's New High School Reader for Advanced Classes, with 200 Classic Exercises.* Cincinnati: W. B. Smith, 1857. Rev. ed. 1885.

———. *McGuffey's New Juvenile Speaker.* Cincinnati: Wilson, Hinkle, 1860.

———. *McGuffey's Rhetorical Guide; or Fifth Reader of the Eclectic Series.* Cincinnati: W. B. Smith, 1844. Rev. ed. 1853.

Monroe, Lewis B. *Monroe's Sixth Reader.* Philadelphia: Cowperthwait, 1872. Reissued 1873.

Moore, J. Hamilton. *The Young Gentleman and Lady's Monitor, and English Teacher's Assistant*. London, c. 1760. 1st American, 1790. Albany, NY: Charles R. and George Webster, 1803. The subtitle describes this volume as a "Collection of Select Pieces from our Best Modern Writers . . . particularly adapted for the Use of our eminent Schools and Academies, as well as private Persons, who have not an Opportunity of perusing the Works of those celebrated Authors." This British collection was widely printed through 1818 in New York, Connecticut, Vermont, Delaware, and Zanesville, OH.

Moore, Mrs. M. B. *The First Dixie Reader; to Succeed the Dixie Primer*. Raleigh, NC: Christian Advocate, 1863.

Murray, Lindley. *The English Reader; or, Pieces in Prose and Poetry*. York, Eng., 1799. 1st American, 1799. Philadelphia: Joseph McDowell, 1829. There were hundreds of printings of this reader across the country through the 1850s, some of which add pronouncing exercises.

———. *Introduction to the English Reader*. York, Eng., 1801. Philadelphia: Benjamin and Jacob Johnson, 1801.

———. *Sequel to the English Reader*. York, Eng., 1800. New York: Isaac Collins, 1801.

New York Reader, Nos. 1–3. New York: Samuel Wood, 1812–15. *Early American Imprints* Ser. 2, microphages 26297, 29358, and 41648.

Oldham, Oliver. *Amusing and Instructive Reader*. New York: Ivison and Phinney, 1854.

Osgood, Lucius. *American Readers: For Schools and Families*. 6 vols. Pittsburgh: A. H. English, 1870–73.

———. *Progressive Readers*. 5 vols. Pittsburgh: A. H. English, 1855–58.

Parker, Richard Green. *Progressive Exercises in Rhetorical Reading*. Boston: Crocker and Brewster, 1836. Although copyrighted in Jan. 1835, a note indicates its publication was delayed until May 1836. Regularly issued through the 1860s.

Picket, Albert. *The Juvenile Mentor*. New York: Smith and Forman, 1809.

Pierpont, John. *American First Class Book*. Boston: Cummings, Hilliard, 1823. This advanced reader remains in print through 1854, as did the subsequent prequels.

———. *Introduction to the National Reader*. Boston: Carter, Hendee, 1828.

———. *The National Reader*. Boston: Richardson, Lord, and Holbrook, 1827.

———. *The New Reader*. Philadelphia: Lippincott, Grambo, 1854. Subtitled "to follow 'The Young Reader' in the Common Schools of the U.S." Some copies titled "Pierpont's Third Reader."

———. *The Young Reader*. 1830. New York: George F. Cooledge, 1835. This first reader is subtitled "to go with the spelling book."

Pinneo, Timothy S. *The Hemans Reader for Female Schools*. New York: Clark, Austin, and Smith; Cincinnati: W. B. Smith, 1847.

Porter, Ebenezer. *The Rhetorical Reader.* 1831. Andover, MA: Gould and New-man; New York: Leavitt, Lord, 1832. This reader went through hundreds of printings, first locally in Andover, then in major markets (New York, Chicago), with a "new and enlarged" edition copyright in 1848. An 1855 edition added 200 pages of "additional exercises" by James N. McElligott. It remained in print through the 1860s.

Riggs, Stephen Return, trans. *Wayawa Tokaheya* [First Reader]. Adapted from *Model First Reader* by J. Russell Webb. Chicago: George Sherwood, 1873. English-language reader adapted with interlined Dakota translations. Both model reader and the Dakota reader have rare colored illustrations.

Robbins, Eliza. *American Popular Lessons: Chiefly Selected from the Writings of Mrs. Barbauld, Miss Edgeworth.* 1820. New York: R. Lockwood, 1829. Reissued often through 1848. A sequel appeared in 1827.

Roemer, Jean. *Polyglot Reader, and Guide for Translation.* 5 vols. New York: D. Appleton, 1855–56. This series prints an English-language reader and four translated volumes, in French, German, Spanish, and Italian. 7 issues through 1890.

Russell, Anna, and William Russell. *Introduction to the Young Ladies' Elocution-ary Reader.* Boston: James Munroe, 1845. Reissued 1857.

———. *The Young Ladies' Elocutionary Reader.* Boston: James Munroe, 1845. 4 reissues through 1853.

Sanders, Charles W. *High School Reader.* New York: Ivison, Phinney, 1856. Reissued through 1864.

———. *School Readers.* 6 vols. New York: Ivison, Phinney, 1840–62. Reissued through 1870s.

———. *Union Fifth Reader.* New York: Ivison, Phinney, 1867. Part of the 5 vol. *Union Series,* in print through 1878. The *Union Fourth* was printed in English in Tokyo in 1882. Sanders also compiled a larger (600-page) *Rhetorical, or Union Fifth Reader* in 1862–66.

———. *Young Ladies' Reader.* New York: Ivison and Phinney, 1855. Reissued through 1866.

Sargent, Epes. *The Standard Speaker.* 1852. Philadelphia: Charles Desilver, 1856. Many issues through 1870. In 1857, Epes added "primary" and "interme-diate" speakers.

Sigourney, Lydia. *Girl's Reading Book.* New York: J. Orville Taylor, 1837. Many issues through 1847. Reissued as *The Girl's Book,* 1852, 4 issues to 1868.

Swinton, William. *Fifth Reader and Speaker.* New York: American Book, 1883.

———. *Seven American Classics: Supplementary to the Fifth Reader.* New York: Ivison, Blakeman, Taylor, 1880. 3 issues to 1908.

Swinton, William, and George Cathcart. *Seven British Classics: Supplementary to the Fifth Reader.* New York: Ivison, Blakeman, Taylor, 1880. Reissued 1908.

Town, Salem. *The Progressive Fourth Reader.* Boston: Sanborn, Carter, Bazin, 1857. Reissued 1864, 1866.

[Warren, Israel Perkins.] *The Freedman's Third Reader.* Boston: American Tract Society, 1866. Rpt. in Morris, *Freedmen's Schools,* vol. 2.

Watson, J. Madison. *Independent Sixth Reader: Containing a Complete Scientific and Practical Treatise on Elocution.* New York, Chicago, and New Orleans: A. S. Barnes, 1871, 1877.

Webb, J. Russell. *Model First Reader.* Chicago: George Sherwood, 1873. This reader, used as a "template" for Stephen R. Riggs's Dakota reader, *Wayawa Tokaheya* [First Reader], has rare colored illustrations.

Webster, Noah. *An American Selection of Lessons in Reading and Speaking. The Third Part of the Grammatical Institute of the English Language.* Hartford, CT: Hudson and Goodwin, 1785.

Wells, William. *Wilmsen's Reader, or, The Children's Friend.* Trans. and adapt. of *Deutsche Kinderfreund für Schule and Haus* by Friedrich P. Wilmsen. Berlin, 1831. Philadelphia: Thomas, Cowperthwait, 1845. Subtitle reads, "adapted to the use of schools in the U.S." F. Wilmsen's textbook is noted as "a work which has long held the first rank in the celebrated schools of Prussia." Reissued 1847, 1854.

Willson, Marcius. *Harper's Sixth Reader of the United States Series.* New York: Harper, 1872. Issues to 1900. Willson also compiled the 6-vol. *Popular Series* (Philadelphia, 1880).

———. *School and Family Readers.* 5 vols. New York: Harper, 1860.

Composition Books

Booth, David. *The Principles of English Composition.* 1831. London: John Taylor, 1840.

Boyd, James R. *Elements of English Composition.* 1860. New York: A. S. Barnes, 1871. Reprinted through the 1880s.

Brookfield, F. *First Book in Composition.* New York: A. S. Barnes, 1855. Other issues in 1856 and 1867.

Chittenden, Lucy A. *The Elements of English Composition.* 1884. Chicago: S. C. Griggs, 1890. At least 7 issues to 1899.

Conklin, Benjamin Y. *A Complete Graded Course in English Grammar and Composition.* 1888. New York: D. Appleton, 1889.

DeGarmo, Charles. *Language Lessons, Book One.* New York: Werner School Book, 1897.

Frost, John. *Easy Exercises in Composition: Designed for the Use of Beginners.* 1839. 2nd ed. (stereotyped). Philadelphia: W. Marshall, 1839. One month after the 1st edition appeared, the (stereotyped) 2nd edition was issued by the same publisher. It adds several illustrations and a short section on dialogue writing. Last published in 1843.

Gideon, Edward. *Lessons in Language.* Philadelphia: Eldredge, 1888.

Hadley, Hiram. *Lessons in Language.* Chicago: Hadley Bros., 1871. Flourished in the 1870s.

Hall, William D. *Rand McNally Primary Grammar and Composition.* Chicago: Rand, McNally, 1897.

Harper, Mary J. *Practical Composition.* New York: Scribner's, 1870.

Hart, John S. *First Lessons in Composition.* 1870. Philadelphia: Eldredge, 1886. Flourished in the 1870s.

Harvey, Thomas W. *First Lessons in the English Language.* Cincinnati: Wilson, Hinkle, 1875. Flourished in the 1870s; last publication was 1903.

Hyde, Mary Frances. *Practical Lessons in the Use of English.* 1887. Boston: D. C. Heath, 1899. Flourished in the 1880s and 1890s.

Kavana, Rose M., and Arthur Beatty. *Composition and Rhetoric.* Chicago: Rand, McNally, 1902.

Keeler, Harriet L., and Emma Davis. *Studies in English Composition: With Lessons in Language and Rhetoric.* Boston: Allyn and Bacon, 1892.

Kerl, Simon. *Elements of Composition and Rhetoric.* New York: Ivison, Phinney, Blakeman, 1869. 2nd issue in 1871.

Knighton, Frederick. *The Young Composer.* Philadelphia: Robert E. Peterson, 1853. The only other year of publication was 1854.

Mead, William Edward. *Elementary Composition and Rhetoric.* Boston: Leach, Shewell, and Sanborn, 1894.

Metcalf, Robert C., and Orville T. Bright. 1889. *Language Lessons.* 2 vols. New York: American Book, 1894–96.

Newcomer, Alphonso. *A Practical Course in English Composition.* Boston: Ginn, 1893.

Parker, Richard Green. *Aids to English Composition.* Boston: Robert C. Davis, 1844. Flourished through the mid-1870s.

———. *Progressive Exercises in English Composition.* 1832. Boston: Lincoln and Edmands, 1833 stereotype ed. A very long run; flourished through the 1870s.

Quackenbos, George Payn. *First Lessons in Composition.* New York: D. Appleton, 1851. Flourished through the 1860s and appears as late as 1886.

Reed, Alonzo, and Brainerd Kellogg. *One-Book Course in English.* 1888. New York: Maynard, Merrill, 1895. In print through 1910.

Rippingham, John. *Rules for English Composition, and Particularly for Themes.* London, 1811? Poughkeepsie, NY: Paraclete Potter, 1816. Several issues to 1820.

Russell, William. *A Grammar of Composition.* New Haven, CT: A. H. Maltby, 1823.

Swinton, William. *Language Lessons: Introductory Grammar and Composition for Intermediate and Grammar Grades.* 1873. New York: Harper, 1877. Flourished in the 1870s.

————. *New Language Lessons: An Elementary Grammar and Composition.* New York: American Book, 1877.

Walker, John. *The Teacher's Assistant in English Composition.* London, 1801; Carlisle, PA: G. Kline, 1804. A London version appeared as late as 1838. Several versions printed with a variant title: *English Themes and Essays, or the Teacher's Assistant.*

Welsh, Alfred H. *English Composition.* 1889. New York: Silver, Burdett, 1896.

Elocutionary Treatises

The Art of Reading: Rules for the Attainment of a Just and Correct Enunciation of Written Language; Mostly Selected from Walker's Elements of Elocution, and Adapted to the Use of Schools. Boston: Cummings, Hilliard, 1826.

Austin, Gilbert. *Chironomia; or a Treatise on Rhetorical Delivery.* London: T. Cadell and W. Davies, 1806; facsim. ed. Ed. Mary Margaret Robb and Lester Thonssen. Carbondale: Southern Illinois UP, 1966.

Bailey, Mark. *Introductory Treatise on Elocution.* Boston: Brewer and Tileston, 1863.

Mason, John. *Essay on Elocution, or Pronunciation.* London, 1748. Boston, 1809. Montpelier, VT, 1819.

Porter, Ebenezer. *Analysis of the Principles of Rhetorical Delivery, as Applied to Reading and Speaking.* Andover, MA: Mark Newman, 1827.

Rush, James. *The Philosophy of the Human Voice.* 1827. 2nd ed. Philadelphia: Grigg and Elliot, 1833. 7 editions to 1879.

Russell, William. *Orthophony, or Vocal Culture.* 1845. Rev. ed. by Francis T. Russell, 1882. Boston: Houghton, Mifflin, 1895. Claims an 82nd printing by 1900.

Sheridan, Thomas. *A Course of Lectures on Elocution.* London: E. Strahan, 1762.

Walker, John. *A Rhetorical Grammar, or Course of Lessons in Elocution.* London, 1785. American eds. from 3rd London. Boston: J. T. Buckingham; Cummings and Hilliard, 1814, 1822. Rpt. Menston, Eng.: Scolar Press, 1971.

Grammars

Brown, Goold. *Catechism of English Grammar.* New York: Samuel Wood, 1827.

Bullions, Peter. *Practical Lessons in English Grammar and Composition.* New York: Pratt, Woodford, Framer and Brace, 1854. There may be an earlier edition.

Burr, Jonathan. *A Compendium of English Syntax.* 3rd ed., rev. and enl. Boston: James Loring, 1818. This 36-pg. compendium was designed as an appendix to Murray's grammar.

Chessman, Daniel. *Compendium of English Grammar.* 3rd ed. corr. Hallowell, ME: Goodale, Glazier, 1821. This 24-pg. compendium of "all that is necessary to be committed to memory by students" is an abridgement from Lindley Murray's "excellent treatise."

Cobbett, William. *A Grammar of the English Language.* London, 1818. New York, 1819. New York: Peter Eckler, 1901.

Fowle, William Bentley. *North American Grammar, Part First.* Boston: Jenks and Palmer, 1842.

Frazee, Bradford. *Improved Grammar of the English Language.* 2nd ed. Philadelphia: Sorin and Ball, 1845.

Frost, John. *Elements of English Grammar with Progressive Exercises in Parsing.* Boston: Richardson, Lord, and Holbrook, 1828.

———. *Five Hundred Progressive Exercises in Parsing.* 2nd ed. Boston: Hilliard, Gray, Little, and Watson, 1828.

———. *A Practical English Grammar.* Philadelphia: Thomas, Cowperthwait, 1842.

Green, Richard W. *Inductive Exercises in English Grammar.* 1829. Philadelphia: Uriah Hunt, 1831.

Greene, Roscoe. *Grammar for Children.* 3rd ed. Boston: Samuel Colman, 1835.

———. *A Practical Grammar of the English Language.* 2nd ed. Portland: Shirley and Hyde, 1830.

Ingersoll, Charles M. *Conversations on Etymology and Syntax.* Philadelphia: Bennett and Walton, 1822.

Jaudon, Daniel. *The Union Grammar.* 1812. Philadelphia: Tower and Hogan, 1828.

Locke, John. *English Grammar for Children.* Cincinnati: W. M. and O. Farnsworth Jr., 1827.

Lowth, Robert. *A Short Introduction to English Grammar.* London 1762. 1st American, 1775. Cambridge, MA: Hilliard and Metcalf, 1811.

M'Culloch, John Murray. *A Manual of English Grammar.* London: Simpkin and Marshall, 1834.

Morley, Charles. *Common School Grammar.* Hartford, CT: Henry Benton, 1836.

Murray, Lindley. *An Abridgment of L. Murray's English Grammar.* York, Eng., 1797. Philadelphia, 1797. Many different abridgments appear throughout the century.

———. *English Exercises, Adapted to the Grammar lately Published by L. Murray.* York, Eng., 1797. Baltimore: Warner and Hanna, 1805. Many versions throughout the century.

———. *English Grammar: Adapted to the Different Classes of Learners.* York, Eng., 1795. 1st American, 1800. New York: Collins, Perkins, 1897. Murray's *Grammar* appeared in many versions throughout the century, including abridgements, compendiums, and exercises. The Nietz Collection, for example, lists many copies of various versions, including 73 grammars, 87 abridgements, 32 exercises, and an 1837 translation into Dutch.

Parker, Richard Green, and Charles Fox. *Progressive Exercises in English Grammar, Part 1: Containing the Principles of Analysis or English Parsing.* Boston: Crocker and Brewster, 1834.

————. *Progressive Exercises in English Grammar, Part 2: Containing the Principles of the Synthesis or Construction of the English Language.* Boston: Crocker and Brewster, 1835.

————. *Progressive Exercises in English Grammar, Part 3: Containing the Rules of Orthography and Punctuation, the Principles of Etymology and the Prosody of the English Language, with an Appendix.* Boston: Crocker and Brewster, 1840.

Wilmer, Lambert. *English Grammar.* Philadelphia: J. W. Macclefield, 1849.

Primers

Claus, Daniel. *Indian Primer.* London: C. Buckton, 1786.

McGuffey's Eclectic Primer for Young Children. Cincinnati: Truman and Smith, 1838. The primer was revised in 1841; in 1849 it was divided into two versions: *Smaller Eclectic Primer* and *Pictorial Eclectic Primer* (Cincinnati: W. B. Smith), which were revised in 1857 as the *Eclectic Primer* and *McGuffey's First Reader* and revised again in 1879.

Murray, Lindley. *A First Book for Children.* York, Eng., 1801. New York: Collins, Perkins, 1805. Reissued steadily in New Eng. and NY; also Richmond, VA; and Charleston, SC, through 1829. Reprinted in Quebec in 1838, 1856.

The New-England Primer. [1697.] Boston: S. Kneeland and T. Green, 1727. N. pag. The 1727 version is the oldest extant copy, although records indicate earlier versions. Multiple versions of the primer were widely published by local printers through 1830, appearing as well in facsimile versions as early as 1848.

Osgood, Lucius. *Osgood's American Primer.* Pittsburgh: H. I. Gurley and A. H. English, 1870.

Willard, Samuel. *The Franklin Primer.* Boston: J. M. Dunham, 1802. Reissued through 1831.

Spellers

Barry, John. *The Philadelphia Spelling Book.* Philadelphia: Joseph James, 1790. Reissued through 1814.

Henderson, N. P. *Test Words in English Orthography.* New York: Clark and Maynard, 1870. Reissued through 1920.

McGuffey's Eclectic Spelling Book. Cincinnati: W. B. Smith, 1838. Rev. ed. 1846. Issued through 1865. *Alternative Spelling Book* printed 1888.

Moore, Mrs. M. B. *The Dixie Speller.* Raleigh, NC: Christian Advocate, 1864.

Murray, Lindley. *An English Spelling-Book: With Reading Lessons.* York, Eng., 1804. Baltimore: G. Dobbins and Murphy, 1806. Reprinted regularly in

Eng. and U.S. through mid-century. Michael claims at least 51 British editions to 1854 and 13 American editions to 1829.

Sheldon's Word Studies: Graded Lessons in the Orthography of Words, and their Correct Use in Sentences. New York and Chicago: Sheldon, 1886.

Stickney, J. H. *Stickney's Word by Word: Advanced.* Boston: Ginn, 1890. Issues through 1898.

Town, Salem. *Spelling and Defining Book.* Portland, ME: Sanborn and Carter, 1838, 1863. Flourished through 1890s.

Warren, Israel Perkins. *The Freedmen's Spelling-Book.* Boston: American Tract Society, 1865. Rpt. in Morris, *Freedmen's Schools,* vol. 2.

Webster, Noah. *The Elementary Spelling Book.* Pt. 1 of Webster's *Grammatical Institute.* Hartford, CT: Hudson and Goodwin, 1783. Reissued as *The American Spelling Book* in 1787, with a major revision in 1829. Commonly referred to by its binding, as Webster's "blue-back speller."

Other Textbooks

Alcott, William A. *Slate and Black-board Exercises.* New York: Mark H. Newman, 1842. Reading, PA: H. A. Lantz, 1857.

Andrews, E. A., and S. Stoddard. *A Grammar of the Latin Language.* Boston: Crocker and Brewster, 1836. This grammar remained in print throughout the century, supplemented by Andrews's *Latin Exercises* (Boston: Crocker and Brewster, 1837), and in 1847 by the first part of Jacobs and Döring's *Latin Reader.*

Bingham, William. *A Latin Reader, Adapted to Bingham's Latin Grammar.* 1869. Rev. by W. Gordon MacCabe. Philadelphia: E. H. Butler, 1886.

Broadus, John. *A Treatise on the Preparation and Delivery of Sermons.* 1870. Rev. ed., by Edwin Charles Dargan. New York: George Doran, 1898. Flourished for some 50 years; a 1926 version claims to be 42nd edition.

Burgess, Walton. *Five Hundred Mistakes of Daily Occurrence in Speaking, Pronouncing, and Writing the English Language, Corrected.* Philadelphia: D. Burgess; J. B. Lippincott, 1856. This 73-page list of mistakes was frequently reprinted. An 1875 version claims to be a "32nd edition."

Campbell, George. *Lectures on Systematic Theology and Pulpit Eloquence.* London, 1807. Boston: W. Wells and T. Ward, 1810.

Child, Lydia Maria. *The [Little] Girl's Own Book.* 1831. Boston: Carter, Hendee, and Babcock. Enl. ed. New York: Clark Austin, 1834. The 1831 edition was bound as *The Little Girl's Own Book,* although the title page, preface, and running heads refer to *The Girl's Own Book,* the title used in subsequent versions.

Comenius, John Amos. *Orbis Sensualium Pictus.* 1658. Trans. Charles Hoole. *The Visible World; A Nomenclature, and Pictures of All the Chief Things That Are in the World.* New York: T. and J. Swords, 1810. 1st American, from the 12th London ed., which describes the translation as "for the use of young Latine-scholars." A 1791 London edition "rendered" the language "easy to the capacities of children".

Ely, John. *The Child's Instructor.* 1802. Philadelphia: Mathew Carey, 1807.

Frost, John. *Pictorial History of the United States.* Philadelphia: B. Walker, 1844. Gordon McGabe. Philadelphia: E. H. Butler, 1886.

Goodrich, Samuel. *Tales of Peter Parley about America.* 1827. 2nd rev. ed. Boston: Carter, Hendee, 1828.

Hart, John. *A Methode, or Comfortable Beginning for All Unlearned.* London, 1570.

Harkness, Albert. *Second Latin Book.* New York: D. Appleton, 1853.

Jacobs, Frederic. *The Greek Reader.* Boston: Hilliard, Gray, Little, and Wilkins, 1827. From the 7th German ed. Various versions of this reader appeared throughout the century, adapted to different Greek grammars, and the book launched a modern imitator, *Elementary German Reader: On the Plan of Jacob's Greek Reader* (New York: D. Appleton, 1857).

Jacobs, Frederic, and Frederic W. Döring. *The Latin Reader, Pt. 1 and 2.* Boston: Hilliard, 1825. Adaptations appeared in 1830, 1837, 1846.

Jenkins, John. *The Art of Writing.* Andover, MA: Flagg and Gould, 1813.

Kames, Lord Henry Home. *Elements of Criticism.* Edinburgh, 1762. Ed. Abraham Mills. Stereotyped in 1833. New York: Huntington and Savage, 1847. 21 issues to 1889.

———. *Elements of Criticism: With Omissions, Additions and a New Analysis.* Ed. James R. Boyd. New York: A. S. Barnes 1855. 19 issues to 1880s.

———. *An Abridgement of Elements of Criticism.* Ed. John Frost. Philadelphia: Towar, J. and D. M. Hogan; Pittsburgh: Hogan, 1831. 12 issues to 1877.

Mayo, Elizabeth. *Lessons on Common Things.* Ed. John Frost. Philadelphia: Thomas T. Ash, 1835.

———. *Lessons on Things.* Ed. John Frost. Philadelphia: Carey and Lea, 1831.

McClintock, John. *Second Book in Latin.* New York: Harper, 1853.

Phelps, Austin. *English Style in Public Discourse with Special References to the Usages of the Pulpit.* New York: Scribner's, 1883. 8 issues to 1915.

———. *The Theory of Preaching: Lectures on Homiletics.* New York: Scribner's, 1881. At least 11 printings to 1914.

Philbrick, John. *The Primary Union Speaker.* Boston: Thompson, Brown. 1866.

Richardson, Charles. *A Primer of American Literature.* 1883. Boston: Houghton, Mifflin, 1891.

Sanders, Charles W. *Sanders' Bilder Fibel.* Trans. of *Pictorial Primer.* New York: Ivison, Blakeman, Taylor, 1846. This German translation reissued 1870, 1890.

Swinton, William. *Harper's School Geography.* New York: Harper, 1876.

———. *Introductory Geography in Readings and Recitations.* New York and Chicago: American Book, and Ivison, Blakeman, 1882.

Todd, John. *The Student's Manual*. 1835. Rev. ed. 1854. Northampton: Bridgman and Childs, 1874. Many issues through 1880s, including London versions in 1839–54.

Trench, Richard Chenevix. *On the Study of Words*. 1832. From 2nd ed. London, 1851. New York: Redfield, 1856. Some 40 American issues from 1852 to 1927.

Walker, Sidney Charles. *The New Latin Reader.* Boston: Richardson and Lord, 1829.

Webster, Noah. *A Grammatical Institute of the English Language.* (part 1) *A Standard of Pronunciation;* (part 2) *A Plain and Comprehensive Grammar;* (part 3) *An American Selection of Lessons in Reading and Speaking.* Hartford, CT: Hudson and Goodwin, 1783. Pt. 1 reissued in 1787 as *The American Spelling Book,* and pt. 3 reissued in 1785 as a reader. Many versions of these various parts and wholes appear through the 1830s.

Wilmsen, Friedrich P. *Der Deutsche Kinderfreund: Ein Lesebuch für Volksschulen.* Berlin, 1830. Philadelphia: German Lutheran, St. Michael and Zion, 1830. 1st American from 6th German ed. Over 200 issues in Germany. Trans. and adapt. by William Wells as *The Children's Friend,* 1845.

Woodbury, W. H. *Eclectic German Readers.* 5 vols. New York: Ivison and Phinney, 1852.

Other Primary Materials

Abbott, Jacob. *Rollo at School*. Boston: T. H. Carter, 1838. Reissued in London, 1839.

———. *Rollo Learning to Read, or, Easy Stories for Young Children*. Boston: Gould, Kendall, and Lincoln, 1835. Reissued in the 28-vol. Rollo series without the subtitle. Many issues, including a London version (1847) through 1870s.

Addams, Jane. *Twenty Years at Hull-House, with Autobiographical Notes*. New York: Macmillan, 1910.

Alcott, Louisa May. *Jack and Jill: A Village Story*. Boston: Roberts Bros., 1880.

———. *Jo's Boys*. Boston: Roberts Bros., 1886.

———. *Little Men: Life at Plumfield with Jo's Boys*. Boston: Roberts Bros., 1871.

———. *Little Women*. Boston: Roberts Bros., 1868.

Alger, Horatio. *Ragged Dick*. Boston: A. K. Loring, 1868.

Barbour, Florus Alonzo. *The Teaching of English Grammar.* Boston: Ginn, 1901.

Barnard, Henry. *American Journal of Education*. 1855–82.

———. *Pestalozzi and His Educational System*. Rpt. of *Pestalozzi and Pestalozzianism*. New York, 1862. Syracuse, NY: C. W. Bardeen, 1874.

Beman, Amos Gerry. "The Education of the Colored People." *Anglo-African Magazine* 1 (1859): 337–40.

Bingham, Caleb. *Juvenile Letters*. Boston: Carlisle, 1805.

[Bowen, Francis]. Review of *Thoughts for the Present Collegiate System in the U. S. 1842*, by Francis Wayland. *North American Review* 67 (Oct. 1842): 302–43.

Burton, Warren. *The District School as It Was*. 1833. Ed. Clifton Johnson. Boston: Lee and Shepard, 1897.

Catalogue of the Officers and Students of the Harvard University in Cambridge. Cambridge: Hilliard and Metcalf, 1820.

Chace, Elizabeth Buffum, and Lucy Buffum Lovell. *Two Quaker Sisters*. New York: Liveright, 1937.

Child, Lydia Maria. *Selected Letters, 1817–1880*. Ed. Milton Meltzer and Patricia G. Holland, with Francine Krasno. Amherst: U of Massachusetts P, 1982.

Clark, Davis W. *Mental Discipline: With Reference to the Acquisition and Communication of Knowledge, and to Education Generally: To Which Is Appended a Topical Course of Theological Study*. New York: Lane and Tippett, 1847. For the Methodist Episcopal Church.

Clark, S. H. *How to Teach Reading in the Public Schools*. Chicago: Scott, Foresman, 1899.

Committee of Ten of the National Education Association (NEA). *Report of the Committee of Ten on Secondary School Studies*. New York: American Book, 1894.

Coolidge, Susan [Sarah Chauncey Woolsey]. *What Katy Did at School*. 1873. Bristol, Eng.: Parragon, 1999.

Cushing, William. *Index to the North American Review, Vols. 1–125, 1815–1877*. Cambridge, MA: John Wilson, 1878. Rpt. in *ATQ* 4 (1969): 83–160.

Dewey, Orville. "Principles of Elocution." *North American Review* 29 (July 1829): 38–67.

"Dewey, Orville." *National Cyclopaedia of American Biography*. New York: J. T. White, 1891. 5: 47–48.

Dillaway, Charles K. "Education, Past and Present. The Rise of Free Education and Educational Institutions." *The Memorial History of Boston, 1630–1880*. Ed. Justin Winsor. Vol. 4. Boston: Ticknor, 1881. 235–78.

Douglass, Frederick. *Narrative of the Life of Frederick Douglass, An American Slave, Written by Himself*. *The Oxford Frederick Douglass Reader*. Ed. William L. Andrews. New York: Oxford UP, 1966. 21–97.

Eggleston Edward. *The Hoosier Schoolmaster: A Story of Backwoods Life in Indiana*. 1871. Rev. New York: Grosset and Dunlap, 1913.

Eliot, Charles W. *Harvard Memories*. Cambridge: Harvard UP, 1923.

———. "Inaugural Address." *Addresses at the Inauguration of Charles William Eliot*. Cambridge, MA: Sever and Francis, 1869. Rpt. in Hofstadter and Smith 2: 601–24.

———. *The Tendency to the Concrete and Practical in Modern Education*. Boston: Houghton Mifflin, 1913.

Emerson, Ellen Tucker. *The Letters of Ellen Tucker Emerson*. Ed. Edith E. W. Gregg. 2 vols. Kent, OH: Kent State UP, 1982.

Emerson, Ralph Waldo. *The Collected Works of Ralph Waldo Emerson*. 6 vols. to date. Ed. Alfred R. Ferguson, Jean Ferguson Carr, Joseph Slater, et al. Cambridge: Harvard UP, 1971–.

———. *The Journals and Miscellaneous Notebooks of Ralph Waldo Emerson*. 16 vols. Ed. William Gilman, Alfred R. Ferguson, et al. Cambridge: Harvard UP, 1965–95.

———. *The Letters of Ralph Waldo Emerson*. 6 vols. Ed. Ralph Rusk. New York: Columbia UP, 1939.

———. "Quotation and Originality." *Letters and Social Aims*. 1876. *The Complete Works of Ralph Waldo Emerson*. Ed. Edward W. Emerson. Boston: Houghton Mifflin, 1904. 8: 175–204.

Fowler, Henry. *The American Pulpit*. Boston: Ticknor and Fields, 1856.

Genung, John F. *Study of Rhetoric in the College Course*. Boston: D. C. Heath, 1887.

Griswold, Rufus. *The Prose Writers of America*. Philadelphia: A. Hart, 1846, 1852. Rpt. New York: Garrett, 1969.

Hall, Baynard. *Teaching, a Science; The Teacher, an Artist*. New York: Baker and Scribner, 1848.

Hall, Samuel. *Lectures on School-Keeping*. Boston: Richardson, Lord, and Holbrook, 1829.

Hart, John S. *In the School-Room: Chapters in the Philosophy of Education*. Philadelphia: Eldredge, 1868.

Hawthorne, Nathaniel. *The Scarlet Letter: A Romance*. Boston: Ticknor, Reed, and Fields, 1850.

Hinsdale, Burke. *Teaching the Language Arts*. New York: D. Appleton, 1896.

Holbrook, Josiah. *American Lyceum, or Society for the Improvement of Schools and Diffusion of Useful Knowledge*. Boston: Marvin, 1829.

Jardine, George. *Outlines of a Philosophical Education*. Glasgow: A. and J. Duncan, 1818.

Johnson, Samuel. *Dictionary of the English Language*. 2 vols. London, 1755.

Jones, Charles C. *The Religious Instruction of the Negroes in the United States*. Savannah, GA: Thomas Purse, 1842.

Jones, William. *Letters from a Tutor to His Pupils*. London: G. Robinson, 1780.

[Kingsley, James Luce]. Review of *A Life of Washington in Latin, for the Use of the Schools*, by Francisco Glass. *North American Review* 43 (July 1836): 28–52.

Krusi, Hermann. *Pestalozzi: His Life, Work, and Influence*. Cincinnati: Wilson, Hinkle, 1875.

Larcom, Lucy. *A New England Girlhood: Outlined from Memory*. Boston: Houghton Mifflin, 1889. Rpt. Boston: Northeastern UP, 1986.

Lawson, John. *Lectures Concerning Oratory.* Dublin: George Faulkner, 1759.

Mann, Horace. *Lectures on Education.* Boston: Ide and Dutton, 1855. Rpt. New York: Arno, 1969.

———. "Prussian School Classification." *Readings in Public Education in the United States.* Ed. Ellwood P. Cubberley, Boston: Houghton Mifflin, 1934. 287–88.

Marvel, Ik [Donald G. Mitchell]. *Dream Life: A Fable of the Seasons.* 1851. New York: Crowell, 1900.

———. *Reveries of a Bachelor: Or, A Book of the Heart.* New York: Baker and Scribner, 1851.

Mason, John. *A Treatise on Self-Knowledge.* London, 1745. Worcester, MA: Isaiah Thomas, 1789.

Matthews, Brander. *Americanisms and Briticisms: With Other Essays on Other Isms.* New York: Harper, 1892.

McGuffey, William Holmes. "Conversation in a Class Room." *Monthly Chronicle of Interesting and Useful Knowledge.* Mar. 1839: 147–49. Rpt. in Westerhoff 194–201.

———. "General Education." *Western Monthly Magazine.* 1834. Rpt. in Westerhoff 164–71.

———. "Lectures on the Relative Duties of Parents and Teachers." *Transactions of Fifth Western Institute and College for Professional Teachers.* Cincinnati: Executive Commission, 1835. 129–51. Rpt. in Westerhoff 171–93.

———. "Report on the Most Efficient Methods of Conducting Exams in Common School High Schools and Academies." *Transactions of Sixth Western Institute and College for Professional Teachers.* Ed. D. C. Talbott. Cincinnati: Executive Commission, 1836. 239–43. Rpt. in Westerhoff 201–6.

McKean, Joseph. *Lectures on Rhetoric and Oratory, 1809–1816.* Lecture XI. *Papers of Joseph McKean, 1816–1818.* Harvard University Archives. Pusey Library. HUG 1546.49.

Murray, Lindley. *Narratives of Colored Americans.* Ed. Alexander Mott [Abigail Field Mott] and M. S. Wood. New York: William Wood, 1877. Rpt. Freeport, NY: Books for Libraries, 1977.

National Education Association Committee of Fifteen Report on Elementary Education. Chicago: American Book, 1895.

Parker, Edward G. *The Golden Age of American Oratory.* Boston: Whittmore, Niles, and Hall, 1854.

Parker, Richard Green. "On the Teaching of Composition in the Schools." *Proceedings and Lectures of the American Institute of Instruction.* Boston: James Munroe, 1838. 182–207.

Payne, George. *Elements of Mental and Moral Science.* London: B. J. Holdsworth, 1828.

Phelps, Elizabeth Stuart. *Gypsy's Year at the Golden Crescent.* Boston: Graves and Young, 1867.

Porter, Noah. *Books and Reading; or, What Book Shall I Read.* New York: Scribner, Armstrong, 1870.

"Reynolds on the Use of the Eyes." Rev. of *Hints to Students on the Use of the Eyes,* by Edward Reynolds. *Biblical Repertory* (July 1833). *American Annals of Education* 5 (Jan. 1835): 35–39.

Roorbach, Orville. *Bibliotheca Americana.* 1852. New York: Peter Smith, 1939.

"School Books in the United States." *American Annals of Education* 2 (July 1832): 371–84. This periodical, edited in 1832 by W. C. Woodbridge, was popularly known as "Russell's Journal of Education," after William Russell, its founder and first editor.

Sedgwick, Catharine Maria. *A New-England Tale.* New York: E. Bliss and E. White, 1822.

Shepherd, William, Jeremiah Joyce, and Lant Carpenter. *Systematic Education.* London: Longmans, 1815.

Stoddard, Elizabeth. *The Morgesons.* New York: Carlton, 1862.

Stowe, Harriet Beecher. *Uncle Tom's Cabin; or, Life among the Lowly.* Boston: John P. Jewett, 1851.

Trollope, Frances. *Domestic Manners of the Americans.* London, 1832. Ed. Donald Smalley. New York: Vintage, 1949.

Walker, John. *A Critical Pronouncing Dictionary, and Expositor of the English Language.* London: G. G. J. and J. Robinson, 1791.

Warner, Susan [Elizabeth Wetherell]. *The Wide, Wide World.* New York: G. P. Putnam's, 1850.

Webster, Noah. *American Dictionary of the English Language.* 2 vols. New York, 1828; Enl. and improved, Chauncey A. Goodrich and Noah Porter. Springfield, MA: G. and C. Merriam, 1866.

———. *Compendious Dictionary of the English Language.* Hartford, CT: Hudson and Goodwin, 1806.

Wells, William Harvey. *Graded Course of Instruction for Public Schools.* 1862. New York: A. S. Barnes, 1877.

White, John Silas. "Oratio." *Addresses at the Inauguration of Charles William Eliot.* Cambridge: Sever and Francis, 1869. 11–13.

Whitney, William Dwight. *Language and the Study of Language.* New York: Scribner's, 1867. At least 20 American issues to 1910.

Wisely, John Benjamin. *Language for the Grades.* Terre Haute: Inland, 1896.

Winsor, Justin. "Libraries in Boston." *The Memorial History of Boston, 1630–1880.* Ed. Justin Winsor. Vol. 4. Boston: Ticknor, 1881. 279–94.

The Young Ladies' Own Book: A Manual of Intellectual Improvement and Moral Deportment. Philadelphia: Thomas, Cowperthwait, 1838.

Secondary Materials

Agnew, Lois. "The Civic Function of Taste: A Re-Assessment of Hugh Blair's Rhetorical Theory." *Rhetoric Society Quarterly* 28.2 (1998): 25–36.

Anderson, Benedict. *Imagined Communities*. 1983. Rev. ed. New York: Verso, 1991.

Anderson, James D. *The Education of Blacks in the South, 1860–1945*. Chapel Hill: U of North Carolina P, 1988.

Apple, Michael. *Teachers and Texts: A Political Economy of Class and Gender Relations in Education*. New York: Routledge, 1986.

Applebee, Arthur. *Tradition and Reform in the Teaching of English: A History*. Urbana: NCTE, 1974.

Austin, J. L. *How to Do Things with Words*. New York: Oxford UP, 1962.

Avery, Gillian. "The Beginnings of Children's Reading to c. 1700." *Children's Literature: An Illustrated History*. Ed. Peter Hunt. New York: Oxford UP, 1995. 1–25.

Axelrod, Rise, and Charles Cooper. *Concise Guide to Writing*. New York: St. Martin's, 1993.

Bailey, Richard. *Nineteenth-Century English*. Ann Arbor: U of Michigan P, 1996.

Baron, Dennis E. *Grammar and Good Taste: Reforming the American Language*. New Haven: Yale UP, 1982.

Berlin, James A. *Writing Instruction in Nineteenth-Century American Colleges*. Carbondale: Southern Illinois UP, 1984.

Bitzer, Lloyd F. "Editions of *The Philosophy of Rhetoric*." *The Philosophy of Rhetoric*. By George Campbell. Ed. Bitzer. Carbondale: Southern Illinois UP, 1988. lii–lv.

Bledstein, Burton. *The Culture of Professionalism: The Middle Class and the Development of Higher Education in America*. New York: Norton, 1976.

Borrowman, Merle. *The Liberal and Technical in Teacher Education: A Historical Survey of American Thought*. New York: Teachers College P, 1956.

Brereton, John. *The Origins of Composition Studies in the American College, 1875–1925: A Documentary History*. Pittsburgh: U of Pittsburgh P, 1995.

Broaddus, Dorothy C. *Genteel Rhetoric: Writing High Culture in Nineteenth-Century Boston*. Columbia: U of South Carolina P, 1999.

Brosterman, Norman. *Inventing Kindergarten*. New York: Abrams, 1997.

Buell, Lawrence. *New England Literary Culture from Revolution Through Renaissance*. New York: Cambridge UP, 1986.

Campbell, JoAnn. "Controlling Voices: The Legacy of English A at Radcliffe College 1883–1917." *CCC* 43 (1992): 472–85.

——, ed. *Toward a Feminist Rhetoric: The Writings of Gertrude Buck*. Pittsburgh: U of Pittsburgh P, 1996.

——. "Women's Work, Worthy Work: Composition Instruction at Vassar College, 1897–1922." *Constructing Rhetorical Education*. Ed. Marie Secor and Davida Charney. Carbondale: Southern Illinois UP, 1992. 26–42.

Carpenter, Charles. *History of American School-books*. Philadelphia: U of Pennsylvania P, 1963.

Carr, Jean Ferguson. "Nineteenth-Century Girls and Literacy." Greer 51–78.

———. "Rereading the Academy as Worldly Text." *CCC* 45 (1994): 93–97.

Carr, Stephen L. "The Circulation of Blair's *Lectures*." *Rhetoric Society Quarterly* 32.4 (2002): 75–104.

Caspar, Scott E. "Defining the National Pantheon: The Making of Houghton Mifflin's Biographical Series, 1880–1900." Moylan and Stiles 179–221.

Casper, Scott E., Joanne D. Chaison, and Jeffrey D. Groves, eds. *Perspectives on American Book History*. Amherst: U of Massachusetts P, 2002.

Chartier, Roger. *Forms and Meanings: Text, Performances, and Audiences from Codex to Computer*. Philadelphia: U of Pennsylvania P, 1995.

Charvat, William. *Literary Publishing in America, 1790–1850*. Philadelphia: U of Pennsylvania P, 1959.

———. *The Origins of American Critical Thought, 1810–1835*. Philadelphia: U of Pennsylvania P, 1936.

———. *The Profession of Authorship in America, 1800–1870*. Ed. Matthew J. Bruccoli. Columbus: Ohio State UP, 1968.

Coleman, Michael. *American Indian Children at School, 1850–1930*. Jackson: UP of Mississippi, 1993.

Commager, Henry Steele. "McGuffey and His Readers." *Saturday Review* 16 June 1962: 50–51, 69–70.

Connors, Robert J. *Composition-Rhetoric: Backgrounds, Theory, and Pedagogy*. Pittsburgh: U of Pittsburgh P, 1997.

———. "Personal Writing Assignments." *CCC* 38 (1987): 166–83.

———. "Writing the History of Our Discipline." *An Introduction to Composition Studies*. Ed. Erika Lindemann and Gary Tate. New York: Oxford UP, 1991.

Corbett, Edward P. J. "Hugh Blair as an Analyzer of English Prose Style." *Selected Essays of Edward P. J. Corbett*. Ed. Robert J. Connors. Dallas: Southern Methodist UP, 1989. 4–13.

Cornelius, Janet D. *"When I Can Read My Title Clear": Literacy, Slavery, and Religion in the Antebellum South*. Columbia: U of South Carolina P, 1991.

Cremin, Lawrence A. *American Education: The Colonial Experience 1607–1783*. New York: Harper, 1970.

———. *American Education: The National Experience 1783–1876*. New York: Harper, 1980.

———. *American Education: The Metropolitan Experience, 1876-1980*. New York: Harper, 1988.

———. *Public Education*. New York: Basic, 1976.

——. *The Transformation of the School: Progressivism in American Education, 1876–1957.* New York: Knopf, 1961.

Crowley, Sharon. *Composition in the University: Historical and Polemical Essays.* Pittsburgh: U of Pittsburgh P, 1998.

——. *The Methodical Memory: Invention in Current-Traditional Rhetoric.* Carbondale: Southern Illinois UP, 1990.

Cuban, Larry. *How Teachers Taught: Constancy and Change in American Classrooms, 1890-1990.* 1984. 2nd enl. ed. New York: Teachers College P, 1993.

Cubberley, Ellwood P. *Changing Conceptions of Education.* Boston: Houghton Mifflin, 1909.

——. *Readings in Public Education in the United States.* Boston: Houghton Mifflin, 1934.

Davidson, Cathy N., ed. *Reading in America: Literature and Social History.* Baltimore: Johns Hopkins UP, 1989.

——. *Revolution and the Word: The Rise of the Novel in America.* New York: Oxford UP, 1986.

Dawson, Melanie. "From Carnival to Nostalgia: The Play of Cultural Literacy in the Nineteenth-Century Parlor." Diss. U of Pittsburgh, 1997.

Denning, Michael J. *Mechanic Accents: Dime Novels and Working-Class Culture.* New York: Verso, 1987.

Dewey, John. *Democracy and Education.* New York: Macmillan, 1916.

Eldred, Janet Carey, and Peter Mortensen. "'A Few Patchwork Opinions': Piecing Together Narratives of U.S. Girls' Early National Schooling." Greer 23–50.

——. *Imagining Rhetoric: Composing Women of the Early United States.* Pittsburgh: U of Pittsburgh P, 2002.

Elson, Ruth Miller. *Guardians of Tradition: American Schoolbooks of the Nineteenth Century.* Lincoln: U of Nebraska P, 1964.

Emig, Janet. "The Relation of Thought and Language Implicit in Some Early American Rhetoric and Composition Texts." *The Web of Meaning.* Ed. Dixie Goswami and Maureen Butler. Upper Montclair, NJ: Boynton, 1983. 3–43.

Falbo, Bianca M. "Authorship and the Circulation of Literate Practices in the Anglo-American Field of Cultural Production, 1790–1860." Diss. U of Pittsburgh, 1997.

Farkas, Angela. "Sensational Tales and Working-Girl Melodrama: Popular Story Paper Fiction and Its Readers in Late Nineteenth-Century America." Diss. U of Pittsburgh P, 2003.

Ferguson, Margaret W. *Dido's Daughters: Literacy, Gender, and Empire in Early Modern England and France.* Chicago: U of Chicago P, 2003.

Finney, Ross. *A Brief History of the American Public School.* New York: Macmillan, 1927.

Fitzgerald, Kathryn. "A Rediscovered Tradition: European Pedagogy and Composition in Nineteenth-Century Normal Schools." *CCC* 53 (2002): 224–50.

Ford, Paul Leicester. Introduction. *The New-England Primer.* 1897. New York: Teachers College P, 1962.

Franklin, John Hope. *From Slavery to Freedom: A History of Negro Americans.* 1947. 8th ed. Rev. ed. by Alfred A. Moss Jr. Boston: McGraw-Hill, 2000.

Fuller, Wayne E. *The Old Country School: The Story of Rural Education in the Middle West.* Chicago: U of Chicago P, 1982.

Fullerton, Hugh S., ed. *Old Favorites from the McGuffey Readers,* New York: American Book, 1936.

Gage, John T. "On 'Rhetoric' and 'Composition.'" *An Introduction to Composition Studies.* Ed. Erika Lindemann and Gary Tate. New York: Oxford UP, 1991. 15–32.

Genette, Gerard. *Paratexts: Thresholds of Interpretation.* Trans. Jane E. Lewin. Cambridge: Cambridge UP, 1997. Trans. of *Seuils.* Paris, 1987.

Gere, Anne Ruggles. *Intimate Practices: Literacy and Cultural Work in U.S. Women's Clubs, 1880–1920.* Urbana: U of Illinois P, 1997.

———. "Kitchen Tables and Rented Rooms: The Extracurriculum of Composition." *CCC* 45 (1994): 75–92.

Gilmore, Michael T. *American Romanticism and the Marketplace.* Chicago: U of Chicago P, 1985.

Gilmore, William J. *Reading Becomes a Necessity of Life: Material and Cultural Life in Rural New England, 1760–1830.* Knoxville: U of Tennessee P, 1988.

Glazener, Nancy. *Reading for Realism: The History of a U.S. Literary Institution, 1850–1910.* Durham: Duke UP, 1997.

Golden, James L., and Edward P. J. Corbett. *The Rhetoric of Blair, Campbell, and Whately.* Carbondale: Southern Illinois UP, 1990.

Goodburn, Amy. "Girls' Literacy in the Progressive Era: Female and American Indian Identity at the Genoa Indian School." Greer 79–102.

Graff, Gerald. *Professing Literature: An Institutional History.* Chicago: U of Chicago P, 1987.

Graff, Harvey. *The Literacy Myth: Literacy and Social Structure in the Nineteenth-Century City.* New York: Academic, 1979.

———. "The Nineteenth-Century Origins of Our Times." *Literacy: A Critical Sourcebook.* Ed. Ellen Cushman, Eugene R. Kintgen, Barry M. Kroll, and Mike Rose. Boston: Bedford-St. Martin's, 2001. 211–33.

Greer, Jane, ed. *Girls and Literacy in America: Historical Perspectives to the Present.* Santa Barbara: ABC-CLIO, 2003.

Groves, Jeffrey D. "Judging Literary Books by Their Covers: House Styles, Ticknor and Fields, and Literary Promotion." Moylan and Stiles 75–100.

Guthrie, Warren. "The Development of Rhetorical Theory in America, 1635–1850." *Speech Monographs* 15 (1948): 61–71.

Hall, David D. *Cultures of Print: Essays in the History of the Book*. Amherst: U of Massachusetts P, 1996.

Halloran, S. Michael. "From Rhetoric to Composition: The Teaching of Writing in America to 1900." *A Short History of Writing Instruction*. Ed. James J. Murphy. Davis: Hermagoras, 1990. 151–82.

Hall-Quest, Alfred Lawrence. *The Textbook*. New York: Macmillan, 1918.

Hart, James D. *The Popular Book: A History of America's Literary Taste*. New York: Oxford UP, 1950.

Heck, William Harry. *Mental Discipline and Educational Values*. New York: John Lane, 1909, 1911.

Herbst, Jurgen. *And Sadly Teach: Teacher Education and Professionalization in American Culture*. Madison: U of Wisconsin P, 1989.

Hewett, Beth L. "Samuel P. Newman's *A Practical System of Rhetoric:* An American Cousin of Scottish Rhetoric." *Scottish Rhetoric and Its Influences*. Ed. Lynee Lewis Gaillet. Mahwah: Hermagoras, 1998: 179–92.

Hirsch, E. D., Jr. *Cultural Literacy*. New York: Vintage, 1988.

Hobbs, Catherine, ed. *Nineteenth-Century Women Learn to Write*. Charlottesville: UP of Virginia, 1995.

Hodges, R. E. "In Adam's Fall: A Brief History of Spelling Instruction in the United States." *Reading and Writing Instruction in the United States: Historical Trends*. Ed. H. Alan Robinson. Urbana: ERIC, 1977. 1–16.

Hofstadter, Richard, and Wilson Smith, eds. *American Higher Education: A Documentary History*. 2 vols. Chicago: U of Chicago P, 1961.

Hoshor, John P. "American Contributions to Rhetorical Theory and Homiletics." *History of Speech Education in America: Background Studies*. Ed. Karl R. Wallace. New York: Appleton-Century-Crofts, 1954.

Howell, Wilbur Samuel. *Eighteenth-Century British Logic and Rhetoric*. Princeton: Princeton UP, 1971.

Hughes, Raymond G. "An Analysis of the Fourth, Fifth, and Sixth McGuffey Readers." Diss. U of Pittsburgh, 1943.

Huston, Jon. "An Analysis of English Grammar Textbooks Used in American Schools Before 1850." Diss. U of Pittsburgh, 1954.

Johns, Adrian. *The Nature of the Book: Print and Knowledge in the Making*. Chicago: U of Chicago P, 1998.

Johnson, Clifton. *Old-Time Schools and School-Books*. New York, Macmillan, 1904. New York: Dover, 1963.

Johnson, Nan. *Nineteenth-Century Rhetoric in North America*. Carbondale: Southern Illinois UP, 1991.

Jolliffe, David. "The Moral Subject in College Composition: A Conceptual Framework and the Case of Harvard, 1865–1900." *College English* 51 (1989): 163–73.

Kaestle, Carl F. *Pillars of the Republic: Common Schools and American Society, 1780–1860.* New York: Hill, 1983.

Kaestle, Carl F., and Eric Foner, eds. *Literacy in the United States: Readers and Reading since 1880.* New Haven: Yale UP, 1991.

Kaser, David. *Books and Libraries in Camp and Battle: The Civil War Experience.* Westport: Greenwood, 1984.

Katz, Michael B. *The Irony of Early School Reform: Educational Innovation in Mid-Nineteenth-Century Massachusetts.* Cambridge: Harvard UP, 1968.

———. *Reconstructing American Education.* Cambridge: Harvard UP, 1987.

Kerber, Linda. *Toward an Intellectual History of Women.* Chapel Hill: U of North Carolina P, 1997.

Kipnis, William. "Propagating the Pestalozzian." Diss. Loyola U of Chicago, 1972.

Kitzhaber, Albert. *Rhetoric in American Colleges, 1850–1900.* Diss. U of Washington, 1953. Dallas: Southern Methodist UP, 1990.

Kolesnik, Walter. *Mental Discipline in Modern Education.* Madison: U of Wisconsin P, 1958.

Krug, Edward A., ed. *Charles W. Eliot and Popular Education.* New York: Teachers College P, 1961.

———. *The Shaping of the American High School, 1880–1920.* Madison: U of Wisconsin P, 1964.

Labaree, David F. *The Making of an American High School: The Credentials Market and the Central High School of Philadelphia, 1838–1939.* New Haven: Yale UP, 1988.

Lehmann-Haupt, Hellmut. *The Book in America.* New York: Bowker, 1939, 1951.

Lehuu, Isabelle. *Carnival on the Page: Popular Print Media in Antebellum America.* Chapel Hill: U of North Carolina P, 2000.

Leichter, Hope Jensen, ed. *The Family as Educator.* New York: Teachers College P, 1975.

Leitner, Gerhard. *English Traditional Grammars.* Amsterdam: John Benjamins, 1991.

Leonard, Sterling Andrus. *The Doctrine of Correctness in English Usage, 1700–1800.* U of Wisconsin Studies in Language and Literature, no. 25. Madison: 1929.

Lindberg, Stanley W., ed. *The Annotated McGuffey: Selections from the McGuffey Eclectic Readers, 1836–1920.* New York: Van Nostrand Reinhold, 1976.

Lindemann, Erika. "True and Candid Compositions: The Lives and Writings of Antebellum Students at the University of North Carolina." Unpublished ms., 2000.

Lindey, Alexander. *Plagiarism and Originality.* New York: Harper, 1952. Westport: Greenwood, 1974.

Lockridge, Kenneth. *Literacy in Colonial New England: An Enquiry into the Social Context of Literacy in the Early Modern West.* New York: Norton, 1974.

Logan, Shirley Wilson. *"We Are Coming": The Persuasive Discourse of Nineteenth-Century Black Women.* Carbondale: Southern Illinois UP, 1999.

Lyman, Rollo. *English Grammar in American Schools Before 1850.* Chicago: U of Chicago Libraries, 1922.

Macksey, Richard. Forward. *Paratexts.* By Gerard Genette. Trans. of *Seuils.* 1987. London: Cambridge UP, 1997.

Madison, Charles. *Book Publishing in America.* New York: McGraw, 1966.

Manguel, Alberto. *A History of Reading.* New York: Viking, 1996.

Martin, Theodora Penny. *The Sound of Our Own Voices: Women's Study Clubs, 1860–1910.* Boston: Beacon, 1987.

Mathews, Mitford M. *Teaching to Read Historically Considered.* Chicago: U of Chicago P, 1966.

McGill, Meredith L. *American Literature and the Culture of Reprinting, 1834–1853.* Philadelphia: U of Pennsylvania P, 2003.

McHenry, Elizabeth. *Forgotten Readers: Recovering the Lost History of African American Literary Societies.* Durham: Duke UP, 2002.

McHenry, Elizabeth, and Shirley Brice Heath. "The Literate and the Literary: African Americans as Writers and Readers, 1830–1940." *Literacy: A Critical Sourcebook.* Ed. Ellen Cushman, Eugene R. Kintgen, Barry M. Kroll, and Mike Rose. Boston: Bedford-St. Martin's, 2001. 261–74.

Michael, Ian. *Early Textbooks of English.* Reading, Eng.: Colloquium on Textbooks, Schools, and Society, 1993.

———. *Literature in School: A Guide to the Early Sources 1700–1830.* Swansea, Eng.: Textbook Colloquium, 1999.

———. *The Teaching of English: From the Sixteenth Century to 1870.* Cambridge: Cambridge UP, 1987.

Mihesuah, Devon A. *Cultivating the Rosebuds: The Education of Women at the Cherokee Female Seminary, 1851–1909.* Urbana: U of Illinois P, 1993.

Miller, Susan. *Assuming the Positions: Cultural Pedagogy and the Politics of Commonplace Writing.* Pittsburgh: U of Pittsburgh P, 1998.

Miller, Thomas P. *The Formation of College English: Rhetoric and Belles Lettres in the British Cultural Provinces.* Pittsburgh: U of Pittsburgh P, 1997.

———, ed. *The Selected Writings of John Witherspoon.* Carbondale: Southern Illinois UP, 1990.

Minnich, Harvey S. *William Holmes McGuffey and His Readers.* New York: American Book, 1936.

Monaghan, Charles. *The Murrays of Murray Hill.* Brooklyn: Urban History, 1998.

Monaghan, E. Jennifer. *A Common Heritage: Noah Webster's Blue-Back Speller.* Hamden: Archon, 1983.

———. *Learning to Read and Write in Colonial America.* Amherst: U of Massachusetts P, forthcoming.

———. "Literacy Instruction and Gender in Colonial New England." Davidson, *Reading in America* 53–80.

———. "The Uses of Literacy by Girls in Colonial America." Greer 1–22.

Monroe, Will S. *History of the Pestalozzian Movement in the United States.* Syracuse: Bardeen, 1907.

Morris, Robert C., ed. *Freedmen's Schools and Textbooks: Black Education in the South, 1861–79.* 6 vols. New York: AMS, 1980.

———. *Reading, 'Riting, and Reconstruction: The Education of Freedmen in the South, 1861–1870.* Chicago: U of Chicago P, 1981.

Mosier, Richard D. *Making the American Mind: Social and Moral Ideas in the McGuffey Readers.* New York: Russell, 1965.

Mott, Frank Luther. *Golden Multitudes: The Story of Bestsellers in the United States.* New York: Macmillan, 1947.

———. *A History of American Magazines, 1741–1850.* 1930. Cambridge: Harvard UP, 1939.

Moylan, Michele, and Lane Stiles, eds. *Reading Books: Essays on the Material Text and Literature in America.* Amherst: U of Massachusetts P, 1996.

Mussey, Barrows. Introduction. *The Tales of Peter Parley about America.* By Samuel Goodrich. 1827. New York: Dover, 1974. v–xxvi.

Myers, Miles. *Changing Our Minds: Negotiating English and Literacy.* Urbana: NCTE, 1996.

Neuburg, Victor. "Chapbooks in America: Reconstructing the Popular Reading of Early America." Davidson, *Reading in America* 81–113.

Newkirk, Thomas. "Barrett Wendell's Theory of Discourse." *Rhetoric Review* 10 (1991): 20–30.

Nietz, John A. *The Evolution of American Secondary School Textbooks.* Rutland: Tuttle, 1966.

———. "Experiences of a Book Collector." *History of Education Quarterly* 8 (1968): 399–403.

———. *Old Textbooks.* Pittsburgh: U of Pittsburgh P, 1961.

———. "Why the Longevity of the McGuffey *Readers*?" *History of Education Quarterly* 4 (1964): 119–25.

Nord, David Paul. "Religious Reading and Readers in Antebellum America." *Journal of the Early Republic* 15 (1995): 241–72.

North, Stephen M. *The Making of Knowledge in Composition: Portrait of an Emerging Field.* Portsmouth: Boynton-Heinemann, 1987.

Nunis, Doyce B., Jr. *Books in Their Sea Chests: Reading along the Early California Coast.* Berkeley: California Library Assoc., 1964.

Nye, Russell Blaine. *Society and Culture in America, 1830–1860.* New York: Harper and Row, 1974.

Paine, Charles. *The Resistant Writer: Rhetoric as Immunity, 1850 to Present*. Albany: State U of New York P, 1999.

Patterson, Lyman Ray. *Copyright in Historical Perspective*. Nashville: Vanderbilt UP, 1968.

Perkinson, Henry J. Introduction. *Early American Textbooks, 1775–1900*. Washington, DC: U.S. Dept. of Education, 1985.

Perrin, Porter. "The Teaching of Rhetoric in the American College Before 1750." Diss. U of Chicago, 1936.

Pooley, Robert C. *Grammar and Usage in Textbooks on English*. Bureau of Educational Research Bulletin, no. 14. Madison: U of Wisconsin, 1933.

Ravitch, Diane. "Where Have All the Classics Gone? You Won't Find Them in Primers." *New York Times Book Review* 17 May 1987: 46-47.

Reese, William J. *The Origins of the American High School*. New Haven: Yale UP, 1995.

Reid, Ronald F. "The Boylston Professorship of Rhetoric and Oratory, 1806–1904: A Case Study in Changing Concepts of Rhetoric and Pedagogy." *Quarterly Journal of Speech* 45 (1959): 239–57.

Reisner, Edward H. *The Evolution of the Common School*. New York: Macmillan, 1930.

Rice, Edwin Wilbur. *The Sunday-School Movement and the American Sunday-School Union*. Philadelphia: Union, 1917.

Rich, Adrienne. "When We Dead Awaken: Writing as Re-Vision." 1971. *On Lies, Secrets, and Silences: Selected Prose, 1966–78*. New York: Norton, 1979. 33–49.

Ricks, Vickie. "'In an Atmosphere of Peril': College Women and Their Writing." Hobbs 59–83.

Rose, Mark. *Authors and Owners: The Invention of Copyright*. Cambridge: Harvard UP, 1993.

Royster, Jacqueline Jones. *Traces of the Stream: Literacy and Social Change among African American Women*. Pittsburgh: U of Pittsburgh P, 2000.

Rudolph, Frederick. *The American College and University: A History*. New York: Knopf, 1962.

———. *Mark Hopkins and the Log: Williams College, 1836–1872*. Williamstown: Williams College, 1996.

Ruggles, Alice McGuffey. *The Story of the McGuffeys*. New York: American Book, 1950.

Russell, David R. *Writing in the Academic Disciplines: A Curricular History*. 2nd ed. Carbondale: Southern Illinois UP, 2002.

Saenger, Paul. *Space Between Words: The Origins of Silent Reading*. Stanford: Stanford UP, 1997.

Salvatori, Mariolina Rizzi, ed. *Pedagogy: Disturbing History, 1819–1929*. Pittsburgh: U of Pittsburgh P, 1996.

Schultz, Lucille M. "Editing *The Jabberwock:* A Formative Experience for Nineteenth-Century Girls." *Blue Pencils and Hidden Hands: Women Editing Periodicals, 1830–1910.* Ed. Sharon Harris. Boston: Northeastern UP, 2004. 3–19.

———. "Letter-Writing Instruction in Nineteenth-Century Schools in the United States." *Letter Writing as a Social Practice.* Ed. David Barton and Nigel Hall. Amsterdam: John Benjamins, 2000. 109–30.

———. *The Young Composers.* Carbondale: Southern Illinois UP, 1999.

Sealts, Merton M., Jr., *Melville's Reading: A Check-List of Books Owned and Borrowed.* Madison: U of Wisconsin P, 1966.

Shankland, Rebecca H. "The McGuffey Readers and Moral Education." *Harvard Educational Review* 31 (1961): 60–72.

Shannon, Patrick. *The Struggle to Continue: Progressive Reading Instruction in the United States.* Portsmouth: Heinemann, 1990.

Silber, Kate. *Pestalozzi: The Man and His Work.* 1960. London: Routledge, 1965.

Simmons, Sue Carter. "Radcliffe Responses to Harvard Rhetoric." Hobbs 264–92.

Simpson, David. *The Politics of American English, 1776–1850.* New York: Oxford UP, 1986.

Sizer, Theodore, Nancy Sizer, Sally Schwager, Lynne Templeton Brickley, and Glee Kreuger. *To Ornament Their Minds: Sarah Pierce's Litchfield Female Academy 1729–1833.* Litchfield: Litchfield Historical Society, 1993.

Smith, Henry Lester, et al. *One Hundred Fifty Years of Grammar Textbooks.* Bloomington: Indiana UP, 1946.

Smith, William E. *About the McGuffeys.* Oxford: Cullen, 1963.

Solomon, Barbara Miller. *In the Company of Educated Women: A History of Women and Higher Education in America.* New Haven: Yale UP, 1985.

Soltow, Lee, and Edward Stevens. *The Rise of Literacy and the Common School in the United States.* Chicago: U of Chicago P, 1981.

Stevenson, Louise. *Miss Porter's School.* New York: Garland, 1987.

———. "The Home, Books, and Reading in an Age of Commerce." *A History of the Book in America.* Vol. 3. Ed. Hugh Amory and David Hall. London: Cambridge UP, forthcoming.

Storr, Richard J. *The Beginnings of Graduate Education in America.* Chicago: U of Chicago P, 1953.

Sullivan, Dolores P. *William Holmes McGuffey: Schoolmaster to the Nation.* Rutherford: Fairleigh Dickinson UP, 1994.

Sullivan, Mark. *American Finding Herself.* New York: Scribner's, 1927. Vol. 2 of *Our Times: The United States, 1900–1925.*

Svobodny, Dolly, ed. *Early American Textbooks: 1775–1900.* Washington, DC: U.S. Dept. of Education, 1985.

Tarver, J. "Abridged Editions of Blair's *Lectures on Rhetoric and Belles Lettres* in America: What Nineteenth-Century College Students Really Learned about Blair on Rhetoric." *Bibliotheck: A Scottish Journal of Bibliography and Allied Topics* 21 (1996): 55–68.

Thomas, Amy M. "Literature in Newsprint: Antebellum Family Newspapers and the Uses of Reading." Moylan and Stiles 101–116.

Thornton, Tamara Plakins. *Handwriting in America: A Cultural History.* New Haven: Yale UP, 1996.

Tolley, Kim. *The Science Education of American Girls: A Historical Perspective.* New York: Routledge, 2003.

Trachsel, Mary. *Institutionalizing Literacy: The Historical Role of College Entrance Examinations in English.* Carbondale: Southern Illinois UP, 1992.

Tyack, David B. *The One Best System: A History of American Urban Education.* Cambridge: Harvard UP, 1974.

Tyler, Priscilla. "Grammars of the English Language to 1850: With Special Emphasis on School Grammars Used in America." Diss. Western Reserve U., 1953.

United States Copyright Office. *Circular 1a.* Washington, DC: Library of Congress, 1995.

Vail, Henry. *A History of the McGuffey Readers.* Cleveland: Burrows, 1911.

Verduin, Kathleen. "Dante in America: The First Hundred Years." Moylan and Stiles 16–51.

Veysey, Laurence R. *The Emergence of the American University.* Chicago: U of Chicago P, 1965.

Welsch, Kathleen A. "Nineteenth-Century Composition: The Relationship Between Pedagogical Concerns and Cultural Values in American Colleges, 1850–1890." Diss. U of Pittsburgh, 1994.

West, Michael. *Transcendental Wordplay: America's Romantic Punsters and the Search for the Language of Nature.* Athens: Ohio UP, 2000.

Westerhoff, John H., III. *McGuffey and His Readers.* Nashville: Abingdon, 1978.

Williams, Susan S. "Manufacturing Intellectual Equipment: The Tauschnitz Edition of *The Marble Faun*." Moylan and Stiles 117–50.

Woods, William. "The Reform Tradition in Nineteenth-Century Composition Teaching." *Written Communication* 2 (1985): 377–90.

Woodson, Carter G. *The Education of the Negro Prior to 1861.* 1917. 2nd ed. 1919. Rpt. New York: Arno, 1968.

Woody, Thomas. *A History of Women's Education in the United States.* 2 vols. 1929. Rpt. New York: Octagon Books, 1966.

Wozniak, John Michael. *English Composition in Eastern Colleges, 1850–1940.* Diss. Johns Hopkins U, 1951. Washington, DC: UP of America, 1978.

Zboray, Ronald J. *A Fictive People: Antebellum Economic Development and the American Reading Public.* New York: Oxford UP, 1993.

Zboray, Ronald J., and Mary Saracino Zboray. *A Handbook for the Study of Book History in the United States*. Washington, DC: Library of Congress, Center for the Book, 2000.

Index

JEAN FERGUSON CARR is associate professor of English and women's studies at the University of Pittsburgh and coeditor of the Pittsburgh Series in Composition, Literacy, and Culture. She was textual editor for two volumes of *The Collected Works of R. W. Emerson* (1979, 1983) and has published essays on Dickens, Austen, autobiography, and women's writing. She is the faculty adviser for the Nineteenth-Century American Schoolbooks, a digital collection at the University of Pittsburgh.

STEPHEN L. CARR is associate professor of English at the University of Pittsburgh. He has published essays on Blake, Blair, and eighteenth-century British art and philosophy.

LUCILLE M. SCHULTZ is professor of English at the University of Cincinnati. Her book *The Young Composers* (1999) won the Nancy Dasher Award in 2000 from the College English Association of Ohio.

Studies in Writing & Rhetoric

In 1980 the Conference on College Composition and Communication established the Studies in Writing & Rhetoric (SWR) series as a forum for monograph-length arguments or presentations that engage general compositionists. SWR encourages extended essays or research reports addressing any issue in composition and rhetoric from any theoretical or research perspective as long as the general significance to the field is clear. Previous SWR publications serve as models for prospective authors; in addition, contributors may propose alternate formats and agendas that inform or extend the field's current debates.

SWR is particularly interested in projects that connect the specific research site or theoretical framework to contemporary classroom and institutional contexts of direct concern to compositionists across the nation. Such connections may come from several approaches, including cultural, theoretical, field-based, gendered, historical, and interdisciplinary. SWR especially encourages monographs by scholars early in their careers, by established scholars who wish to share an insight or exhortation with the field, and by scholars of color.

The SWR series editor and editorial board members are committed to working closely with prospective authors and offering significant developmental advice for encouraged manuscripts and prospectuses. Editorships rotate every five years. Prospective authors intending to submit a prospectus during the 2002 to 2007 editorial appointment should obtain submission guidelines from Robert Brooke, SWR editor, University of Nebraska–Lincoln, Department of English, P.O. Box 880337, 202 Andrews Hall, Lincoln, NE 68588-0337.

General inquiries may also be addressed to Sponsoring Editor, Studies in Writing & Rhetoric, Southern Illinois University Press, P.O. Box 3697, Carbondale, IL 62902-3697.